For Reference

Not to be taken from this room

*Newbery and Caldecott Medal Books
1976-1985*

Newbery and Caldecott Medal Books 1976-1985

edited by Lee Kingman

with Acceptance Papers, Biographies, and Related Material chiefly from
THE HORN BOOK MAGAZINE

THE HORN BOOK, INCORPORATED • BOSTON • 1986

Copyright © 1986 by The Horn Book, Inc.

All rights reserved. No part of this book may be reproduced or utilized in any form or by any means, electronic or mechanical, including photocopying, recording or by any information storage and retrieval system, without permission in writing from the Publisher. Inquiries should be addressed to The Horn Book, Inc., Park Square Building, 31 St. James Avenue, Boston, MA 02116.

Printed in the United States of America

Library of Congress Cataloging-in-Publication Data

Newbery and Caldecott medal books, 1976–1985.
   Includes indexes.
   1. Newbery medal books.   2. Caldecott medal books.
3. Literary prizes.   4. Children—Books and reading.
5. Children's literature—History and criticism.
I. Kingman, Lee.   II. Horn book magazine (Boston, Mass. : 1945)

Z1037.A2N49   1986   028.5′079   86-15223
[PN1009.A1]
ISBN 0-87675-004-8

The permissions acknowledged on pages 355 to 358 constitute an extension of this copyright page.

Contents

PREFACE	ix
THE NEWBERY MEDAL BOOKS 1976–1985	1

1976 THE GREY KING   3
by *Susan Cooper*
MEDAL ACCEPTANCE 6 · SUSAN COOPER
BY *Margaret K. McElderry* 12

1977 ROLL OF THUNDER, HEAR MY CRY   18
by *Mildred D. Taylor*
MEDAL ACCEPTANCE 21 · MILDRED D. TAYLOR
BY *Phyllis J. Fogelman* 31

1978 BRIDGE TO TERABITHIA   35
by *Katherine Paterson*
MEDAL ACCEPTANCE 38 · KATHERINE PATERSON
BY *Virginia Buckley* 45

1979 THE WESTING GAME   50
by *Ellen Raskin*
MEDAL ACCEPTANCE 51 · THE RASKIN CONGLOMERATE
BY *Dennis Flanagan* 58

1980 A GATHERING OF DAYS: A NEW ENGLAND
GIRL'S JOURNAL, 1830–32   62
by *Joan W. Blos*
MEDAL ACCEPTANCE 65 · JOAN W. BLOS BY *Betty Miles* 70

1981 JACOB HAVE I LOVED   74
by *Katherine Paterson*
MEDAL ACCEPTANCE 76 · KATHERINE PATERSON BY *Gene Inyart Namovicz* 86

1982 A VISIT TO WILLIAM BLAKE'S INN: POEMS
FOR INNOCENT AND EXPERIENCED
TRAVELERS 93
by *Nancy Willard*
MEDAL ACCEPTANCE 94 · NANCY WILLARD BY *Barbara Lucas* 99

1983 DICEY'S SONG 105
by *Cynthia Voigt*
MEDAL ACCEPTANCE 107 · CYNTHIA VOIGT BY *Elise K. Irving* 116 · *Cynthia Voigt* BY *Jessica Voigt* 118

1984 DEAR MR. HENSHAW 120
by *Beverly Cleary*
MEDAL ACCEPTANCE 122 · BEVERLY CLEARY BY *David Reuther* 132

1985 THE HERO AND THE CROWN 136
by *Robin McKinley*
MEDAL ACCEPTANCE 138 · ROBIN MCKINLEY BY *Terri Windling* AND *Mark Alan Arnold* 149

NEWBERY MEDAL BOOKS 153
by *Zena Sutherland*

THE CALDECOTT MEDAL BOOKS 1976–1985 167

1976 WHY MOSQUITOES BUZZ IN PEOPLE'S EARS 169
illustrated by *Leo and Diane Dillon*
retold by *Verna Aardema*
MEDAL ACCEPTANCE 170 · LEO AND DIANE DILLON BY *Phyllis J. Fogelman* 175

1977 ASHANTI TO ZULU: AFRICAN TRADITIONS 181
illustrated by *Leo and Diane Dillon*
written by *Margaret Musgrove*
MEDAL ACCEPTANCE 181 · DIANE DILLON BY *Leo Dillon* 188 · LEO DILLON BY *Diane Dillon* 190
LEO AND DIANE DILLON BY *Lee Dillon* 191

CONTENTS / vii

1978 NOAH'S ARK 193
illustrated by *Peter Spier*
MEDAL ACCEPTANCE 193 · PETER SPIER BY *Janet D. Chenery* 201

1979 THE GIRL WHO LOVED WILD HORSES 204
written and illustrated by *Paul Goble*
MEDAL ACCEPTANCE 205 · PAUL GOBLE BY *Joseph Epes Brown* 208

1980 OX-CART MAN 210
illustrated by *Barbara Cooney*
written by *Donald Hall*
MEDAL ACCEPTANCE 211 · BARBARA COONEY BY *Constance Reed McClellan* 216

1981 FABLES 220
written and illustrated by *Arnold Lobel*
MEDAL ACCEPTANCE 220 · ARNOLD LOBEL BY *Elizabeth Gordon* 226

1982 JUMANJI 229
written and illustrated by *Chris Van Allsburg*
MEDAL ACCEPTANCE 230 · CHRIS VAN ALLSBURG BY *David Macaulay* 234

1983 SHADOW 238
translated and illustrated by *Marcia Brown*
from the French of *Blaise Cendrars*
MEDAL ACCEPTANCE 239 · MARCIA BROWN BY *Janet A. Loranger* 250

1984 THE GLORIOUS FLIGHT: ACROSS THE CHANNEL WITH LOUIS BLÉRIOT JULY 25, 1909 254
written and illustrated by *Alice and Martin Provensen*
MEDAL ACCEPTANCE 255 · ALICE AND MARTIN PROVENSEN BY *Nancy Willard* 259

1985 SAINT GEORGE AND THE DRAGON 263
illustrated by *Trina Schart Hyman*
retold by *Margaret Hodges*
MEDAL ACCEPTANCE 264 · TRINA SCHART HYMAN
BY *Katrin Hyman* 275

THE CALDECOTT SPECTRUM 279
by *Barbara Bader*

THE NEWBERY MEDAL HONOR BOOKS 315

THE CALDECOTT MEDAL HONOR BOOKS 319

A DECADE OF CHILDREN'S BOOKS:
A CRITIC'S RESPONSE
by *Ethel L. Heins* 323

Index of Titles Mentioned 343

Index by Author of Titles Mentioned 347

Preface

Many changes have taken place in the publishing of children's books since the establishment of the Newbery and Caldecott Medals. One element, however, has remained constant: The medals are presented for the books considered "the most distinguished." Members of every committee appointed to choose the Medal and Honor books have brought their different backgrounds, experiences, tastes, and knowledge to bear in applying that difficult standard "distinguished"; yet, although the requirement of distinction has not changed, perhaps the perception of what should be meant by it has been developing over the decades. In 1986 we are not as a people as naive as we were in 1922 or in 1938. Today we want books for children to do so much more than they needed to do in the past: not only to offer memorable characters and stories and to provide sensible and interesting information, but to inspire and nurture children's creativity; we want books that will give solace and comfort in an unstable world; and, perhaps currently the most difficult, we want books that will compete with the new media — television and video cassettes — for a significant share of our children's attention. At least we must hope that books today will deliver all this because children have less time to be children, and we are aware that the span of time in which to develop a hunger for books is so short.

It is at best a paradox, at worst an awkward situation, when celebration and criticism of a medal-winning book appear in the same volume. However, the purpose of this series of Newbery and Caldecott Medal books is to present not only the acceptance speeches of the authors and artists given at the time of their awards and the biographical material written about them which appeared in *The Horn Book Magazine,* but to present as well an evaluation of the books as seen in the perspective of the decade. To quote from the preface to *Newbery and Caldecott Medal Books 1966-1975,* "Books by professionals, chosen to be honored by professionals in their field of library work, deserve professional criticism."

A high professional standard has indeed been achieved by the three essayists who have evaluated books for this volume. Zena Sutherland, who has written about the Newbery Medal books, has been a contributing book review editor for the *Saturday Review* and the *Chicago Tribune;* she earned a master's degree in library science at the University of Chicago and for many years has been editor of that university's *Bulletin of the Center for Children's Books*. She has also been an associate professor at the Graduate Library School of the University of Chicago. A member of several Newbery-Caldecott Medal Committees, she chaired the 1975 committee. Barbara Bader, who wrote the essay on the Caldecott awards in *Newbery and Caldecott Medal Books 1966-1975,* has made an evaluation of the Caldecott awards given from 1976 to 1985. At the University of Chicago and the Institute of Fine Arts, New York University, she studied art history. She obtained a degree in library science at Pratt Institute and was a children's librarian for several years. She has also been an associate editor in charge of reviewing children's books at *Kirkus Reviews*. In 1976 her extensive study, *American Picturebooks from Noah's Ark to the Beast Within,* was published by Macmillan. The difficult task of presenting an overview of the thousands of books published for children from 1975 through 1984 (the Newbery and Caldecott Medal books are chosen each year from the previous year's publications) has been ably done by Ethel Heins. After receiving her degree from Douglas College, she served as a children's librarian at the New York Public Library and as a school librarian in Lexington, Massachusetts. From 1974 through 1984 Ethel Heins was editor of *The Horn Book Magazine*. As an adjunct professor, she has given courses at the Center for the Study of Children's Literature, Simmons College, and was recently honored by Simmons with a degree, Doctor of Children's Literature. She has served on four Newbery-Caldecott Medal Committees and on one Caldecott Committee.

The format of this volume contains one change from that of previous books in this series. Now that there are lengthy periods of time when even medal-winning books are out of stock and sometimes out of print, it seems more useful to include a précis of each book rather than a quote of one or two pages from each book which might not serve to reveal much more than the author's style.

My special thanks go to Karen Jameyson of The Horn Book staff for her cheerful assistance in the preparation of this book.

Lee Kingman

The Newbery Medal Books
1976-1985

The Newbery Medal 1976

THE GREY KING

written by SUSAN COOPER

published by ATHENEUM PUBLISHERS 1975
 A MARGARET K. MCELDERRY BOOK

BOOK NOTE

Will Stanton, whose experiences in three previous volumes of *The Dark Is Rising* sequence have shown him to be not just the young boy he seems but also one of the immortal Old Ones, has come to Wales to regain his health. At his uncle's farm he is welcomed by his Aunt Jen, his Uncle David, his cousin Rhys, and their sheepherder, John Rowlands. The welcome is a warm one compared to the stare given him by a strange man, Caradog Prichard.

During a giddy spell when he is in the Church of St. Cadfan, Will remembers fragments from a poem that haunted him during his illness, and he realizes that the name Cadfan's Way is important. He meets a dog, Cafall, and his master, Bran, a boy about Will's own age, and knows that even though Bran is an albino he is the "raven boy" of the poem. Bran, whose name means *crow* in Welsh, also has powers, and he knows that Will is the Old One he has been told to await. To prove that he is not an enemy from the Dark, Bran recites part of the poem and describes the man who taught it to him and who told him to help Will in his quest for a golden harp. Will recognizes the man as his master, Merriman, the oldest and wisest of the Old Ones, and then he recalls all of the vital poem. Bran's knowledge of Welsh helps as they puzzle over it.

They are interrupted by Caradog Prichard who accuses Cafall of worrying his sheep and threatens to shoot him. When Will helps John Rowlands herd his sheep, one of them is attacked by what appears to be a gray dog. The injured ewe is left inside a deserted cottage, but when they return for her, she has vanished. Some sheep are found to be killed, and the shepherds fear dogs have done it. But Bran suggests it is the work of gray foxes. Will knows then than they are creatures of the Grey King, an enemy from the Dark.

Trees and bracken on the mountain catch fire, threatening grazing animals and fields. Even Caradog Prichard, who is enraged by the slaughter of his sheep, has to stop accusing Cafall and fight the fire, which Will fears is the work of the Grey King and the Dark. As he and Bran fight their way up a ridge, they are surrounded by fire on one side and ghostly gray foxes, the sheep-killers, on the other. Cafall challenges the leader; Will invokes a spell, and he, Bran, and the dog find themselves transported—through another time and place and a trip into starry heavens—to a great chamber where three Lords of High Magic, robed and hooded, are enthroned. Using the clues he has found in the poem, Will explains that he is accompanied by the raven boy and has come for the golden harp. The men test Will and Bran with three riddles. When they answer correctly, one Lord reveals himself as Merriman, but another, a Lord of the Dark, gives a cry of rage and disappears when Will takes up the golden harp. Bran is able to play the magic harp to save them from the fury of the Grey King's north wind as they return to the Welsh valley, and they hide the harp as they come down the mountain.

Before they reach home, Caradog Prichard shoots Cafall when he sees the dog leaping toward a sheep. Only the boys could see that a gray fox, Cafall's target, was attacking the sheep, and only John Rowlands notices there is no sheep's blood on the dead dog. Bran's despondency over the loss of his dog brings up the strange circumstances of his arrival in the valley as a baby, brought by his mother, Gwen. John Rowlands tells Will as much as he knows of the story—that Bran's mother had vanished, leaving her baby behind. Owen Davies, who loved Gwen, adopted Bran.

When Will goes to fetch the harp, he is confronted by Prichard and uses his powers as an Old One to put the man under a spell. But Will, in turn, is confronted by the voice of the Grey King, who warns that the Dark is rising. At the farm Prichard insists that the Evans's sheep dog Pen is the one attacking his sheep. Will knows it is one of the Grey King's foxes turning itself into Pen's black shape. To protect Pen, Will and John Rowlands take the dog to Idris Jones's farm. On the way John, who seems aware of Will's double role, points out that good people in the valley can be hurt by the Light's pursuit of its goal. Will, as a boy, thinks of Bran's loss of his dog; but as an Old One, he thinks of his master, Merriman, and tells John there is only one destiny for the Light: to save the world from the Dark—at times, despite the individual cost.

At the farm of Idris Jones, Will finds that the neighboring lake has a name in the poem. Idris tells him a dead sheep is on the mountain, and they climb up to discover the body of the ewe that vanished. On starting down, Will has a serious fall. He is resting in a field when Bran appears to warn him that Caradog Prichard is coming to shoot Pen. The boys try to intercept Prichard at the cottage from which the sheep disappeared—the same cottage, Will now knows, in which Gwen abandoned Bran. But the power of the Grey King has transfixed Pen flat to the floor. Will tries a spell to release Pen, but it only reveals the presence of a warestone belonging to the Dark—a pebble that conveys information to, and power from, the Grey King.

Will leaves Bran with Pen and bicycles to the Evans's farm for the golden harp. He tells Owen Davies where Bran is, and the man goes to the cottage, fearing the same power which took Gwen away will take Bran. Owen shows the boy the note his mother left, and Bran then has a vision of Merriman taking his mother away. Feeling a new power in himself, Bran calls out to Pen, and the dog leaps up and they run to the moor. Owen Davies drives off to the Jones's farm. When Will reaches the cottage, it is empty except for the warestone which he appropriates. Through it he learns more about Bran and his mother and then bicycles to the Jones's farm by the lake.

Prichard lies in wait for Will. The man grabs for the bundle containing the harp, and Will immediately becomes an Old One in a full blaze of power—which calls up the wrath of the Grey King. Prichard is caught between the two powers, as six swans seem to warn him and a great wave on the lake threatens to inundate everything. Will watches Prichard accept help from the Dark and knows he must use the harp. As Will plays, the lake calms and he sees six horsemen, the Sleepers, ride out of the mountain toward Bran, who is waiting on a ledge. They salute Bran and disappear. Prichard also sees Bran, with Pen beside him and

Owen Davies nearby. Prichard tears the harp away from Will, throws it into the lake, and tries to shoot Pen. John Rowlands stops him, however, and in the accusations that follow, Will learns that Prichard had long ago seen Gwen playing the harp and had wanted Bran's mother for himself and that Prichard believed Cafall to be a dog belonging to Bran's father. This statement makes Bran aware that his father had a dog named Cafall; and it reminds Will that a great king, Arthur, had had a dog named Cafall. Will realizes that Bran must truly be the Pendragon, the son of Arthur and Guinevere. Prichard attacks Bran and Owen Davies, but John Rowlands knocks him down and, abandoned by the Dark, Prichard falls from the mountain, while Will watches the ghost foxes rush into the lake and disappear.

Newbery Medal Acceptance

by Susan Cooper

This year marks the centennial of the American Library Association and the bicentennial of the United States of America. It says a great deal for the rugged independence of the Children's Services Division that they should choose such an anniversary to award the Newbery Medal to a Limey.

A very nervous Limey, too. Not for that reason: I do, after all, live near Boston, where the history of the wicked British pursues me at every turn. Especially as recounted by my American children. No. My problem is one aspect of the Newbery familiar to those of you who have attended this ceremony before—the fact that the winner, accustomed to solitude as a hermit to his cell, can traditionally be expected to stand up here, before two thousand faces, absolutely rigid with fear.

I did think I'd found a way to overcome this problem. I happen to be very, very short-sighted. I should need only to remove my glasses, I thought, to be unable to see any one of these unnerving faces. I might even see something quite different. As one of my fellow-sufferers, James Thurber, once said, "Those of us who are half blind are luckier than you think. Where the rest of you see a paper bag blowing down the street, we see an old lady turning somersaults."

I gave up the idea about the glasses when I realized that if I couldn't see my audience, equally I shouldn't be able to see my speech. But Thurber's remark stuck in my head. He might just as well have been talking about another kind of minority group than the myopic: those of us who write books—like *The Grey King*—which are classified as fantasy. We live in the same world as the rest of you. Its realities are the same. But we perceive them differently.

We see around corners. It's a little like abstract painting, or poetry—and not at all like the realistic novel. The material of fantasy is myth, legend, folk tale; the mystery of dream, and the greater mystery of Time. With all that haunting our minds, it isn't surprising that we write stories about an ordinary world in which extra-ordinary things happen.

Nor is it surprising that we should be read, today, mainly by children. Most of us, mind you, have no idea whether we are writing books for children or for adults. We write the book that wants to be written, and let our publishers tell us what it is. (And there I am luckier than most, since Margaret McElderry is the wisest and most sensitive editor-publisher I have ever known, anywhere.) But even though more adults are reading fantasy these days—in a flight, perhaps, from the realities of the machine back to the older realities of myth—even so, children are the natural audience for fantasy. They aren't a different species. They're us, a little while ago. It's just that they are still able to accept mystery. They don't bat an eye when you present them, within the framework of the world they know, with things like a flying horse, candles which burn bitter cold, a house in which yesterday will take place tomorrow. Nothing shakes them. Experience hasn't yet interrupted their long discovery. They still know the essence of wonder, which is to live without ever being quite sure what to expect. And therefore, quite often, to encounter delight.

Those of us who work in the arts—people like Leo and Diane and me—we never know quite what to expect either. Once upon a time, when I was about twenty-five years old, writing features for the Sunday *Times* in London, the Literary Editor of the paper came into my office one day and dropped a press release on my desk. He said, "Read that. You ought to try it."

It was a notice from an English publishing house called Ernest

Benn Limited. They'd been the original publishers of E. Nesbit, and in her honor they were offering a prize for what they called "a family adventure story." There was a deadline, and being a journalist I liked deadlines. (Needed them. I still do.) And it sounded like fun—so I did try. I invented three children called Simon, Jane, and Barney, and a rather vague plot about villainy and hidden treasure. And I wrote a first chapter in which they traveled down from London to Cornwall by train for a summer holiday, as my brother and I had done as children.

And then a funny thing began to happen. The story, somehow, took over. My children were met at their destination by a very strange great-uncle named Merriman (why did I call him Merriman? I didn't know) and before I quite knew what I was doing, the plot began to change completely. I forgot all about the E. Nesbit prize and the family adventure story—and the deadline. And I found I was writing a fantasy, full of images which had haunted me since childhood but which I'd never thought to put into fiction. In the final version I even cut that first deliberate chapter. And there I was with a book called *Over Sea, Under Stone*. Which turned out to be the first movement in a symphonic pattern of five books—one of which is the reason I'm here today.

The pattern didn't emerge for a long time. I had no intention then of writing a sequel to *Over Sea*—though I did leave it open-ended, since I'd grown fond of the characters, especially the Merlin-figure called Merriman, and I didn't want to cut myself off from them forever.

About five years went by, in the space of which I married, came to America to live, wrote a couple of adult books, and had a baby. Then one snowy day I was cross-country skiing with my husband in Massachusetts, where we live. Now skiing is not a sport which produces great conversation. You just get the odd word, like "Help!" So I was tramping along in silence, looking at the snowdrifts, seeing small trees sticking up out of the snow and thinking they looked like the antlers of deer—and then for no good reason at all, I suddenly knew that I was going to write a book, set for the most part in thick snow like this, about a small boy who woke up one birthday morning and found he was able to work magic.

I wrote the idea down, and forgot about it. I wrote two more adult books and had another baby, and three more years went by.

Then one day, something sent me back to reread the first children's book, *Over Sea, Under Stone*. Perhaps it was all my endless reading about Britain, prehistory, Britain, myth, folk tale, Britain.... This went on all the time, because I'd never really mastered my homesickness, and I suppose I never shall. I reread something I'd had the old man Merriman say, about the constant recurrence in the history of Britain of the battle between the Dark and the Light. He'd said,

"[T]he struggle between good and evil ... goes on all around us all the time, like two armies fighting. And sometimes one of them seems to be winning and sometimes the other, but neither has ever triumphed altogether. Nor ever will ... for there is something of each in every man. . . ."

And out of the shadows came again the image of the snow and the antlered snowdrifts, and the boy waking to find himself with powers he hadn't had before. And I started thinking, and scribbling, and I found coming into my head the pattern not only of that book but of the overall sequence of five, each dealing with different aspects of the long struggle. One was already written, four more were to come. So I made an outline of each, characters and plot and setting, and before I started to write the second, *The Dark Is Rising*, I wrote the last page of the very last book. That's still sitting in my file, and I shall use it—unchanged—when I find myself reluctantly reaching the place where it belongs later this year.

I would not have predicted all of that.

But of course, the whole process is a mystery, in all the arts. Creativity, in literature, painting, music. Or in performance: those rare lovely moments in a theater when an actor has the whole audience in his hand suddenly, like *that*. You may have all the technique in the world, but you can't strike that spark without some mysterious extra blessing—and none of us knows what that blessing really is. Not even the writers, who talk the most, can explain it at all.

Who knows where the ideas come from? Who knows what happens in that shadowy part of the mind, something between Plato's cave and Maeterlinck's Hall of Night, where the creative imagination hides? Who knows even where the words come from, the right rhythm and meaning and music all at once? Those of us who make books out of the words and ideas have less of an answer than anyone. All we know is that marvelous feeling that comes, sometimes, like a break of sunshine in a cloud-grey sky, when through all the research and concentration and slog—suddenly you are writing, fluently and fast, with every sense at high pitch and yet in a state almost like trance. Suddenly, for a time, the door is open, the magic is working; a channel exists between the page and that shadowy cave in the mind.

But none of us will ever know why, or how.

Just one thing can, perhaps, be charted, and that's the *kind* of stories that are told. If only by looking back over your own work after you've done it, you can find some thread that runs through, binding it all together. The underlying theme of my *Dark Is Rising* sequence, and particularly of its fourth volume *The Grey King,* is, I suppose, the ancient problem of the duality of human nature. The endless coexistence of kindness and cruelty, love and hate, forgiveness and revenge—as inescapable as the cycle of life and death, day and night, the Light and the Dark.

And to some extent, I can see its roots. My generation, especially in Britain and Europe, was given a strong image of good and bad at an impressionable age. We were the children of World War II. Our insecurities may not have differed in kind from those of the modern child, but they were more concrete. That *something* that might be lurking in the shadow behind the bedroom door at night wasn't, for us, a terrible formless bogeyman; it was specific—a Nazi paratrooper, with a bayonet. And the nightmares that broke into our six-year-old sleep weren't always vague and forgettable; quite often they were not only precise, but real. We knew that there would indeed be the up-and-down wail of the air-raid siren, to send us scurrying through a night criss-crossed with searchlights, down into the shelter, that little corrugated iron room buried in the back lawn, and barricaded with sandbags and turf. And then there would be the drone of the bombers, the thudding of anti-aircraft fire from the guns at the end of the road, and the crash of bombs coming closer, closer all the time.

We took it all for granted, of course, like the gas masks we carried to school each day, the bits of shrapnel we collected after every air raid, the sight of Father's rifle and steel helmet in the polite English umbrella stand. And many families, like my own, were lucky; we were never physically hurt, we simply had a rather noisy war. But I don't think the sensation of threat, of an incomprehensible looming menace, ever went away.

The experience of war, like certain other accidents of circumstance, can teach a child more than he or she realizes about the dreadful ubiquity of man's inhumanity to man. And if the child grows up to be a writer, in a world which seems to learn remarkably little from its history, then the writing will be haunted.

Haunted, and trying to communicate the haunting. Whether explicitly, or through the buried metaphor of fantasy, it will be trying always to say to the reader: Look, this is the way things are. The conflict that's in this story is everywhere in life, even in your own nature. It's frightening, but try not to be afraid. Ever. Look, learn, remember, this is the kind of thing you'll have to deal with yourself, one day, out there.

Perhaps a book can help with the long, hard matter of growing up, just a little. Maybe, sometimes.

Thank you for giving me the Newbery Medal. The encouragement it brings is impossible to describe. But don't forget, Newbery winners come and go. Midsummer monarchs, that's what we are: set up, and honored, and then, by a natural rhythm, replaced. The real continuity, in this matter of keeping a channel between the imagination of the writer and the development of the child, is made year in and year out by you—librarians, teachers, storytellers, publishers. You remember—every one of us here does—that wonderful feeling of going into a library when you're young and have much yet to read. It's like entering Aladdin's cave: all those books, all that delight, waiting. And someone there to say, "Hey—try this one. It's good."

That's the channel of communication that *you* keep open, and without it we the writers would be powerless. The centennial of the American Library Association makes a happy moment to celebrate the fact. So—happy birthday, ladies and gentlemen. Please keep up the good work for at least another hundred years.

BIOGRAPHICAL NOTE

Zoe Dominic

Susan Cooper
by Margaret K. McElderry

Susan Cooper is one of the small and very select company of writers who—somehow, somewhere—have been touched by magic; the gift of creation is theirs, the power to bring to life for ordinary mortals "the best of symbolic high fantasy." Where does such a gift originate? How is it manifested? These are questions never wholly answerable since they lead back to the ultimate mystery of birth, but they are intensely interesting to pursue, and the pursuit is infinitely rewarding though never concluded. The impact of Susan Cooper's writing, like the impact of meeting her in person, sends one off on this pursuit, to seek answers to the unanswerable, to gain insight and treasure along the way.

Modest, reserved, with a quick, shy smile, and filled with ready wit and humor, Susan conveys immediately a shining sense of life, of sharp, clear individuality, of intense and brilliant inner resources, of strong purpose and definite intention—all firmly controlled by a well-disciplined, well-schooled mind and heart. To know her, to work with her is an unending, constantly renewing joy and delight.

Aware that Susan had broken off an extremely successful

career in journalism as a feature writer for the eminent Sunday *Times* of London when she married a distinguished American scientist and came to live in the United States, I wondered why someone who has been recognized on both sides of the Atlantic as an outstanding creative writer had chosen journalism at the start. Though not mutually exclusive, the two kinds of writing are not as a rule equally attractive to writers, who tend to find their niche early in one field or the other. How had Susan been led to the Sunday *Times*?

The first eighteen years of her life were spent in Buckinghamshire, England, the setting of *The Dark Is Rising* (Atheneum), the second book in her five-book sequence called by the same title. She grew up knowing that reading was an important part of life. Her home was full of books and music, reflecting her parents' interests. Despite World War II and its aftermath, she and her brother, as children, were taken to London to the pantomime, to the theater for such plays as *Peter Pan,* to concerts, and to Gilbert and Sullivan operettas. But looking back, she realizes that radio was an important part of her life, too. At that time—in the 1940s—*Children's Hour* was a regular program on the BBC. It featured "marvelous and intelligent dramatizations of books," Susan recalls. She remembers particularly John Masefield's *The Midnight Folk* and *Box of Delights.* Programs like these played a great part in awakening her imagination. Years later, as a journalist, she met David Davies who planned the music for *Children's Hour,* produced plays for it, and in time ran the program. It was a curious sensation to hear his voice in the present as an echo from the time when she was a ten-year-old.

Susan has no conscious recollection of learning the old tales and legends of Buckinghamshire. They seem always to have been a part of her, acquired "by osmosis," as she puts it. The great oak tree of Herne the Hunter, the tree where Will Stanton and the Hunter meet in *The Dark is Rising,* was a familiar sight; so were Bronze Age barrows and Saxon and Norman churches. "It's all part of daily living in England," Susan says. "There were tramps and there was a Tramps Alley, as in *The Dark Is Rising.* There were Roman villas nearby where we went on school trips." Her strong imagination was nurtured by the ancient land in which she lived. An extra influence at this time was *The Land,* a book by

Jacquetta Hawkes about England—the long and ancient history of its countryside, the land itself.

At eighteen, Susan left Buckinghamshire to become an undergraduate at Oxford in Somerville College, studying for an honors degree in English Language and Literature. Two of the professors whose lectures she was to attend were C. S. Lewis and J.R.R. Tolkien.

In the great tradition of English universities, extracurricular activities for undergraduates are fully as important as lectures and study. Lacking the self-confidence to become involved in her deepest interest—the theater—Susan chose instead the university undergraduate newspaper, *Cherwell*, and won a place on it as a reporter, thus beginning her journalistic pursuits. In time she became the first woman editor of *Cherwell*. All of this gave her valuable experience, and she also got to know some of the top London newspaper people who came to lecture at Oxford.

By the time she graduated, Susan was totally committed to writing. The only way to earn a living by writing, however, was journalism—not by writing books or plays—so against everyone's advice she set out to find a job in London. A Saturday job with one of the large London tabloids was terminated because Susan was not aggressive enough as a reporter. She refused to climb over the wall of a country estate, where Arthur Miller and Marilyn Monroe were staying, to get an interview! On weekdays, she worked for a man who was publishing lists of jobs for university graduates. Then came an offer from the Sunday *Times* to cover the rose growers' annual show in London as a free-lance assignment. It was fun to meet and talk to the growers, but Susan could not find a real lead with which to begin her story. Just as she was leaving the show, she heard an old lady inquire of a grower, "How far apart should I keep my Passions?" Susan had her lead and went off triumphantly! The Sunday *Times* liked her piece, and she was offered a job by Ian Fleming, who was writing the "Atticus" column for the paper at that time. "He was a tall, elegant man with a bow tie," Susan says. "A poppet—but I was scared to death of him!" This was the beginning of her years as reporter, staff writer, and eventually feature writer for the Sunday *Times*, which was just at the start of an exciting period of expansion and development.

Susan's first writing for children began by happenstance. The art editor started a feature called "Mainly for Children." It was illustrated with photographs or drawings, and staff members took turns writing it. Susan's first article for it was based on Malory (a great love of hers at Oxford) and was called, "Who Was King Arthur?" Other subjects ranged from pantomime to steam-engine railway trains. Because her father, grandfather, and great-grandfather had all worked for the Great Western Railway, Susan was allowed to ride from London to Bristol, standing on the footplate of a steam engine with the driver and fireman, the only woman ever permitted to do so except Princess Elizabeth.

This work led Susan toward the world of children's books, and before long she began to write *Over Sea, Under Stone* (Harcourt), the first book in her five-book sequence. Because Jonathan Cape Ltd. was the publisher of Arthur Ransome's books, which Susan had loved as a child, she sent her manuscript to Cape. It was accepted—and it was published in England (1965) just after Susan Cooper married Nicholas Grant and moved to this country.

Her adult science fiction novel, *Mandrake,* had come out in England just before that (1964). *Dawn of Fear* (Harcourt), her second book for children, was published first in the United States (1970) and later in England. A powerful, realistic story of wartime England, it is not part of the sequence. By then Susan had published two other books for adults: *Behind the Golden Curtain* (Scribner, 1965), a study of the U. S. A., and *J. B. Priestley* (Harper, 1970), a biography of a long-time friend, the English writer.

It was here, in the United States, that the rest of the five-book sequence took shape in her imagination. Susan likens the books to the movements of a symphony. Each is set in a specific season—Lammas, Christmas, Halloween, Midsummer—times when magic is strong over the land. Susan made voluminous notes to herself on images from myth and folklore, reflections on good and evil, interlaced with jottings about possible scenes, character interactions, and plot developments. Eventually, she wrote the last page of the fifth and last book in the sequence, *Silver on the Tree.* Then she began to write *The Dark Is Rising.*

To have *The Dark Is Rising* (1973) singled out as the only Newbery Honor Book in 1974 was a tremendously encouraging event for Susan, who was still undergoing a process of adjustment in her new country. She was also still shy. When she attended the Newbery-Caldecott banquet at ALA in New York City that year, after one unbelieving look at the nearly 2000 people in the audience, she turned to me and whispered, "I don't believe I ever want to win the Newbery!"

There followed *Greenwitch* (Atheneum, 1974), a shorter, less dense book, which Susan considers to be a sort of rondo in her sequence. Its setting is again Cornwall. In *The Grey King* (Atheneum, 1975), the setting changes to North Wales, the third important geographic location in Susan's life. It was her grandmother's home—and is now her parents'—and, as with Buckinghamshire and Cornwall, Susan knows it well. The fifth and last book of the sequence, *Silver on the Tree* (to be published in 1977 by Atheneum), also takes place in Wales.

Her years as a writer, both in and out of journalism, have given Susan Cooper a sure command of the English language. She uses it as a fine instrument to achieve her purpose. But the deep, subconscious well-springs from which her true creation comes are not subject to command. Susan likens the sense of revelation that comes at moments of imaginative breakthrough to Will Stanton's opening the great carved doors on the snowy hillside that led him into the vast hall where he first met Merriman Lyon and the Lady in *The Dark Is Rising*.

Though England is the home of powerful, ancient magic, here in our own United States the magic still goes on for Susan and for those near her. On a lovely May evening last year, she and I were walking through a meadow that borders a salt marsh pond near my home in Rhode Island. Susan had mentioned earlier that the first chapter of *Silver on the Tree,* all she had written so far, was giving her some trouble, and she wondered if we might have half an hour the next morning to talk about it. But this evening, in the long, lingering light, we were relaxed and peaceful. As we neared the pond, we saw two lovely white swans in stately transit through the still water.

"There are two swans in my first chapter," Susan said quietly. A few minutes later she exclaimed—with a sense of urgency that surprised me—"Look at that huge bumblebee out so late." It *was* a big bee, but I was mystified by her excitement. "There's a bumblebee in my first chapter," she said. We walked on. I began telling her casually of a black fisher, a kind of mink, that we had seen only once in that same meadow, a species of animal that had never before or since been known in that area. She was silent for a moment. Then, "But there's a black mink in my first chapter," Susan said. The next morning, when I came downstairs, she was already outside, cutting dead blossoms from the daffodils.

"When do you want to talk about the first chapter?" I asked.

"Oh," she replied airily, "last night's magic worked. It all came right this morning and I've worked it out. There *is* magic here, you know."

Music and song, old tales and legends, prose and poetry, theater and reality, imagination and intellect, power and control, a strong sense of place and people both past and present—all are part of the magic that has touched Susan Cooper. She is undismayed by the challenge of crossing borders old and new, physical and metaphysical. Her journeys add great luster to the world of literature.

The Newbery Medal 1977

ROLL OF THUNDER, HEAR MY CRY

written by MILDRED D. TAYLOR

published by THE DIAL PRESS 1976

BOOK NOTE

Cassie Logan lives in rural Mississippi near Vicksburg with Big Ma, her grandmother; her brothers, Stacey, Christopher-John, and Little Man; and Mama. Papa is often away laying railroad track. Despite the Depression the family feels more secure than other Black families because they are landowners and with hard work can pay their taxes and mortgage. Mama teaches at Great Faith Elementary and Secondary School, which the Logan children attend. At first their problems seem no more complex than being splashed by the bus carrying white children; sorting out the slippery behavior of their schoolmate, T.J. Avery; or handling the unsought attention of a white boy who wants to make friends. The children are aware, however, that two men named Berry have been doused with kerosene and badly burned by the keepers of the local store, the Wallaces.

On the first day of school Little Man refuses to take a book because it is so dirty. Cassie objects, too, when she finds lists showing that each book has been handed over in "very poor" condition to the "nigra" race after long use in white schools. Little Man is switched by his teacher, and Cassie is reprimanded. Before Mrs. Logan hands similar books to her class, she pastes brown paper over the offensive lists.

Papa returns for a quick visit and brings a strong Black man, Mr. Morrison, to stay on the farm. Before Papa leaves he forbids the children to go to the Wallace store. During the autumn rains, the bus for the white children drenches the Logans one time too many. At lunch hour they dig a ditch across the road, and the driver mires the bus in it. The white kids have to slog home, but the elation Cassie and her brothers feel is short-lived: A neighbor tells the family the "night-men" are riding, and Cassie wonders if it is because of the bus accident. Later she watches the parade of cars start to turn into their yard; when they leave, she sees Mr. Morrison cross the yard carrying a shotgun. Cassie's sick feeling is not cured by hearing, through T.J., that the night-riders went on to tar and feather a Black man who had a complaint against a storekeeper, Jim Lee Barnett, in Strawberry.

Stacey is caught in class with cheat notes that T.J. tricked him into holding, and he is whipped by the teacher—his mother. After school T.J. takes refuge at the Wallace store, but the Logan kids disobey their father and go looking for him. Stacey and T.J. fight until Mr. Morrison breaks it up and takes the Logan kids home. There they find that Harlan Granger, the white man who owns most of the nearby land and wants their property, has been hassling Big Ma. Stacey confesses that he went to find T.J. at the Wallace store, and the next day Mama takes the children on a long wagon ride to see the barely surviving Mr. Berry. The children then understand about boycotting the store and about Mama's stopping at each farm on the way back to urge that none of the children go there. She also urges that they buy their supplies in Vicksburg but finds too many families are on credit at Wallace's and are continually getting deeper in debt.

Big Ma takes Cassie, Stacey, and T.J. to Strawberry on market day. The children take their family shopping lists into Barnett's store, but the man keeps waiting on white people, and when Cassie objects, Barnett asks "whose little nigger" she is. Cassie makes a scene, and Stacey gets her out of the store quickly. Then she accidentally bumps into a white girl, Lillian Jean Simms, who demands an apology and tells her to get off the sidewak. Cassie apologizes but won't step down into the mud. Lillian Jean's father shoves her down, and Cassie feels further betrayed when Big Ma forces her, as a crowd gathers, to apologize to *Miz* Lillian Jean. Cassie won't accept Stacey's explanation that Big Ma had no choice.

Uncle Hammer Logan arrives from the North in his silver Packard for his Christmas visit and has to be restrained from going after Mr. Simms when he hears about Cassie's humiliation. Mama tries to convince Cassie that white people believe they are better than Blacks but that Blacks do have some choice as to what they make of their lives despite their circumstances.

Cassie and the boys enjoy dressing up and going to church in Uncle Hammer's car. Stacey looks particularly fine in a warm coat, a gift from Uncle Hammer. Later he unfortunately lets T.J. con him out of the coat.

While Papa is home for Christmas, Big Ma has the white lawyer Mr. Jamison come, and she deeds over the land to her two sons. The men and Mama tell Mr. Jamison how they want local families to boycott the Wallace store but in order to do that, they would all need to have their credit backed in Vicksburg. They want to put the land up, but Mr. Jamison, a sympathetic man who doesn't like what the Wallaces and the night-riders are doing, says he'll back the credit. When Harlan Granger hears what the Logans are doing, he threatens them and says they'll lose their land anyway.

Meanwhile the children are involved in their own problems. Cassie works out a scheme to get even with Lillian Jean. After pretending to be her willing slave, she takes her into the woods and beats her up. T.J. is caught cheating by Mrs. Logan, who punishes him; but then Kaleb Wallace, Mr. Granger, and the rest of the school board fire Mrs. Logan because T.J. has reported she destroyed school property—when she pasted over the objectionable lists in the books. Stacey convinces the kids at school to boycott T.J., and he starts hanging around with two older white boys, R.W. and Melvin Simms.

By late spring Harlan Granger and the other landowners raise what they take from the Black sharecroppers from fifty to sixty per cent because they are shopping in Vicksburg. Most families can't live on forty per cent, but Papa finds some who can still cooperate. He and Stacey and Mr. Morrison go to Vicksburg for supplies, and on their return they are attacked by the Wallaces. Papa is shot and then run over by the wagon. Later the Wallaces hassle Mr. Morrison when he has Cassie and her brothers in the wagon, but Mr. Morrison strong-arms their truck off the road.

While Papa is recovering, the Logans learn that T.J. is up to no good with the Simms brothers. Tensions are already high when the bank in Strawberry notifies the Logans they will have to pay off the rest of their mortgage on the land immediately. Papa phones Uncle Hammer who has gone up North, and he sells his car to pay off the mortgage.

One night T.J., badly hurt, comes to Stacey for help. The Simms brothers and T.J. broke into Barnett's store, and when Mr. Barnett discovered them, one of the brothers hit him with an axe. Then the Simms boys beat up T.J. so he wouldn't tell who did it. T.J. wants to get home before the sheriff from Strawberry comes to find him. A thunderstorm is working up as Stacey, Cassie, and the two younger Logans help T.J. home. They start back from the Averys' just as a parade of night-riders arrives, including the Simms brothers. The children hide, but they can see all the Averys being dragged out and know that T.J. is about to be lynched.

Suddenly Mr. Jamison arrives and tries to get the night-riders to turn T.J. over to him and the sheriff. Frustrated, the mob threatens to go after the other troublemakers, Papa and Mr. Morrison. Stacey stays to see what happens to T.J. but sends Cassie and the younger boys to warn Papa. Papa and Mr. Morrison leave the house, and soon after, Cassie realizes the woods and the cotton fields are on fire. Everyone—white, Black, landowner, sharecropper, adult, child—turns out to fight the fire and save the cotton crop. The Logans have lost a good bit of their cotton, but Cassie realizes her father set the fire to stop the lynching; although T.J. does have to go to jail, his life has been saved. Cassie comes to understand the inequities and hardships of the world she lives in and what difficult things people often have to do to survive.

Newbery Medal Acceptance
by Mildred D. Taylor

As a small child I loved the South. I used to look forward with eager anticipation to the yearly trips we took there when my father would pack the car and my mother would fry chicken, bake a cake and sweet-potato pies, stir up jugs of ice water and lemonade, and set them all in a basket on the back seat of the car between my sister and me. In my early years the trip was a marvelous adventure, a twenty-hour picnic that took us into another time, another world; down dusty red roads and across creaky wooden bridges into the rich farm country of Mississippi, where I was born.

And life was good then. Running barefoot in the heat of the summer sun, my skin darkening to a soft, umber hue; chasing butterflies in the day, fireflies at night; riding an old mule named Jack and a beautiful mare named Lady; even picking a puff of cotton or two—there seemed no better world. And at night when neighboring relatives would gather to sit on the moonlit porch or by the heat of the fire, depending on the season, talk would turn to the old people, to friends and relatives who then seemed to have lived so long ago. As the storytellers spoke in animated voices and enlivened their stories with movements of great gusto, I used to sit transfixed, listening, totally engrossed. It was a magical time.

Yet even magical times must end.

I do not remember how old I was when the stories became more than tales of faraway people, but rather, reality. I do not remember when the twenty-hour picnic no longer was a picnic, the adventure no longer an adventure. I only remember that one summer I suddenly felt a climbing nausea as we crossed the Ohio River into Kentucky and was again admonished by my parents that my sister and I were now in the South and must remain quiet when we pulled into the gas stations, that we must not ask to use the restrooms, that they would do all the talking.

That summer and the summers to come I grew to realize that the lovely baskets of food my mother always packed for the trips, she prepared because we could not eat in the restaurants; that the long overnight ride was because we could not sleep in the motels; that the jugs of water and lemonade were because we could not drink at the water fountains—at least not the fountains marked "White Only," which were usually newer and cleaner. I was to learn the fear of the police siren. I was to learn to hate the patrolmen who frisked my father and made him spread-eagle—all because of thirty-five miles per hour. I was to learn the terror of the back road and the long, long wait for morning while my father, exhausted from the drive, tried to sleep as my mother watched guard.

Those were hard things for a child to learn. But I was blessed with a special father, a man who had unyielding faith in himself and his abilities, and who, knowing himself to be inferior to no one, tempered my learning with his wisdom. In the foreword to *Roll of Thunder, Hear My Cry* I described my father as a master storyteller; he was much more than that. A highly principled, complex man who did not have an excellent education or a white-collar job, he had instead strong moral fiber and a great wealth of what he always said was simply plain common sense. Throughout my childhood he impressed upon my sister and me that we were somebody, that we were important and could do or be anything we set our minds to do or be. He was not the kind of father who demanded A's on report cards, although he was pleased when we got them, or ranted and raved if there was a D or two. He was more concerned about how we carried ourselves, how we respected ourselves and others, and how we pursued the principles upon which he hoped we would build our lives.

There was never a moment when he was too busy or too tired to share my problems or to give guidance to my sister and me. Through him my growing awareness of a discriminatory society was accompanied by a wisdom that taught me that anger in itself was futile, that to fight discrimination I needed a stronger weapon. When my family was refused seating in a Wyoming restaurant, he taught me that I must gain the skill to destroy such bigotry; when "For Sale" signs forested the previously all-white neighborhood into which we had moved, he taught me pride in our new home as well as in myself by reminding me that how I saw myself was more important than how others saw me; and when I came home from school one day versed in propaganda against the Soviet Union, he softly reminded me that Black people in the United States of the fifties had no more rights than I had been told the citizens of the Soviet Union had. From that I learned to question, to reason.

The effects of those teachings upon me are evident to anyone reading *Roll of Thunder, Hear My Cry*. Also evident are the strong family ties. Through David Logan have come the words of my father, and through the Logan family the love of my own family. If people are touched by the warmth of the Logans, it is because I had the warmth of my own youthful years from which to draw. If the Logans seem real, it is because I had my own family upon which to base characterizations. And if people believe the book to be biographical, it is because I have tried to distill the essence of Black life, so familiar to most Black families, to make the Logans an embodiment of that spiritual heritage; for, contrary to what the media relate to us, all Black families are not fatherless or disintegrating. Certainly my family was not.

During my childhood a family that offered aunts and uncles who were second parents, and cousins who were like brothers and sisters, was as natural to me as a mother and father are to most children. Even today the family remains a tight, extensive group, as Phyllis Fogelman, editor-in-chief of Dial, found out in early February when we were both in Washington celebrating the announcement of the Newbery-Caldecott awards with the Dillons and the rest of the Dial family. As Phyllis continued to glow from the yet unbelievable reality of the Dial sweep, I innocently asked her how many invitations I could have for the American Library Association banquet in June. Phyllis, unsuspecting, said that of course my mother and sister would be invited to the banquet as Dial's guests.

My heart quickened. Only two? To Phyllis, I said: "But I'll need more than two."

Phyllis, now becoming aware of what I was leading up to, looked a bit apprehensive, but asked pleasantly, "How many will you need, Mildred?"

I began to make a silent count, coming up with a number that I didn't have the heart to hit Phyllis with on her great day. "I'll let you know," I said.

A few days later when I was settled back in the comfort of my own home with the typewriter in front of me, I brazenly typed the number I had not had the courage to speak: thirty. I could picture Phyllis falling out of her chair when she saw the letter but consoled myself with the fact that I had trimmed the list as much as I could. After all, no one could expect me to exclude these essential people, people who have supported me not only in the writing of the books but throughout my life. Phyllis, upon receiving the letter, must have sensed this, for after recovering from her initial shock she began to make arrangements for the seating of the clan.

And tonight to my great delight there sits before you and me the core of the Taylor-Davis family.

It is good to see them there, for their gathering now is exemplary of the many gatherings we had when I was a child. At those gatherings there was always time for talk, and when we children had finished all the games we could think to play, we would join the adults, soon becoming enraptured by their talk, for it would often turn to a history which we heard only at home, a history of Black people told through stories.

Those stories about the small and often dangerous triumphs of Black people, those stories about human pride and survival in a cruelly racist society were like nothing I read in the history books or the books I devoured at the local library. There were no Black heroes or heroines in those books; no beautiful Black ladies, no handsome Black men; no people filled with pride, strength, or endurance. There was, of course, always mention of Booker T. Washington and George Washington Carver; Marian Anderson and occasionally even Dr. Ralph Bunche. But that hardly compensated for the lackluster history of Black people painted by those books, a history of a docile, subservient people happy with their fate who did little or nothing to shatter the chains that bound them, both before and after slavery. There was obviously a terrible contradiction between what the books said and what I had learned from my family, and at no time did I feel the contradiction more than when I had to sit in a class which, without me, would have been all white, and relive that prideless history year after year.

As I grew, and the writers of books and their publishers grew, I noticed a brave attempt to portray Black people with a white sense of dignity and pride. But even those books disturbed me, for the Black people shown were still subservient. Most often the Black characters were housekeepers and, though a source of love and strength to the white child whose story it was, they remained one-dimensional because the view of them was a white one. Books about Black families by white writers also left me feeling empty, not because a white person had attempted to write about a Black family, but because the writer had not, in my opinion, captured the warmth or love of the Black world and had failed to understand the principles upon which Black parents brought up their children and taught them survival. It was not that these writers intentionally omitted such essential elements; it was simply that not having lived the Black experience, they did not know it.

But I did know it. And by the time I entered high school, I had a driving compulsion to paint a truer picture of Black people. I wanted to show the endurance of the Black world, with strong fathers and concerned mothers; I wanted to show happy, loved children about whom other children, both Black and white, could say: "Hey, I really like them! I feel what they feel." I wanted to show a Black family united in love and pride, of which the reader would like to be a part.

I never doubted that one day I would grasp that bright spark of life in words for others to see, for hadn't my father always said I could do anything I set my mind to do? But as the years passed and what I wrote continued to lack the vitality of the world I knew, there began to grow within a very youthful me an overwhelming impatience, and the question: *when?*

Well, the *when* was not to come until almost four years ago, after I had seen much of the world, returned to school for graduate study, and become a Black student activist. It was then that on a well-remembered day in late September a little girl named Cassie Logan suddenly appeared in my life. Cassie was a spunky eight-year-old, innocent, untouched by discrimination, full of pride, and greatly loved, and through her I discovered I now could tell one of the stories I had heard so often as a child. From that meeting came *Song of the Trees*.

If you have met Cassie and her brothers—Stacey, the staunch, thoughtful leader; Christopher-John, the happy, sensitive mediator; and Little Man, the shiny clean, prideful, manly six-year-old—then perhaps you can understand why, when I sent that manuscript off to Dial, I did not want to give them up. Those four children make me laugh; they also make me cry, and I had to find a way of keeping them from fading into oblivion. In August, 1974, came the answer: I would write another book about the Logans, one in which I could detail the teachings of my own childhood as well as incorporate many of the stories I had heard about my family and others. Through artistic prerogative I could weave into those stories factual incidents about which I had read or heard, as well as my own childhood feelings to produce a significant tapestry which would portray rural Black southern life in the 1930s. I would write *Roll of Thunder, Hear My Cry*.

Writing is a very lonely business. It is also a very terrifying one emotionally if a writer knows and cares about the people of her novel as well as I know and care about the Logans. Cassie's fears were my fears and what she feared from the night men, so did I. More than once my dreams were fraught with burnings and destruction, with faceless men coming in the night, with a boy being beaten, with a boy about to die. In September 1975, the month I had promised Phyllis and Regina Hayes, my editors, the first draft of the book, I found I could not write the final chapters, all of which dealt with explicit violence. I wanted to forget about the book. I began to wish that I had never gotten into it, that I had never signed a contract which obligated me to finish it, for I hate violence and I dreaded writing about it. But with October on its way, I knew I had to force myself to write those chapters. Feeling the pressure of my own deadline, I worked and worked with the final pages trying to make them catch fire and burn with passions of fear and anger and hate—but they still had no life.

Finally one Saturday afternoon after I had retyped the manuscript to send to Phyllis and Regina, I looked once more at those chapters. Frustrated and angry with myself because my words were too limited, my power too weak to convey what I knew the Logans felt, because I had failed where I could not fail, my mind seemed to snap. Rage welled within me, and I sent all two-hundred-plus sheets of the manuscript spinning into the air. Then I began to let fly everything I could lay my hands on. It was not until I had broken a precious irreplaceable treasure, a brightly painted ostrich egg brought from Africa, that my rage passed and was replaced by an aching sorrow. Holding the pieces of that broken egg I cried for the loss of it, and for my inability to write what was inside me.

Sleep has always been a great healer for me, and I slept almost the entire weekend. Late Sunday evening I awoke perfectly calm, renewed, and with a tugging thought that I knew *why* what I had written was wrong. I had attempted to make Cassie play too big a part in the climax. I had wanted her to be with David when his leg was broken, to be with him when the fire started, to fight the fire. After all, it was she who had to tell the story and how could she if she wasn't there? But the character of David Logan wouldn't let me put her into the center of the action. I thought of my own father and what he would have done. He, like David, would never have taken his young daughter on such dangerous missions. It was clear to me now. All I had to do was allow my characters to remain true to themselves; that was the key.

I believe that that key served me well in the writing of *Roll of Thunder, Hear My Cry,* and I hope that it will continue to guide me through the next two books about the Logans, which will chronicle the growth of the Logan children into adolescence and adulthood. Winning this distinguished award makes me shiver more than a little as I realize how difficult it will be to live up to readers' expectations as well as my own. Yet I will continue the Logans' story with the same life guides that have always been mine, for it is my hope that these four books, one of the first chronicles to mirror a Black child's hopes and fears from childhood innocence to awareness to bitterness and disillusionment, will one day be instrumental in teaching children of all colors the tremendous influence that Cassie's generation—my father's generation—had in bringing about the great Civil Rights movement of the fifties and sixties. Without understanding that generation and what it and the generations before it endured, children of today and of the future cannot understand or cherish the precious rights of equality which they now possess, both in the North and in the South. If they can identify with the Logans, who are representative not only of my family but of the many Black families who faced adversity and survived, and understand the principles by which they lived, then perhaps they can better understand and respect themselves and others.

As we all know, Cassie's South of the thirties is no more. The changes have come hard but sure, and even at this moment continue. Those changes have been heralded by Black people everywhere, but most of all I think, by the thousands like my father who left the South during and after World War II. Now many of those same thousands speak with longing of returning to that land of their childhood.

My father, too, had wanted to return.

He believed that as the North in the years following the War had held opportunities for Blacks, now the opportunities were in the South and he had, even in his last days, the dream of "going back home." He had never forgotten the feel of the soft red earth. He had never forgotten the goodness of walking on acres of his own land, of knowing that land had a history that stretched back over many generations. There, next to the house which my great-grandfather had built, he hoped to build his own house, surrounding it with flowers and fruit trees, with horses and cows, tending his land with the love he had felt for it as a boy.

Yet even as he dreamed, he knew it would not be so. Once as he lay in his hospital bed, he confided to me that he would never see the land again. I protested, for I never believed that he would die, not when he was only fifty-six, not he who was so strong, the rock upon which so many of us who loved him leaned for strength and guidance. But he was wiser than I, and speaking in that voice which I had heard too often of late, a voice which held confidence and sadness but not fear, which echoed of good-bye, he said: "You know, I've always tried to be a good father. Sometimes I was hard on you and your sister, but I did what I thought was right." He paused and then spoke slowly words which I shall always remember: "You and your sister," he said, "I'm so proud of y'all."

There is a great loneliness tonight in accepting this award, for my father, the person who would have rejoiced most at my receiving it, is not here to share the moment of triumph. He once told me that I had been given a great gift by knowing how to write. He also told my uncle that I had a special mission to fulfill. I don't think he ever realized how much he contributed to either that gift or to that mission, if that mission is to open to boys and girls, men and women, another dimension of the Black experience. While he lived, there were no banquets in his honor, no awards for his achievements. Instead, his awards and his honors have come through me and I feel loving pride that I can offer them to his memory.

There are others to thank for my receiving this award—Phyllis Fogelman and Regina Hayes, editors who have been more than editors, but rather trusted friends, whose insight into what I have attempted to portray and whose faith in me has been paramount in making reality believable; my dear mother, who has always urged perseverance; my sister, grandparents, aunts, and uncles, all the family. But it is my father to whom I owe most, for without his teachings, without his words, my words would not have been. Therefore, it is now with greatest gratitude that I accept in the name of my father, Mr. Wilbert Lee Taylor, the Newbery Medal from the American Library Association for *Roll of Thunder, Hear My Cry,* one of four books drawn from his legacy.

BIOGRAPHICAL NOTE

Mildred D. Taylor
by Phyllis J. Fogelman

"A natural writer" is an overused expression I don't particularly like, but in speaking of Mildred Taylor it seems absolutely appropriate. Mildred's words flow smoothly, effortlessly, it seems, and they abound in richness, harmony, and rhythm. Her stories unfold in a full, leisurely way, well suited to and evocative of her Southern settings. Her ability to bring her characters to life and to involve her readers is remarkable. In short, Mildred is one of the few people of whom I have felt: This woman was born to write. So I was astonished when one day she confessed she had never particularly liked writing, nor did she feel she was exceptionally good at it. "But," she added, "once I had made up my mind, I had no doubts about doing it. It was just something that would happen someday. By the time I entered high school, I was confident that I would be a writer." It is this combination of natural gift and determination, a complete kind of knowing, that makes Mildred such a remarkable and forceful storyteller.

As an editor, I am tempted to go on talking about Mildred Taylor, the author, forever, but it seems more appropriate here to set forth some facts about her life. Mildred was born in Jackson, Mississippi. When she was three weeks old, her father was involved in a racial incident that brought home to him once again the precarious position of Blacks in Mississippi, and on the same day he decided to leave the South. Although her mother cried, taking things out of his suitcase as fast as he put them in, he would not change his mind; and that night he was on a train headed for Toledo, Ohio. By the time Mildred was three months old, he had found a job and sent for his wife and two young daughters.

Consequently Mildred grew up in Toledo, but the family's roots were in the South, where they returned as often as possible. Mildred attended Toledo schools which, although integrated city-wide at the high-school level, used a system of grouping by so-called ability levels that worked against Black children coming from inferior neighborhood schools. As a result she often found herself the only Black student in the college preparatory courses, and because of this she competed all the harder. English was her best subject, and her senior class prophecy was certainly on target: "The well-known journalist Mildred Taylor," it read, "is displaying her Nobel Prize winning novel...."

As Mildred tells it, "I'm afraid I was one of those students who was a class officer, an editor of the school newspaper, and a member of the honor society, when what I really wanted to be was a cheerleader. I remember how disappointed I was when I failed to make the cheerleading squad and my father telling me that I had greater things cut out for me. Believe me," she adds, "that wasn't much consolation then!"

Mildred often speaks of her father as a determining factor in her life, the person who more than anyone else gave her a sense of worth and conviction, and this was particularly true during the years when she was becoming aware of the different directions her life might take. He taught her that all possibilities were open to her if she made up her mind that she could accomplish what she wanted.

Mildred has said that looking back she can see she made all her important decisions about life while she was quite young. The first, of course, was about writing—made when she was nine or ten. She was also determined to see the world; at sixteen she decided she would join the Peace Corps upon graduation from college. She wanted very much to be sent to Ethiopia, and from then until she was graduated from the University of Toledo, she devoured everything she could get her hands on about the Peace Corps and Ethiopia. Going to college wasn't really a decision; it was just something "I always took for granted, for I needed those four years of study to achieve my other two goals."

As it turned out, the Peace Corps did send Mildred to Ethiopia, where she taught English and history, and she recalls those years as the happiest in her adult life. She fell in love with Africa—the variety of the landscape, the sound of singing in the fields, the people who accepted and cared for her—and she has always hoped to return. As the end of her stay in Ethiopia approached, Mildred had terrible nightmares about having to leave, only to awaken each morning filled with joy that she was still there.

When she returned to the United States, Mildred recruited for the Peace Corps and then taught in one of its training programs. The following year she enrolled in the School of Journalism at the University of Colorado. Black Studies programs were just getting underway and upon receiving her master's degree, she worked in the Black Education Program as study skills coordinator.

Mildred had continued to write all along, but it wasn't until after two years in the Black Education Program that she realized she needed to concentrate more on her writing. She wanted a change of scene as well, so she moved to Los Angeles and found an eight-to-five job that called for minimum effort during the day and left her evenings free for creativity. During the California period she found out how very lonely writing is. Mildred totally separated herself from people—she went to work, she returned home, she wrote—and found that she needed something else. As she puts it, "Writing alone made me too weak emotionally; I needed an outside social force, something in which I could also be creative but which would be people-oriented in a different way. It was then that I decided to return to school to receive a degree in international training." Mildred is currently doing an internship at an international house, learning the complete operation of it so that she can set up such a house sometime in the future.

It was before Mildred returned to the east coast to begin her studies in international training that she came to our attention at Dial. She had entered the Council on Interracial Books for Children competition and won first prize in the African-American category in 1973 for *Song of the Trees*. The winning manuscripts were sent to a number of publishers, and while Mildred was in New York for the awards ceremonies, she visited several who had expressed interest in her manuscript. Dial was one. We felt an immediate rapport with Mildred, a feeling that was evidently mutual. We were immensely impressed with her dignity and self-possession and with her seriousness and sense of responsibility to herself as a writer. She not only was willing to make revisions, she welcomed any suggestions she felt would improve her book.

Her growth as a writer has been extraordinary and wonderfully exciting for us. Every small bit of editorial guidance offered was eagerly received and acted upon. When revisions on *Roll of Thunder, Hear My Cry* were complete, all of us who read the manuscript were struck by the dramatic way in which Mildred's talent had come to fruition. Her power as a writer was astonishing even to us. In retrospect one can see how the first book was the seed, the preparation for the second, but at the time we marveled at her growth. The ability to grow so remarkably attests once again to Mildred's determination and discipline.

Which brings me back to Mildred Taylor, the person. Working with Mildred over the past few years, Regina Hayes and I have learned to appreciate the great warmth and richness and humor of her nature. She is a person of strong convictions and loyalties—particularly to her unique and marvelous extended family.

Sitting at lunch a few months ago, Mildred held both of us totally spellbound as she described a Taylor family Christmas—the mouth-watering spreads of homemade pies and cakes, hams and turkeys each branch of the clan prepared; the visits throughout Christmas week to each household; the stories and anecdotes told around the fire; the hoghead *souse*—a special delicacy which her father had always prepared for the holidays. When she finished, we heaved great sighs of regret knowing we'd never experience such a holiday. So you can imagine our reaction when Mildred called recently to invite "the whole Dial family" to be guests of the Taylor family in Toledo following the ALA convention this summer. A chance to be part of that clan even for a day is an irresistible invitation!

The Newbery Medal 1978

BRIDGE TO TERABITHIA

written by KATHERINE PATERSON

illustrated by DONNA DIAMOND

published by THOMAS Y. CROWELL COMPANY 1977

BOOK NOTE

Jesse Oliver Aarons, Jr., is out in the cow pasture early in the August mornings practicing his sprints. When school starts, he wants to be the fastest runner in the fifth grade at Lark Creek Elementary School. Running and drawing animals are the two things that make him happy in an otherwise impoverished life. He has two bickering older sisters; a pestering smaller sister, May Belle; and a baby sister, Joyce Ann. His mother is disorganized and tired. His father commutes to a laborer's job in Washington, D.C. Jesse is responsible for milking the cow, Miss Bessie, and helping his mother with other chores his sisters avoid.

When a family moves into the nearby Perkins place, someone totally different comes into his life. He is unable to tell if it is a girl or a boy sitting on the fence watching him run one morning. It turns out to be Leslie Burke, a girl his age who is so self-confident that when she arrives at school wearing faded denim cut-offs, a blue tank-top, and sneakers with no socks and finds all the other kids dressed in clean Sunday best for the opening day, it doesn't bother her.

At lunch hour it is traditional for the fourth- and fifth-grade boys to run races. Jesse is eager to show how fast a runner he has become. There are so many boys that they divide into heats, and Leslie—the only girl ever to intrude—gets into his heat. Jesse is appalled when Leslie wins the heat, but he stands up for her right to run in the finals. She wins, and that is the beginning of the end of the boys' races.

The only other thing Jesse has looked forward to at school is the once-a-week music class with Miss Edmunds, who plays the guitar and teaches them songs. She is young and wears jeans, and she has praised his drawings.

Leslie's composition about her scuba diving reveals how different her background and experience has been. But when Mrs. Myers assigns a Cousteau TV program as homework, Leslie has to admit that her parents do not have, and do not want, a TV in their house. She has told Jesse that her parents, both writers, have moved to the country to reassess their "value structure." When Leslie is teased about not having a TV, Jesse feels sorry and is ready to be her friend.

After school they swing across the dry creek below the Perkins place on a rope they find hanging from an apple tree. They land by a woods and declare it a secret place. Leslie tells Jesse about fantasy kingdoms like Narnia and names their kingdom Terabithia. They build a castle from scrap wood and during the autumn spend their free time at Terabithia. When winter sets in, Jesse's friendship for Leslie is tested by his sisters and his mother; they make it uncomfortable if the girl stops by his house, and he feels out of place at her house. But Leslie is delighted by his Christmas gift of a puppy. The puppy is named Prince Terrien and made a guardian of Terabithia. Leslie gives Jesse tubes of water-color paint, brushes, and art paper, which more than make up for his otherwise difficult and disappointing family Christmas.

After the holidays, however, Jesse feels left out as Leslie helps her father refinish a room in their house. When he complains that she is always busy, she tells him to come and help. Gradually he feels easier about being with the Burkes and comfortable with their talk and their music. He works hard, stripping wallpaper and showing how handy he is with practical things. After they have sanded the floor and painted the walls gold, he realizes it is a beautiful and special room.

At Easter Leslie asks if she can attend church with the Aarons family, and Jesse's mother agrees to include her if she'll wear a dress. Leslie conforms, wearing appropriate clothing, but her reaction, relayed later to Jesse and May Belle, is that she doesn't believe everything in the Bible or that God damns people to hell if they don't believe the Bible. May Belle is worried. " 'What if you *die*?' " she asks Leslie. " 'What's going to happen to you if you *die*?' "

It is an extremely rainy spring, and the creek bed over which Jesse and Leslie swing to reach Terabithia is full of racing water. Despite this, they visit their secret kingdom often during their vacation, and Leslie, enjoying the fantasy, inquires at their sacred grove as to why evil spirits are sending such extraordinary rain. As the water keeps rising, Jesse's fear of the creek also rises. He plans to tell Leslie he will not visit Terabithia again until the creek goes down.

He has just come in from milking the cow early in the morning, when Miss Edmunds phones to invite him to go to Washington with her and see the paintings at the National Gallery. On their way Jesse thinks of how nice it would have been if Leslie were invited, too, and he looks forward to telling her about it all. He has a wonderful time and returns feeling it is the one perfect day of his life so far, only to find his whole family gathered to tell him the news: Leslie is dead. The rope broke while she was swinging across to Terabithia.

Although his parents try to be understanding and helpful, Jesse cannot face the reality and finality of Leslie's death. The three of them go to the Burke house to pay their respects. Jesse is confused by his thoughts—his wondering how Leslie would look laid out: Was she wearing blue jeans or a dress? He doesn't want to see Bill, Leslie's father, crying. Jesse is mad at Leslie for dying just when he needed her most, when he needed to conquer his fear about the creek. At home he hits May Belle hard when she asks if he saw Leslie laid out. Then in his despair he throws the paints and paper Leslie gave him into the creek.

When the Burkes take their daughter's ashes to Pennsylvania, they leave the dog, P.T., with Jesse. On a morning walk the boy and the dog find the creek is down a little and the hard rains have left a tree limb across it. Jesse crosses to Terabithia; P.T. follows him. Jesse makes a funeral wreath for the kingdom's queen, Leslie, and leaves it in the sacred grove. This makes him feel better, and when he returns to the creek to find May Belle crying with fright, halfway across the water on the limb, he patiently helps her to safety.

At school he is upset to find Leslie's desk already removed from the classroom but comforted that their teacher, Mrs. Myers, understands how he feels. When the Burkes return to move out of the Perkins place, they reclaim P.T. Jesse must rely on what Leslie did—teaching him about a new and shining kingdom—as his memory of her: "It was up to him to pay back to the world in beauty and caring what Leslie had loaned him in vision and strength." He builds a bridge across the creek and takes May Belle across it to discover Terabithia.

Newbery Medal Acceptance
by Katherine Paterson

The day after my early-morning call telling me that *Bridge to Terabithia* had won the Newbery Medal, a scene from my childhood kept replaying itself in my head. A chubby-faced eight-year-old is telling her older brother and sister what she desperately hopes is a very funny story.

"Katherine," they ask sweetly when she finishes, "did you make that up all by yourself?"

"Yes." She nods eagerly.

"Sounded like it."

You cannot see my eight-year-old self, but I promise you, she is here tonight as I accept your honor for this funny little wounded story which I made up myself and which sounds like it. It is a marvelous thing to know that it has been heard and not despised. Thank you.

When I say I made it up all by myself, that is not really true. I know how very many people are a part of its making: Lisa Hill, from whose life and death the story sprang; my husband John, who loved it first; our children, Lin, John, David, and Mary; the Womeldorf family in which I, like Jesse Aarons, was the middle child of five; the sixth-grade class I taught, or who taught me, in rural Virginia more than twenty years ago; Virginia Buckley, my editor and my friend, along with all my fellow workers at Thomas Y. Crowell; Donna Diamond with her delicate but, at the same time, powerful illustrations. My new friends at Crowell and Harper understand that I need to say a special thanks to Ann Beneduce and Sophie Silberberg, whose love and concern not only for my work but for me has meant so much to my life.

I was told that I could make a long speech, but if I mention everyone who has helped me, we'll be in Chicago until the next blizzard. So, my loving and beloved ones, I am very grateful.

The summer our son David was three years old he fell in love with bridges. I understood just how he felt, being a lover of bridges myself, and coming home from Lake George, the whole family took delight in the bridges along the way. We were spending the night with our Long Island cousins; it was well after dark, and everyone was getting cranky by the time the last bridge was crossed.

"When is the next bridge, Mommy?" David asked.

"There aren't any more," I told him. "We're almost at Uncle Arthur's house now."

"Just one more bridge, Mommy, please, just one more bridge," he said, believing in his three-year-old heart that mothers can do anything, including instant bridge building.

"There aren't any more bridges, sweetheart, we're almost there."

He began to weep. "*Please,* Mommy, just one more bridge."

Nothing we said could console him. I was at my wits' end. Why couldn't he understand that I was not maliciously withholding his heart's desire—that there was no way I could conjure up a bridge and throw it in the path of our car? When would he know that I was a human being, devoid of any magic power?

It was later that night that I remembered. The next day I could give him a bridge, and not just any bridge. The next day I could give him the Verrazano Bridge. I could hardly wait.

That is the last and only time I was given credit for building the Verrazano Bridge, but it occurs to me that I have spent a good part of my life trying to construct bridges. Usually my bridges have turned out looking much more like the bridge to Terabithia, a few planks over a nearly dry gully, than like that elegant span across the Narrows. There were so many chasms I saw that needed bridging—chasms of time and culture and disparate human nature—that I began sawing and hammering at the rough wood planks for my children and for any other children who might read what I had written.

But of course I could not make a bridge for them any more than I could conjure one up that night on Long Island. I discovered gradually and not without a little pain that you don't put together a bridge for a child. You become one—you lay yourself across the chasm.

It is there in the Simon and Garfunkel song—"Like a bridge over troubled waters/I will lay me down." The waters to be crossed are not always troubled. The land on the other side of the river may be flowing with joy, not to mention milk and honey. But still the bridge that the child trusts or delights in—and in my case, the book that will take children from where they are to where they might be—needs to be made not from synthetic or inanimate objects but from the stuff of life. And a writer has no life to give but her own.

My first three novels were set in feudal Japan, but I never considered them remote from my life. I had left Japan seven years before I wrote the first of them, but in writing them, I had a chance to become almost Japanese again, and if you know me, you know that Muna and Takiko and Jiro are me as well. Yet of all the people I have ever written about, perhaps Jesse Aarons is more nearly me than any other, and in writing this book, I have thrown my body across the chasm that had most terrified me.

I have been afraid of death since I was a child—lying stiffly in the dark, my arms glued to my sides, afraid that sleep would seduce me into a land of no awakening or of wakening into judgment.

As I grew up, the fear went underground but never really went away. Then I was forty-one years old with a husband and four children whom I loved very much, my first novel published, a second soon to be and a third bubbling along, friends I cared about in a town I delighted to live in, when it was discovered that I had cancer. I could not in any justice cry "Why me?"—for no one had been given more of the true wealth of this world than I. Surely as a card-carrying member of the human race some dues must be paid.

But even though the operation was pronounced successful and the prognosis hopeful, it was a hard season for me and my family, and just when it seemed that we were all on our feet again and beginning to get on with life, our David's closest friend was struck and killed by lightning.

If the spring and summer had been hard, they were nothing compared to the fall. David went through all the classical stages of grief, inventing a few the experts have yet to catalog. In one of these he decided that since Lisa had been good, God had not killed her for her sins but as a punishment for him, David. Moreover, God would continue to punish him by killing off everyone he loved. I was second on the list, right after his sister Mary.

We listened to him and cried with him, but we could not give Lisa back to him, these mere mortals that he now knew his parents to be.

In January I went to a meeting of the Children's Book Guild of Washington at which Ann Durell of Dutton was to speak. By some chance or design, depending on your theology, I was put at the head table. In the polite amenities before lunch someone said to me: "How are the children?"—for which the answer, as we all know, is "Fine." But I botched it. Before I could stop myself I began really to tell how the children were, leading my startled tablemates deep into the story of David's grief.

No one interrupted me. But when I finally shut up, Ann Durell said very gently, "I know this sounds just like an editor, but you should write that story. Of course," she added, "the child can't die by lightning. No editor would ever believe that."

I thought I couldn't write it, that I was too close and too overwhelmed, but I began to try to write. It would be a kind of therapy for me, if not for the children. I started to write in pencil on the free pages of a used spiral notebook so that when it came to nothing I could pretend that I'd never been very serious about it.

After a few false starts, thirty-two smudged pages emerged, which made me feel that perhaps there might be a book after all. In a flush of optimism I moved to the typewriter and pounded out a few dozen more, only to find myself growing colder and colder with every page until I was totally frozen. The time had come for my fictional child to die, and I could not let it happen.

I caught up on my correspondence, I rearranged my bookshelves, I even cleaned the kitchen—anything to keep the inevitable from happening. And then one day a friend asked, as friends will, "How is the new book coming?" and I blurted out—"I'm writing a book in which a child dies, and I can't let her die. I guess," I said, "I can't face going through Lisa's death again."

"Katherine," she said, looking me in the eye, for she is a true friend, "I don't think it's Lisa's death you can't face. I think it's yours."

I went straight home to my study and closed the door. If it was my death I could not face, then by God, I would face it. I began in a kind of fever, and in a day I had written the chapter, and within a few weeks I had completed the draft, the cold sweat pouring down my arms.

It was not a finished book, and I knew it, but I went ahead and did what no real writer would ever do: I had it typed up and mailed it off to Virginia before the sweat had a chance to evaporate.

There is no span of time quite so eternal as that between the mailing of a manuscript and the reception of an editor's reply. I knew she hated it; that's why she hadn't written or called. It was weird and raw and no good, and she was trying to think of some kind way to tell me that I was through as a writer.

Finally she called. "I laughed through the first two thirds and cried through the last," she said. So it was all right. She understood, as she always has, what I was struggling to do. And although she did not know what was happening in my life, she did not break the bruised reed I had offered her but sought to help me weave it into a story, a real story, with a beginning, a middle, and an end.

"We need to see Leslie grow and change," she said. And suddenly, from the ancient dust of the playground at Calvin H. Wiley School, there sprang up a small army of seventh-grade Amazons led by the dreadful Pansy Something-or-Other, who had terrorized my life when I was ten and not too hard to terrify.

"You must convince us," Ann Beneduce added, "that Jesse has the mind of an artist." This seemed harder, for I certainly don't have Ann's kind of artistic vision. I started bravely, if pompously, reading the letters of Vincent Van Gogh, and when they didn't help, I went, as I often do, to my children.

"David," I asked, feeling like a spy, "why don't you ever draw pictures from nature?"

And my nine-year-old artist nature-lover replied, "I can't get the poetry of the trees." It is the only line of dialogue that I have ever consciously taken from the mouth of a living person and put into the mouth of a fictitious one. It doesn't usually work, but that time it seemed to.

I have never been happier in my life than I was those weeks I was revising the book. It was like falling happily, if a little crazily, in love. I could hardly wait to begin work in the morning and would regularly forget about lunch. The valley of the shadow which I had passed through so fearfully in the spring had, in the fall, become a hill of rejoicing.

This time when I sent the manuscript off to Virginia I said: "I know that love is blind, for I have just mailed you a flawless manuscript."

In time, of course, my vision was restored. I no longer imagine the book to be without flaws, but I have never ceased to love the people of this book—even the graceless Brenda and the inarticulate Mrs. Aarons. And, oh, May Belle, will you ever make a queen? I still mourn for Leslie, and when children ask me why she had to die, I want to weep, because it is a question for which I have no answer.

It is a strange and wonderful thing to me that other people who do not even know me love Jesse Aarons and Leslie Burke. I have given away my own fear and pain and faltering faith and have been repaid a hundredfold in loving compassion from readers like you. As the prophet Hosea says, the Valley of Trouble has been turned into the Gate of Hope.

Theodore Gill has said, "The artist is the one who gives form to difficult visions." This statement comes alive for me when I pore over Peter Spier's *Noah's Ark*. The difficult vision is not the destruction of the world. We've had too much practice imagining that. The difficult vision which Mr. Spier has given form to is that in the midst of the destruction, as well as beyond it, there is life and humor and caring along with a lot of manure shoveling. For me those final few words "and he planted a vineyard" ring with the same joy as "he found his supper waiting for him and it was still hot."

In talking with children who have read *Bridge to Terabithia*, I have met several who do not like the ending. They resent the fact that Jesse would build a bridge into the secret kingdom which he and Leslie had shared. The thought of May Belle following in the footsteps of Leslie is bad enough, but the hint that the thumb-sucking Joyce Ann may come as well is totally abhorrent to these readers. How could I allow Jesse to build a bridge for the unworthy? they ask me. Their sense of what is fitting and right and just is offended. I hear my young critics out and do not try to argue with them, for I know as well as they do that May Belle is not Leslie, nor will she ever be. But perhaps some day they will understand Jesse's bridge as an act of grace which he built, not because of who May Belle was but because of who he himself had become crossing the gully into Terabithia. I allowed him to build the bridge because I dare to believe with the prophet Hosea that the very valley where evil and despair defeat us can become a gate of hope—if there is a bridge.

In closing, I want to explain the Japanese word on the dedication page of *Bridge to Terabithia*. The word is *banzai,* which some of you will remember from old war movies. I am very annoyed when writers throw in Italian and German phrases that I can't understand, but suddenly as I wrote the dedication to this book, *banzai* seemed to be the only word I knew that was appropriate. The two characters which make the word up say, "all years," but the word itself combines the meanings of our English word *Hooray* with the ancient salute to royalty, "Live forever!" It is a cry of triumph and joy, a word full of hope in the midst of the world's contrary evidence. It is the word I wanted to say through *Bridge to Terabithia*. It is a word that I think Leslie Burke would have liked. It is my salute to all of you whose lives are bridges for the young.

Banzai!

BIOGRAPHICAL NOTE

Katherine Paterson
by Virginia Buckley

Katherine Paterson likes to tell the story of how the night of the National Book Award ceremonies for *The Master Puppeteer* (Crowell) last year, she and her husband were in their hotel room when out of the darkness they heard a voice intone: "I want to be a spy—for h-o-p-e." It was their son, John, Jr., mimicking a line from her acceptance speech, and as Katherine imitates *him,* she dramatically lowers her voice. Katherine's knack for telling anecdotes is part of her gift as a writer. As you get to know her, you realize that the quick wit and strong loyalties with which she endows her characters are qualities that she herself possesses and extends to her family, friends, and the people she works with—even chance strangers.

In January this year, bound for blizzard-crippled Chicago for the announcement of the Newbery-Caldecott awards, Katherine's airplane was forced to land in Kansas City. But she struck up an acquaintance with two women, one of whom was laden with a baby and lots of luggage. It is typical of Katherine to say that they aided her as much as she them. And I was touched when I learned of her concern for me, when I temporarily disappeared and my plane was diverted to Tulsa, Oklahoma. "You always end up with something different from what you expect," says Katherine, and wisely so.

Katherine's two awards in consecutive years are in many ways a classic success story. Married to a minister, she began writing fiction when her four children were still quite young. She has always loved to read and says that she started writing because as a harassed mother she wanted to have something at the end of the day which had not been eaten up or dirtied up or torn apart. Her first novel of feudal Japan, *The Sign of the Chrysanthemum* (Crowell), was written a chapter a week for an adult education course in writing for children. It was then sent, unsolicited, to Thomas Y. Crowell, where it was picked out by an editorial reader. Two more novels of Japan followed, *Of Nightingales That Weep* (Crowell) and *The Master Puppeteer*, which besides winning the National Book Award also received an Edgar Allan Poe Special Award from the Mystery Writers of America. These earlier novels were all based on Katherine's knowledge of Japan, where she lived for four years. Her most recent novels, *Bridge to Terabithia*, the Newbery Medal winner, and *The Great Gilly Hopkins* (both Crowell), just published this spring, have contemporary settings in Maryland and in northern Virginia, where Katherine has lived.

For Katherine writing is a cooperative endeavor. Before sending a manuscript to the publisher, she gives it to her husband to read—and listens to his criticism. Editing her books is one of my greatest pleasures, and our long discussions by phone and by letter have resulted in a fine friendship. Our editorial offices light up whenever Katherine visits, and at a recent sales conference, where she presented her latest book, she delighted the whole sales and children's editorial staff when she quipped, "The last time I spoke to a group of men after lunch, they all fell asleep." This was a reference to a time years ago when she taught a class after lunch at a boys' school.

The wellspring of Katherine's ability to relate instantly to others can be traced back to an unusual childhood. Born in Tsing Kiang pu, China, on Halloween, she was the middle one of five children of missionary parents serving with the Presbyterian Church, U.S. When she was four, China's war with Japan started, which forced her family to make their first refugee trip back to the United States via Southeast Asia and Europe. "I visited the zoo in every port city in the world," she says. For a year the family lived in Lynchburg and in Richmond, Virginia, but they all felt like foreigners. "I hated America. When I was in first grade I didn't get any valentines. I don't think I was disliked. I was totally overlooked." She was happy to go back to China a year later, but again war intervened. She remembers being terrified watching the Japanese soldiers practicing for the invasion of San Francisco on the beach behind their summer house. "I was out playing and heard this blood-chilling sound. Soldiers wearing only a loincloth and carrying guns with bayonets were coming up our yard. I grabbed my little sister's hand and ran for all I was worth."

Forced to flee China permanently, the family then returned to the United States and moved to various locations in Virginia, North Carolina, and West Virginia. Again Katherine was the outsider, a refugee who did not fit in. "I was a weird little kid and was called a Jap. In fifth grade one day I got straight A's, and then I knew I could make it. I was very verbal and started writing plays. The kids respected this. I loved acting and was the evil fairy in 'The Sleeping Beauty.' "

By the time she graduated summa cum laude from King College, a small Presbyterian college in Bristol, Tennessee, she had attended thirteen different schools. Then, after a year teaching the sixth grade in Virginia, she enrolled in the Presbyterian School of Christian Education in Richmond, from which she obtained a master's degree in English Bible.

At the end of that summer, in 1957, Katherine made a decision that most directly influenced her writing career. She had always wanted to go back to China and had considered Taiwan, but upon a friend's advice she went to Japan, instead. There she spent two years studying at the Japanese Language School in Kobe and then worked for two years as a Christian Education Assistant to a group of eleven pastors in rural Tokushima Ken on Shikoku Island. "It would be hard to overestimate the effects of these four years in Japan in making me the person I am. To become a mute illiterate simply by crossing an ocean is a shattering and instructive experience. But to be able to go beyond those first humiliations and frustrations, to be allowed to come alive among a people like the Japanese, is a gift beyond the telling."

When asked why she chose to write about feudal Japan in her novels, Katherine answered that as a Southerner she felt kin to the Heike Clan who rose to power and were destroyed during the twelfth century. She also wanted to say something about the waste and futility of war and about what you become being more important than your family tree. Civil strife is in the background of all three of her Japanese novels, and it must also reflect the terror she herself felt when the Japanese soldiers stormed her beach.

Given a fellowship to Union Theological Seminary in New York upon her return to this country, Katherine made another decision that influenced her life. For it was during this time that she met and married (on Bastille Day) John Barstow Paterson. Their eldest daughter Elizabeth PoLin (Chinese for "Precious Life") was born in Hong Kong and came to them six months after their son John, Jr., was born. Then David was born, and about two years later the family was completed by Mary Katherine Nah-he-sah-pe-che-a (Apache for "a young Apache lady").

John is the pastor of the Takoma Park Presbyterian Church in Maryland, where the family has lived for the past twelve years. Katherine enjoys singing in the choir and teaches the fifth- and sixth-grade church school class. "I love and believe the Biblical story of God's unfailing grace, and I am more and more aware of the truth of the Apostle's words that 'we are members one of another.'" Katherine has also written several curriculum materials for the Presbyterian Church, U.S., and for the National Council of Churches. She has two curriculum units in the works.

One would think that managing a large household, writing five highly acclaimed novels in almost as many years, and being involved in church-related activities would be enough to keep this spirited author occupied. But Katherine is also this year's president of the Children's Book Guild of Washington, D.C., an organization devoted to children's literature and comprising authors, artists, and librarians. The Patersons also served as temporary foster parents of two Cambodian children, an experience that found its way into Katherine's latest book, about a foster child.

Every time I reread one of Katherine's novels, I find something new of value. Most recently I became aware of her abiding sympathy for the underdog, the lowly of this earth. Now that I think of it, that sympathy might be the ripening of this mature, engaged, and engaging woman with the ready laugh, who can still recall that when she was a child in Shanghai, she and her friends dramatized over and over *The Wizard of Oz*—but that she was never allowed to play Dorothy and was always a Munchkin.

The Newbery Medal 1979

THE WESTING GAME

written by ELLEN RASKIN

published by E. P. DUTTON 1978

BOOK NOTE

In Westingtown on the shore of Lake Michigan, Sunset Towers is a new building in which the six apartments have been rented to people who do not realize they have been specially selected as tenants. Among them are the Wexlers—Dr. Jake Wexler, a podiatrist whose office is in the building; his wife Grace; and their two daughters, the beautifully perfect Angela and the often ignored Turtle—and the Theodorakis family who run a coffee shop in Sunset Towers: mother, father, and two teen-age sons. Other tenants in the building are Sydelle Pulaski, a secretary; Flora Baumbach, a dressmaker; J. J. Ford, a judge, who is not only female but black; and the Hoo family, whose Chinese restaurant is on the top floor, where Mr. Hoo waits in vain for customers. Madame Hoo speaks no English, and Doug Hoo is a high school track star. Also living there in a tiny room is a cleaning lady, Berthe Erica Crow, referred to by all as Crow. A delivery boy, age sixty-two, is Otis Amber, whose errands seem to involve him continually in the affairs of the Sunset Towers tenants. Dr. D. Denton Deere, a plastic surgeon, also is in and out of the building because he is engaged to Angela Wexler. Keeping an eye on the building and its tenants is the doorman, Sandy McSouthers. Offstage, more or less, are Barney Northrup, rental agent for Sunset Towers; Samuel W. Westing, the missing millionaire who founded the gigantically successful Westing Paper Products Corporation; Julian R. Eastman, the president of the corporation; and Dr. Sidney Sikes, an old friend of the eccentric millionaire.

 The long-empty and spooky Westing mansion is next to Sunset Towers. Turtle makes a bet that she can stay for a certain length of time in the house at night. She finds a body, and it is believed to be that of Samuel W. Westing, who had disappeared thirteen years before. His obituary in the newspaper tells the tragic story of his daughter Violet, who drowned on the eve of her wedding, and of his then being deserted by his wife. Sixteen people, including some of the residents of Sunset Towers, plus Sandy McSouthers, Dr. Deere, Otis Amber, and Crow, are named as beneficiaries in Samuel Westing's will and invited by an attorney to the Westing mansion for the reading of the will.

The will states that Samuel Westing did not die of natural causes; that one of the heirs is responsible, and it sorts the sixteen people into pairs of players, giving each pair a series of words as clues. Who is the guilty person? Who will win the "windfall" mentioned in the will?

Although all the heirs are important to the puzzle, Turtle emerges as the instigator of much of the action. The pairings of partners works in mysterious ways to each one's final advantage; and the intricate interweaving of the relationships of the heirs and their relationship to Samuel Westing, along with attempts to solve their clues, leads to the surprising solution.

Newbery Medal Acceptance
by Ellen Raskin

With deepest gratitude and everlasting astonishment I accept the 1979 John Newbery Medal and the awesome covenant it exacts, on behalf of my young, my dedicated, my loyal readers.

I had dreamed of this moment many times, but this is nothing like my dream. There, in vain reverie, I would stand before a cheering but faceless crowd, outside of time, outside of space, flaunting the Caldecott Medal.

As proof to the paucity of my imagination, here I stand in an ideal setting, at a perfect time, celebrating the honor of the Newbery Medal with friends, colleagues, and the worshiped idols of my childhood: librarians—librarians who unlocked their treasure chest of riches to the lost child that I was and who now add my small gift to their miraculous hoards. And my family is here: my husband Dennis Flanagan, my daughter and son-in-law Susan and Jim Metcalfe, who have given me so much love that I had plenty left over to lavish on the characters in *The Westing Game.*

This, indeed, is not a dream. On the other hand, this moment is too good to be real. Life, quirky though it may be, does not improve upon dreams. Life is not this generous with its rewards.

Then what place is this that is neither reverie nor reality? I seem to be somewhere where anything can happen, somewhere deeper than dreams and truer than life. This somewhere could only be a book. I stand here in a book, written by an author who has bestowed upon this middle chapter the happiest of interim endings; an author whose profound and satiric wit, whose flawless sense of time and place make me gasp in admiration.

This ceremony could have been set in Milwaukee, my home town, or in Pittsburgh, the home of the dedicatees of my book and the Westinghouse Corporation; but that would have been too obvious. (As my readers can tell you, I have a strong aversion to the obvious.) Dallas is just right. Here I was warmly welcomed before any medal came my way by the children of the Richardson and the Garland schools, who read books, talked books, bought books. Besides, in this fantasy of fantasies, what better place to celebrate a book about money and millionaires than Texas?

If the locale is ideal, the timing is exquisite: one week from the Fourth of July in the International Year of the Child. To be honored for my contribution to American literature for children in this year of all years is cause for wonder. I do write books for children consciously and proudly, but now I must ask myself: Why? What? How?

To me, writing for a reading child does *not* mean preaching or teaching (I leave that to the more qualified). It does *not* mean prescriptive formula (if I had the need for formulas I would write for adults). It does *not* mean catering to arbitrary reading levels or age groups; my readers have one thing in common: They are young enough or curious enough to read slowly, and the slower the better for my books.

The one literary concession I do make, one that forces me to eliminate words here and add sentences there, is to the look of the book. I write and design my book to look accessible to the young reader; it will have less than two hundred pages, and there will be no endless seas of gray type. I plan for margins wide enough for the hands to hold, typographic variations for the eyes to rest, decorative breaks for the mind to breathe. I want my children's book to look like a wonderful place to be.

But why? Why, as an adult, do I write books for children? I have thought long and hard about this too-often-asked question, and the only answer I can come up with is: maybe because I'm short.

I may not appear short to some of you; but, believe me, I have spent most of my years looking up people's noses. As a child, being school-bright was little compensation for being a year younger than my Nordic classmates. Great expectations were had of me when I was skipped to the third grade, but then and there my string of perfect report cards was broken. I flunked posture! A shy child, I lacked the courage to explain that I *was* standing up straight; I was just shorter than everyone else. To add injury to insult, the geography books I had to balance on my head probably squashed me down another two inches. And not having eyes on the top of my flattened skull, I could no longer name the states that border on the Mississippi.

I did have a brief respite from shortness. Having grown up as far as I could, I left the tall state of Wisconsin to launch a successful career as a free-lance illustrator, eye-to-eye with the average-sized natives of New York City. Then one unforgettable afternoon Susie left her house key at school, and I was soon to step back into the frustrations of the undersized. The doorbell rang, I rose from my drawing boards, crossed the room, opened the front door, and looked *up* at my twelve-year-old daughter. Up, not down.

Short again and forevermore, I started my first children's book. With the comfort of hindsight I could look back and smile at my early moping self. Lucky adult that I became, I offered *Nothing Ever Happens on My Block* (Atheneum) to the right editor—Jean Karl. To Jean, many thanks for showing me the way into children's literature; and to Suzanne Glazer, many kisses for the boundless enthusiasm that has kept me there.

Switching from commercial art to picture books is plausible, but what about from picture books to the novel? Simple. All it takes is a brilliant editor, Ann Durell, who in a rare lapse into looniness asked this illustrator to write a long book; and who, a year later when the moon again was full, confronted by the unlikeliest of novels (not-what-she-had-in-mind-at-all, she-may-be-crazy-but-the-author's-even-nuttier) had the courage to publish it. Thank you, Ann, for letting me keep this medal; at least half of it belongs to you and to the other good people at E. P. Dutton: Julie Ziercher and Riki Levinson, who worked with such devotion on *The Westing Game,* and Mimi Kayden. Mimi, my love for all the little things and all the big things you did to help our books find their readers.

Had Ann Durell and I had our wits about us, we might not have been so surprised at my funny way with words. Those years of art training, those many more years of sketching and drawing sharpened my eye to the out-of-scale, the out-of-proportion. (Everything looks weird if you stare long enough.) The visual artist looks and can see beauty in the absurd, magic in the mundane. What varies from the norm describes the norm, and how much easier it is to tell those meanings in words. In words. With words. Words about words. Words are adaptable tools to a dedicated reader; to the illustrator words become tools as brushes have been, and brush strokes are meant to be visible.

If that is not reason enough for my wordplay, I happen to be married to the word-master of all time. After living almost twenty years with a man who never lets a word pass by without twisting it, refining it, defining or redefining it, a bit of his mastery should have rubbed off on me. Thanks, Dennis.

Well, the words kept coming: *The Mysterious Disappearance of Leon (I mean Noel),* then *Figgs & Phantoms,* then *The Tattooed Potato and Other Clues* (all Dutton); and then three years ago I sat down at the typewriter with no wisp of an idea, just the urge to write another children's book. It will have a story. It will have a character with whom my readers can relate. And, because of who I am and was, and out of my compassion for the hurts and hazards of childhood, it will have a happy ending. But what shall I write about?

It is 1976, the Bicentennial year. My story will have a historical background; its locale, the place I know best: Milwaukee. I now have my first character: Lake Michigan.

Recalling that Amy Kellman's daughter asked for a puzzle-mystery, I decide that the format of my historical treatise will be a puzzle-mystery (whatever that is). I type out the words of "America the Beautiful" and cut them apart.

Meanwhile on television, between re-created Revolutionary battles blasting and fireworks booming, come reports of the death of an infamous millionaire. Anyone who can spell *Howard Hughes* is forging a will. Good, I'll try it, too.

Now I have Lake Michigan, a jumbled "America the Beautiful," the first draft of a very strange will, and a dead millionaire—a fine beginning for a puzzle-mystery, but where is the historical background? Wisconsin abounds in labor history; therefore, my millionaire will be an industrialist, murdered because—let me see, because he was a notorious strikebreaker. Old man Kohler! I shift the scene sixty miles north to my father's hometown, Sheboygan, which borders on the Kohler company, factory, and town. I cannot use the name Sheboygan (my readers will think I'm trying to be funny), and I certainly cannot use the name Kohler (they're still making toilets up there). Instead, I raise the shore of Lake Michigan, and my industrialist, named Samuel W. Westing, will die in his mansion on the cliff called the Westing house.

Now I need heirs, lots of them. Since my books collect characters, invited or not, I plan for a goodly number at the start. Sixteen seems a goodly number, almost too good; I will pair them: eight pairs of heirs. Imperfect heirs. My characters will be imperfect, each handicapped by some physical, emotional, or moral defect. Defects which will make them easier to remember, imperfect because aren't we all?

And in honor of the Bicentennial, they will be melting-pot characters: Polish, Jewish, German, Greek, Chinese, Black. With the blind arrogance of the possessed, I devise sixteen imperfect ethnics. Ordinary folk: dressmaker, judge, cook, podiatrist, maid, inventor, secretary, student—this is getting boring—a reluctant bride-to-be, a bird watcher in a wheelchair, a thirteen-year-old girl who plays the stock market—still boring—a bookie, a burglar, a bomber—that's better. And the murderer will limp. Out of respect for plodding, rereading readers who never miss a clue, if the murderer limps, I must make most of my characters, at one time or another, limp.

I am off and typing. I still do not know who is the bookie, who is the bomber, who killed Sam Westing, or why everyone is gimping around, but no matter. The characters will shape the action; the action will shape the characters. My characters will show me the way. And so they do.

" 'Grownups are so obvious,' " Turtle says in my book. That may be, but I am quick to scoff at others' faults before they scoff at mine. With time I tolerate the imperfections of the stranger; with acquaintance I begin to understand; with caring the faults fall away, and I perceive, in rare times touch, the true being of a friend. So, too, when I write. Those characters, whom I myself create and name, begin as strangers. Slowly, slowly, they take shape and grow and cast shadows on one another and on me. I learn to like them, to love them. Although I rewrite my story many times, I try not to alter this fragile metamorphosis. I would like my readers to share the joy of watching those ridiculous strangers become good friends.

Unfortunately, I end up loving all of my characters. None of them could possibly be a murderer. And mean old Sam Westing isn't so mean after all, once you get to know him. I cannot let him die. Now I really have a problem: How can there be a will if nobody died?

It is rewrite time. The plot thickens and thickens but refuses to jell, and I refuse to give up; two hundred million dollars is at stake, and I want to win. Knitting and unraveling, knotting and unknotting, I rewrite the manuscript again. And again. At last (hallelujah at last!) I find the answer to the question I forgot to ask. The plot comes full circle; all points of the compass are touched; the game is won. My book is done.

Sam Westing, the rascal, almost outwitted me with not one but four disguises. I almost outwitted myself; my tribute to American labor history ended up a comedy in praise of capitalism. In the larger sense, however, it did turn out to be exactly what I wanted it to be—a children's book.

It is the book that is the important thing, not who I am or how I did it, but the book. Not me, the book. I fear for the book in this age of inflated personalities, in which the public's appetite for an insight into the lives of the famous has been whetted by publicity-puffers and profit-pushers into an insatiable hunger for gossip. I worry that who-the-writer-is has become of more interest than what-the-writer-writes. I am concerned that this dangerous distortion may twist its way into children's literature.

I do understand the attempt to introduce books to children through their authors, and in my travels I have seen it done effectively and well. I salute all efforts to encourage reading. But an author is not a performer; meeting a writer is not a substitute for reading a book. It is the book that lives, not the author. It is not I that is being honored here tonight; it is my book.

What becomes of Ellen Raskin is of little matter on this occasion. What does matter, what we are celebrating here tonight, is that Turtle and Angela and Chris and Sydelle, all sixteen of my beloved characters are alive and well and forevermore will be playing The Westing Game. I hold the Newbery Medal in my hand, but the shinier one is on the book.

For this great honor I am deeply grateful to Dr. Cianciolo, the members of the Newbery-Caldecott Awards Committee, and the Association for Library Service to Children. I am indebted to so many for their continued support and encouragement—librarians, teachers, reviewers—that it is impossible to single out any one person. However, I would like to repeat the tribute that recurred in each of my dream-speeches, for it seems even more appropriate now: To Mary Elizabeth Ledlie, thank you for letting me and my books come home again. Thank you all and a very happy Fourth of July.

BIOGRAPHICAL NOTE

The Raskin Conglomerate
by Dennis Flanagan

It is widely assumed that Ellen Raskin, whose book *The Westing Game* recently won the John Newbery Medal, is one person. There is much evidence to the contrary. It points toward a loosely associated group of artists, perhaps organized into a corporation. Consider the following:

Ellen Raskin the Writer of Children's Books

Here the evidence is straightforward and reasonably well known. This Ellen Raskin has written fifteen books: *Nothing Ever Happens on My Block; Silly Songs and Sad; Spectacles; Ghost in a Four-Room Apartment; And It Rained; The World's Greatest Freak Show; A & The, or William T. C. Baumgarten Comes to Town; Franklin Stein; Who, Said Sue, Said Whoo?: Twenty-two, Twenty-three* (all Atheneum); *Moose, Goose & Little Nobody* (Parents); *The Mysterious Disappearance of Leon (I mean Noel); Figgs & Phantoms; The Tattooed Potato and Other Clues;* and *The Westing Game* (all Dutton). These books have received twenty-three awards, including the Newbery Medal and the Boston Globe-Horn Book Award.

It has been a productive career, by no means as productive as some, but surely not one suggesting that the writer could have had a lot of time for other pursuits. Now, however, we come to another Ellen Raskin.

Ellen Raskin the Illustrator and Designer

This Ellen Raskin began her career as a student of fine arts at the University of Wisconsin. Thereafter she went to New York and set up shop as a free-lance commercial artist. It would not be possible to catalog her production here. Suffice it to say that she has made more than a thousand illustrations of all kinds, including those for some fifteen children's books not written by the preceding Ellen Raskin. One of her main activities has been the design and illustration of book jackets, and here again she has made more than a thousand of them. These numbers are not figures of speech but are assignments duly entered in the logbook. Rapid calculation will indicate that if she did nothing but make one book jacket a week, it would take her about twenty years to make a thousand of them. As a maker of book jackets, she has been recognized by fifteen major awards and exhibitions. Clearly she could have had little time for any other line of work.

Ellen Raskin the Musician and Composer

This Ellen Raskin has been less productive than the others, perhaps even something of a recluse. Her career began with the piano in her parents' home in Milwaukee, which at a tender age she played incessantly in order to escape imperfect reality. She achieved a substantial skill and a good knowledge of music, but her progress was interrupted when the piano was removed by the finance company. Some years later, with the setback still rankling, she acquired a harpsichord and a leading teacher and assaulted baroque music with fierce intensity. At this point a literary interest intersected her musical ones. A long-time admirer of William Blake, she discovered that his *Songs of Innocence* had originally been set to music. Blake had sung them to a musical friend, whose transcriptions were then lost. Ellen Raskin, inhabiting Blake's mind after one hundred seventy-seven years, re-created the music and published it (*Songs of Innocence,* Doubleday). It is not easy to see how this could have been managed by any of the other Ellen Raskins.

Ellen Raskin the Finance Capitalist

This Ellen Raskin is not an artist at all, except in the sense of possessing skill, but there can be no doubt that she exists. Her main activity is in the stock market, where at any one time she maintains a portfolio of some twenty-five holdings. Her office is an icon of the environment of the financial operator: electronic machines, thick loose-leaf tomes filled with numbers in agate type, hardbound ledgers inscribed with long columns of digits in a neat bookkeeper's hand, charts with jagged curves rising and falling like the Himalayas. For many stock-market operators the moment of truth is the "takeover," when the stock of a company zooms upward as it appears that the company is about to be taken over by another company. By this standard Ellen Raskin has done well: She has had six takeovers in the past two years. (She attributes her keen sense of when to sell to a repetitive experience of her early childhood. When she accompanied her father to crap games, she kept a running account in her head, and then when he was comfortably on top, she would sob: "I want to go home.") Her broker has taken to calling her for tips. To witness her wolfish grin as she talks with him on the telephone is to doubt that she can even be an acquaintance of the other Ellen Raskins.

Ellen Raskin the Housewife

This Ellen Raskin has a full-time job. Indeed, she avers that it leaves her no time for anything else. Married to a captain of industry, she presides over a busy two-family house in Greenwich Village. Not for her the professional woman's "Honey, let's catch a bite out tonight." Afternoons are reserved for brooding over the evening feast, even unto banquets for the multitude featuring beef Wellington or poached striped bass. Accountancy, landlordism, the subcontracting of carpentry and plumbing, and other aspects of household management are as second nature. In the summertime on Long Island the garden blooms with tomatoes, corn, squash, asparagus, snow peas, raspberries, zucchini, rutabaga, kohlrabi. The Ellen Raskin in this role seems totally out of keeping with the others: a taciturn peasant with muddy boots, matted hair, broken fingernails and a small cigar pendent from her lower lip.

There are still other Ellen Raskins: Ellen Raskin the sports nut (currently about twenty nights per winter at Madison Square Garden, living and dying with the New York Rangers), Ellen Raskin the immoderate hero-worshiper (Piero della Francesca, Velazquez, Milton, Franz Shubert, Henry James, Joseph Conrad), Ellen Raskin the bibliophile (specializing in first editions of James and Conrad), Ellen Raskin the zoological-park freak (hasn't missed one from Tokyo to Barcelona), Ellen Raskin the gamester (a passionate wordist and an assassin at the evening chessboard), Ellen Raskin the tap-dancer (an automatic response to any charge of flagging spirits), Ellen Raskin the easel painter (a busy new career launched well ahead of Grandma Moses'). One of her most important roles is Ellen Raskin the mother; her daughter Susan Metcalfe is a highly successful businesswoman, a sure sign of sound upbringing. Finally, there are Ellen Raskin of the beautiful face and smashing form and Ellen Raskin the lover (of the fortunate husband who writes this piece).

The Newbery Medal 1980

A GATHERING OF DAYS: A NEW ENGLAND GIRL'S JOURNAL, 1830-32

written by JOAN W. BLOS

published by CHARLES SCRIBNER'S SONS 1979

BOOK NOTE

When Catherine Hall begins writing in her journal in October 1830, she is thirteen, the oldest daughter of Charles Hall, a farmer living in Meredith, New Hampshire. She has a younger sister, Matty; her mother and a baby brother have died several years before. Although she attends the village school, Catherine is responsible for many household tasks: cooking, preserving food, sewing, knitting, mending, and cleaning. Her closest friend, Cassie Shipman, who is a year older, lives on the neighboring farm with her parents and three brothers, David, Asa, and Willie.

Catherine's journal progresses through day-to-day events at home and at school, reflecting the strong educational and religious tone of community life, not only on the Sabbath but in the precepts set as school lessons and in the moral stories told by adults. When Catherine sees a shadowy figure of a man in the woods, she first remembers a story told to show that intelligence should prevail over ignorant fear and reasons that it is a man, not a phantom. In the newspaper she sees advertisements about runaway slaves, and she hears her father say that it would be wrong to meddle in any such matter and only right to turn a runaway back to his master.

With the arrival from Salem of Cassie's Aunt Lucy, bringing trunks of clothing and copies of *Godey's Lady's Book,* there is diversion for the girls; and there is much cooking in preparation for Thanksgiving, which the Halls and the Shipmans celebrate together.

On her way home from school Catherine forgets her writing book when she puts it down to pick some weed pods; when she looks for it the next day, it is gone. This worries her, as does a visit on a feeble excuse from unmarried Aunt Lucy to her father.

Catherine likes their home and pattern of life the way it is.

The writing book reappears by the woods, and written inside is a message: "PLEEZ MISS TAKE PITTY   I AM COLD." Snow has fallen; it is the season for logging and skating. Catherine is relieved to find that Asa is also aware of the runaway in the woods, has seen the message in her book, and says they must help him. Some pies are stolen from the Shipmans, and Asa is accused and thrashed. When he doesn't tell about the runaway, Catherine wraps some food in one of her mother's quilts and, with Cassie, leaves the bundle in the woods. Christmas, marked only by a church service, passes; Asa reports the bundle has disappeared, and Catherine often wonders in the months to come how the runaway fares.

The highlight of January occurs after a great snowstorm, as ox teams and men with shovels break out the roads and entire families follow to gather in the nearest town. Teacher Holt is admonished by the community for bringing Garrison's newspaper, *The Liberator,* to school and discussing slavery and abolition; Catherine worries again if she did right or wrong. The teacher is turned out of his lodgings, but the Shipmans take him in. In March Catherine turns fourteen; the maple sugaring begins. In April school closes with recitations before parents, and poems and remembrances—especially beribboned locks of hair—are exchanged by the students. Mr. Hall drives a team to Boston to trade furs, maple sugar, and straw brooms for food staples and cloth. In a week he comes home with the news that he has met a widow and will soon return to marry her and bring home not only a new wife but a stepson who is Catherine's age. The girl writes in her journal: "I will not call her Mother."

With the arrival of Ann and her son Daniel, Catherine has much to cope with, from her stepmother's earnest moral sayings to her directions for spring cleaning. Catherine is afraid she will be questioned as to why there are only eleven quilts when every household should have a dozen. But there are pleasures, too—the admiration of the new mural stenciled on the Shipmans' parlor wall; the start of summer school in June with a new teacher, a woman. Unexpectedly, it is Matty who mentions the missing quilt, and Catherine has to confess to her stepmother that she took it and tell why. Ann reflects upon a punishment and says

Catherine must make a quilt to replace it. She chooses to do "Mariner's Compass" and soon learns what a long and painstaking task it is to cut all the pieces and sew the blocks together.

July the Fourth, the most celebrated holiday of the year, brings all the families to town to see the militia parade and hear the Declaration of Independence read, followed by prayers and an oration, picnics, and fireworks. July also brings the announcement that Aunt Lucy and Teacher Holt are to marry and move to Exeter where he will teach at the boys' academy. Catherine, at last, begins to call her stepmother Mammann.

As summer progresses, the women suffer from the extreme heat, since all the cooking and preserving must be done on hot wood stoves. Cassie is taken ill with a fever and treated by a doctor with leeches to bleed her. In a few days she is dead. The loss of her dearest friend is hard for Catherine to bear as she realizes its permanence. Her other close friend, Sophy, leaves school at age fifteen to work in the mills in Lowell. Aunt Lucy dyes all her frocks black since she is in mourning when she marries Teacher Holt.

In the post one day a package arrives from Canada for Catherine, containing two pieces of crocheted lace and the message: "SISTERS BLESS YOU. FREE NOW. CURTIS." After keeping the lace a while, Catherine wraps them and leaves them on Cassie's grave. She finishes her quilt, and in the spring she leaves for Exeter, where she will help Aunt Lucy with her new baby and Teacher Holt will continue her education with private lessons. Here her journal concludes.

Newbery Medal Acceptance
by JOAN W. BLOS

It is an awesome thing to be told that you have made a distinguished contribution to children's literature.

I learned that I had won the Newbery Medal late in January. The actual moment of notification—suitably close to midnight—was an event of transformative proportions, having all the trappings of magic, and not to be believed. Until that moment I had been a teacher of children's literature, a reviewer and critic of children's books, and an editor of half of a quarterly, the other half being British. I had done these things because they were my work, because they were important to me and I liked doing them. In a substantially different way, my husband, our children, my mother, and our friends were important to me, also. Even our cat and our shaggy black dog, the birth of whose puppies two days before Christmas verged on the disconcerting, were significant parts of my life. There was also this thing called My Writing, which never seemed quite to fit in. It was true that I had published a book in the fall. But that one was out in the world, on its own. I hadn't yet started another.

And then, the transformative telephone call. Words. Exclamations. Laughter. None of it real in the night. Next morning when I reawakened, I was the winner of the Newbery Medal: not only from that day to this, but happily ever after.

In the days which followed I tried to explain to others what had happened in ways they would understand. To colleagues at the large midwestern university where I teach and which is known for its athletic prowess: "It's going to the Rose Bowl and *winning,* and you hadn't even known that you were on the plane!" To the mother of a seven-month-old baby: "It's waking up to a seven-month-old baby and finding yourself its mother!"

As rational beings we have come to expect development through stages or something like orderly growth: from football practice to victory and thus to cheering throngs. The rhyme we chanted as children taught that first comes love, and then comes marriage, and then comes whoever and the baby carriage.... When events defy our expectations and we cannot locate the causes of effects, we start to think of magic. However, as readers of fairy tales know, magic, however magical, doesn't begin from scratch. Magic is merely a method of change, the means by which something existing in state A is made to assume state B. Pumpkin to coach or prince to frog; Joan Blos to Newbery winner. But the prince was a prince before he was a frog, and the pumpkin will soon be a pumpkin again. And I, most of all, am my everyday self, a teacher of children's literature. And I must ask your forgiveness if I sometimes sound like one!

I have long believed that children's books are best when they are the work of those who share the essential, ancient, and parental need to cherish and inform the young. This does not mean that the books which they write must all be serious! Our first delight in the infant is the smile, and language itself arises in pleasure, in the aahs and coos of the baby at rest; for anger the scream suffices.

Be that as it may, *A Gathering of Days* began in facts which I had collected about a particular New Hampshire house, its region, and its past; for example, that in 1809, ten years prior to his marriage, the builder of the house had purchased the homestead from an elder brother. He died at the age of thirty-seven in 1825. The will he wrote commenced as follows: "I," and then his name was given, "being sound of mind but weak in boddy [sic]...." *The Grafton Journal* is said to have published a notice of the death. Initially random, my set of notes began to suggest certain patterns and include most distant events. It was at this time that I first suspected that I might have a book on my hands. I determined that it would be nonfiction; perhaps I would call it something like *The New Hampshire Book*. Time passed, and despite the oppressive title, the thought to write endured. Meanwhile, the book decided for itself that fiction would serve the content better than the document I had planned. "The wind roared up the hill," I wrote, "and flung itself at the white painted house." *Was* it white then? Would it have been red? I soon discovered to my chagrin that I did not know the color of the house toward which the wind roared up the hill and, furthermore, did not care. As truth exists in different forms, it was not exterior coloration but life as human experience that mattered most to me.

In the end this same impression—the house withstanding the wintry blast—turned up in two passages in the finished book. One was assigned to January 6:

It [the newly fallen snow] is fully up to the sills in front and well over that at the back of the house *where the wind blows up from the hill.*

For another entry I wrote:

Friday, October 22, 1830. We had a visitor today but nearly failed to admit him. No callers, surely, were expected. And peddlers, tinkers, and the like will not come by till Spring. Thus we ignored the rattling latch—*at times the wind will mislead us so*—until a voice called out.

Looking back, I can now discern at least three kinds of truthfulness with which I was concerned: the *social truthfulness* of the situation, the *psychological truthfulness* of the characters, and the *literary truthfulness* of the manner of telling. A three-year-old child I once heard about was delighted to have discovered that they call it Orange Juice because it is orange, and juice. I, with equal earnestness, had just reinvented Historical Fiction. The story is what resulted. "How much of it is true?" I am asked. "I tried to make it truthful," I reply, "but not much of it is true."

The story's characters are the people who stare and stare from New England portraits by artists who left no names. Its location is rural New Hampshire. It was therefore important that the tone be closer to *Leavitt's Almanac,* for farmers, than to *Godey's Lady's Book.* Both the form and style of my book were suggested by period writings. It therefore pleases me very much when people comment on the book's resemblance to actual family journals, or offer to share them with me.

Contemporary literature—post-Freudian and post-Joycean—has come to rely on open introspection to chart the changes in characters who are gifted self-observers. Within the journal form I had chosen lay an unexpected problem: how to present psychological change in persons not psychologically minded in the modern sense. I had to make two assumptions: first, that any report of events is going to be selectively determined by the reporting person; second, that that selectiveness is itself determined by inner priorities and needs, and so can represent them. These were enabling insights for me; and thereafter much of the work became the arrangement, in sequence, of such events as my diarist might record. She could then reveal herself without violation or contradiction; as she changed responsively it would show how she was changing. So it is that early in the book Catherine, the heroine, busily reports:

Only three more weeks remain until Thanksgiving Day! I must attach my new lace collar to my Sabbath dress. Also, it being snug for me, I must take up the patterned frock which I have given to Matty. She can use it nicely, I think, together with her new knit stockings and the red Morocco boots that were mine once also.

Domestic details preoccupy her. Catherine, although but a child herself, is full of motherly cluckings and concerns about the younger sister for whom she has been made responsible by their mother's death.

One year later she writes of a friend:

Sophy, once so flibbertigibbet, sends good earnings home. All of the mill girls protested their pay, and as 'tis known no girl in New England would take a place till the issue's resolved, the owners knuckled under rather than stop the mill.

The larger world impinges on Catherine's, while at home her father's remarriage proves a circumstance of importance. Through the difficult accommodation, through challenge, loss, and learning to trust, Catherine is able to achieve more lasting and more genuine growth.

Will young readers be aware of such aspects of the story? I am less worried about reader awareness, in the sense of articulate response, than hopeful that the inner story will generate understanding of others and of the self. Will some find the book old-fashioned, and thus irrelevant? Circumstances explored by the book are pertinent today: sex as well as its consequences, the challenge to children when respected adults hold conflicting opinions, the making of new families out of shattered parts, the personal responsibility that lies between the socially accepted and the morally right. All of these are as centrally placed in my historical fiction as in more topical novels for children and for young adults. In a sense my book was made possible by the books which recently, cogently, and usefully have enlarged the realm of the permissible in children's literature. The freedom which their authors won benefits others as much as themselves. I needed and I used that freedom; I gladly acknowledge that debt.

I would like, at this happiest of moments, to acknowledge indebtedness of a rather more personal sort. But those who have helped me the longest and the most are as modest as they are giving. Perhaps I can honor both qualities best by voicing my love, and my gratitude, but making no mention of names.

And so to a final comment.

On hearing about the book's award, a friend asked one of our children, "Is it another story in which someone somewhere grows up? I always used to notice," he said, "that all the Newbery books I read turned out to be about that." Well, of course, for what other subject can and will so lastingly appeal to those who write for children out of their adult lives? As parent, teacher, yes, *and writer,* I can comprehend the bond which derives from the age-old wish to encourage, literally meaning to *fill with courage,* those who are still young. The Medal, as at last I understand, exacts rededication even as it rewards. In that spirit I accept it with pride, believing in its magic, persuaded that it is true.

BIOGRAPHICAL NOTE

Joan W. Blos
by Betty Miles

Joan Blos has been involved with words and books, with children and books for children, for much of her life. Having been an avid reader as a child, a writer in school and at work, a student of child development, and a parent, she rediscovered the world of children's books as a volunteer reviewer in 1954. "From that time on," she says, "I never thought of other work, and I doubt that I ever will."

For most of her career she has thought of herself primarily as a teacher, and she is a good one. Her love of language, her knowledge of psychology and child development, her demanding standards, her humor and easy personal style make children's literature enjoyable and important for her students in education and—through them—for the children they will teach. She takes children and children's books seriously though never pretentiously—unlike the young student who applied for admission to her writing seminar some years ago. "Oh, Mrs. Blos," this untried writer exclaimed. "I've always wanted to write children's literature!"

Despite her amusement at the ingenuous remark, it is apparent that Joan Blos has, in fact, done just that; she has written children's literature. The field in which she has served as scholar, critic, and teacher is now enriched by her own contribution to its source. She thinks of her book as "one part of her life." Now this book—this gathering of days—will become, in turn, a part of the lives of many people. And her own regard for self-understanding, for empathy, and for realized growth, quietly stated in her nineteenth-century heroine's clear voice, will encourage and move young readers for many years to come. Tying together the past, the present, and the promise of the future in a tale that confirms human bonds—this is what Joan Blos, as a teacher, has always believed to be the role of literature. Her book is true to that belief and to her life.

Joan Blos has said that the nineteenth-century New England family imagined in *A Gathering of Days* represents "a borrowed past" for someone who, as a child, knew only two grandparents and who even now knows nothing of those who went before. That the Holocaust obliterated any chance to trace her own roots perhaps accounts for her deep interest in continuities and connections and in the relationship of apparently disparate people's lives to one's own.

"I see the writing of *A Gathering of Days* as an extension of the rest of my life," she says. "It's not something that makes it all worthwhile; not some culmination. It's one *part,* and I hope that new things are going to come from it."

New things *will* come of it; new things always come to Joan Blos. She invites them. But before she moves on, the happy occasion of the Newbery Medal provides a pause in which to honor not only this "part of her life" but all the rest that is reflected in it.

Joan Blos grew up in New York City, the daughter of Charlotte Winsor, a teacher who attained national prestige in the field of teacher education, and Max Winsor, a physician interested in the problems of juvenile delinquents. Her parents read aloud to her when she was small; later, having neither brothers nor sisters, she read aloud to the two younger cousins with whom she was closely raised. Until she was thirteen, she attended City and Country School, where the sunny library with its wicker chairs was a favorite place. She has said, "Favorite books at that time included *Caddie Woodlawn, Roller Skates, Hitty: Her First Hundred Years* and *The Trumpeter of Krakow.* All were read in those wicker chairs; all were Newbery winners." At night she fell asleep listening to the boats on the river. Of the same experience E. B. White wrote in *Here Is New York* (Harper) "I heard the Queen Mary blow one midnight . . . and the sound carried the whole history of departure and longing and loss."

Her first published writing, a poem, appeared in the school magazine when she was ten. In high school she wrote plays as well as poems, participated in a science project on the automobile, and received twenty-five dollars for a short story published in a national magazine. A physiology major at Vassar College, she earned a graduate degree in clinical psychology at The College of the City of New York, with a thesis on young children's responses to stories. She was working as a research assistant at the Child Study Center of Yale University when she met her husband, then a medical student and now a psychoanalyst engaged in private practice and research. Stephen Blos was born while they lived in New Haven; Sarah Blos was born two years later after their move to New York City. In the fall of 1958 Joan Blos joined the staff of Bank Street College of Education. That pioneering institution for the study of child development and education was founded by Lucy Sprague Mitchell, whose study of children's language and literature has influenced generations of writers for and about children, among them Margaret Wise Brown, Irma Simonton Black, Claudia Lewis, and Joan Blos herself.

As a member of the Publications Department at Bank Street, she was an instructor in children's literature, a staff member of the Writers' Laboratory, and an associate editor of the Bank Street Readers. At that time I, too, had begun to work at Bank Street. Joan and I became colleagues and, quickly, friends—a relationship that has deepened over twenty-three years. It is an honor for me to say publicly how proud I am of her now—and have always been. During the Bank Street years she wrote several picture books for children and began to publish the critical articles about children, books, and reading for which she has become well known.

Since 1970 Joan Blos has taught children's literature at the University of Michigan, focusing on books for the prereading child. She is the United States editor of the quarterly *Children's Literature in Education* and writes frequently for other journals.

She has been a sought-after speaker for parent and professional groups, a role now intensified by the announcement of her Newbery Medal.

But what is she *like*? What is often called, with curious deprecation, the "human side" of any person is always the hardest to describe. Close friendship does not make it easier but simply enlarges the data bank of observed characteristics—including in this case an addiction to Mallomars and a pleasant tendency to turn silly on occasion. To summarize, Joan Blos is likable, funny, smart, *caring*. She cares about her husband; they have been married and happy and colleagues for twenty-seven years. During long hours at the dinner table, while the dishes lay unwashed, they discussed books and the ideas that result in them as well as the concerns and insights that bridge their two professions. She cares about her children and their work; they reciprocate with pride. She cares about her friends and their children, about her wide networks of colleagues, about language and books, about old houses and new ideas. She cares about how things look—a child's profile, flowers in vases, a well-designed book. The precisely observed detail in *A Gathering of Days* is predictable from someone who cares, as she does, about the color of wooden beads against a dress or of a picnic cloth spread on meadow grass. On being asked to describe herself for young readers, Joan Blos says that she likes to take long walks with her husband, to knit, and to make soup and that she doesn't like mean jokes, scary movies, or blueberries cooked into muffins.

She says (and knowing her genuine modesty, I believe her) that she is absolutely astonished to have won the Newbery Medal. I say, with the pride and pleasure of long acquaintance, that it is an honor worthy of her.

The Newbery Medal 1981

JACOB HAVE I LOVED

written by KATHERINE PATERSON

published by THOMAS Y. CROWELL COMPANY 1980

BOOK NOTE

Louise Bradshaw, born moments before her twin sister Caroline, is ever aware of how her supposedly frail but musically talented sister has absorbed all of her family's attention and support. Their father is a waterman, who tongs for oysters and traps crabs in Chesapeake Bay. Their mother, formerly a school teacher, takes Caroline from their home on Rass Island on many ferry trips to the mainland for her singing lessons. Also in the household is their difficult, disagreeable grandmother. Louise, at thirteen, contributes to the family income by crabbing with a fourteen-year-old boy, Call Purnell. It is in this year of 1941, as America becomes involved in World War II, that Louise realizes she is unhappy; that resentment at her family's attitude toward her—she has never given them "a minute's worry," so they take her for granted—rankles the pride she has felt in her sister's talent; and that Caroline, who calls her Wheeze, is the center of all attention.

    When Hiram Wallace, who left the island almost fifty years before, returns to live in his long-deserted family home, Louise imagines he is a spy and persuades Call to spy on him with her; but they soon become his friends. Brought up in a strict Methodist church, Louise often wrestles with her growing hate for her twin as well as her irritation with Grandma's insistent Bible-quoting about sex and sin. She begins working longer and putting aside money for herself, hoping she can afford boarding school on the mainland. After Louise discovers that old Auntie Braxton has had a stroke and gets her to a hospital, she cleans up the cat-ridden house; then, despite Louise's hard work, it is Caroline's charm that finds homes for the sixteen cats. A hurricane disrupts the island, damaging land, houses, and boats. Midstorm Louise persuades Captain Wallace to take refuge with the Bradshaws, and he stays a few days with them when his house is destroyed. Louise is shaken as she senses her strong physical attraction to the Captain despite the great difference in their ages. At fourteen, she is upset and bewildered by her feelings and taunted by Grandma who observes them. The girl cannot talk about it with her mother or twin and is relieved when the Captain moves to Auntie Braxton's empty house. Island morality being so strong, Caroline and Call suggest that Captain Wallace marry Trudy Braxton so he can stay in the house when she returns from the hospital. He does, and Louise goes through a miserable time. The storm has given the Bradshaws financial problems. Caroline's voice and piano lessons are sacrificed, but Louise cannot bring herself to give up her hard-earned savings. During the winter, Call leaves school and helps Mr. Bradshaw tonging oysters. When Trudy Braxton dies, Grandma, bringing her skewed religion and hate into the open, accuses Louise of helping the Captain kill his wife. Yet Louise's spirit is really broken when Captain Wallace wishes to use his wife's legacy to send Caroline to music school in Baltimore, and Grandma quotes from the Bible, "Jacob have I loved, but Esau have I hated." In her despair Louise refuses her mother's suggestion they try to send her to boarding school, even though that had been her own goal. Caroline leaves for music school; Call joins the navy; and as the war continues in 1943 and 1944 Louise leaves school and works with her father. But her mother insists on giving her lessons at home so she can graduate from high school. In 1945 the war ends, and as Caroline plans to go on to Juilliard School of Music on a full scholarship, Louise waits for Call to come home, hoping he not only will help her father again but will be the man for her. She and Call visit the Captain, and Call reveals that he has seen Caroline; that he plans to live in New York and he and Caroline will marry. When the wedding takes place before Christmas in 1946, Louise stays on Rass Island to take care of Grandma so her parents can go to New York. She invites Captain Wallace to Christmas dinner, and he makes her realize her future has always been in her own hands; she can no longer blame others for what she has not done for herself. She must decide what she wants and then do it.

When her mother finally reveals that it is Louise she will miss more than Caroline, Louise feels she has overcome her twin's shadow and can leave the island. She goes to college on the mainland and studies to be a nurse-midwife. Working in the Appalachian mountains, she finds a busy life as well as a husband and three stepchildren, and eventually she has a son. Mr. Bradshaw dies; Caroline has a successful operatic career; Louise plans to bring her mother to live with her. Yet the final resolution in her life is accomplished when, as a midwife, she succeeds with the difficult delivery of twins and conveys her concern that both twins, the strong one and the weak one, are to be cared for with equal love.

Newbery Medal Acceptance
by Katherine Paterson

I was thrilled, honored, gratified, not to say shocked, to learn that *Jacob Have I Loved* was to be given the 1981 Newbery Medal. But there was a problem. "What shall I say in San Francisco?" I cried out to my husband. "I don't know what to say." He proposed: "Thank you." Yes, but what next? A writer I know suggested that it was time I said to the American Library Association, "We have got to stop meeting like this." I was sorely tempted, but these speeches tend to get preserved, and who wants to appear flippant to posterity? I complained to another friend that everything I thought of sounded either coy or dumb, and she replied, "Well, I don't think you need to worry about coy. It's just not your style to be coy." It took me several seconds to get it. Call Purnell would have caught on sooner. Into the midst of all this inner turmoil there came one cool, clear voice. It had a distinct Chesapeake Bay island ring to it. "Oh, my blessed. Wouldn't you know? Here I bring up a prize catch, and the fool's fixing to ruin it for me."

So with Sara Louise Bradshaw prodding me at the end of her skiff pole, I was made to turn from the frazzled writer to the book. How could I forget that it is books which are being honored, books for children? And who could be happier than I to join in the sixtieth anniversary of such a celebration?

Those who know me best will testify that I am far more of a

reader than I am a writer. If you understand that, you will understand something of what it means to me to be sharing this occasion with Jane Langton and Madeleine L'Engle, writers whose extraordinary vision lighted many of those dark days when I was still struggling to write fiction that someone would find worth publishing. And Arnold Lobel. There we are—Lin, John, David, Mary, and I—all crowded onto one bed, five heads poked together over the pictures, warming ourselves on Frog and Toad, delighting in them and in each other. In those days before I had ever met any real writers, much less become one, the books of these three were among those wonderful works that were enriching my life and the lives of our children. If Arnold will allow me to steal a phrase, it is a moment of true happiness to find myself in this distinguished company. And, speech or no speech, I am very grateful to Ginny Kruse and the members of the Newbery Committee as well as all of you in the Association for Library Service to Children who have made this possible.

Thank you, John Paterson, for your love and patience and unswerving conviction that I can, too, write another book. Thank you, Lin, John, David, and Mary, for all the joy you bring us as well as your total lack of reverence, which keeps me anchored to the real world of gallon milk jugs and swimming meets and socks that never match.

Thank you, Harper and Row. Thank you, Crowell. You know how I love you all. Pat Allen, thank you for liking my peculiar title and insisting that it stay on the book. And Virginia Buckley. What more can I say to you, Virginia? Surely you know that any honor that comes to a book we have done together is more than half yours. And Gene Namovicz. One book will never repay you for all the wear and tear of friendship, but it was all I had. Thank you for liking it even before it had a gold seal. I'm glad your name is in it. And, finally, the Womeldorfs. Thank you, each one. I am proud as well as grateful that we have belonged to one another.

But this speech must be concerned not with me and my myriad debts but with a book. One of you asked me three years ago what I wanted to do next, and I, seeing not the glamour of an awards ceremony but the pile of mess upon my desk back home, said: "All I want to do is write a publishable book." At the time my aim seemed far in excess of my grasp. Lauren Wohl and Bill Morris would call me on your behalf, asking me to speak, and I would whine: "Oh, Lauren, oh, Bill, please. I've got this book I want to write." That sounds pretty convincing for a few months, but when more than two years go by and there is no tangible evidence that any such book exists, someone might begin to think of the tailors who toiled night and day on a magnificent new wardrobe for a certain emperor. But neither Lauren nor Bill ever pried, or even raised an eyebrow. There were times when I suspected that they had more faith in this invisible book of mine than I did.

At one point, near desperation, I said to Virginia Buckley: "If I ever finish this book, Virginia, I'm going to mail it to your home address in a plain brown wrapper. And you must promise me that if it is no good, you will not only refuse to publish it, but that you will never tell another soul that it exists." Virginia, being a gracious person as well as a great editor, did not even point out whose integrity was being impugned by such a demand. She took all my melodrama with a simple nod and one stipulation. "Just don't put a pseudonym on it," she said. I didn't have the nerve to tell her I'd seriously considered it.

Then there were those of you who would ask most politely the perfectly logical question "What are you working on now?"—only to receive a snarl or a disconsolate mutter in reply. Well, this is it. This is the book that I would not talk about for so long even with my husband or my editor or my closest friends, the book that took me months to begin and that I often wondered if I could ever finish. This is *Jacob,* whom I have loved off and on for years.

Whenever I speak, one of the questions sure to be asked during the question-and-answer time is "How long does it take to write a book?" as though books, like elephants or kittens, have a regular and therefore predictable gestation period. Often I will begin my reply by asking, "Which book?" trying to indicate that each book is different and has its own unique history. There is, however, one answer that would be true in every case, but whenever I try to put it into words I find myself swimming in pomposity. The correct answer, you see, is this: It has taken all my life to write this book. Maybe longer.

The conflict at the core of *Jacob Have I Loved* began east of Eden, in the earliest stories of my heritage. Cain was jealous of his brother, and, we are told, "Cain rose up against Abel his brother and slew him." If, in our Freudian orientation, we speak of the basic conflict as that between parent and child, the Bible—which is the earth from which I spring—is much more concerned with the relationships among brothers and sisters. "A friend loveth at all times," says the writer of Proverbs, "but a brother is born for adversity." They never taught us the second half of that verse in Sunday School.

The fairy tales, too, are full of the youngest brother or sister who must surpass his supposedly more clever elders or outwit the wicked ones. In *The Uses of Enchantment* (Knopf) Bruno Bettelheim suggests that a great deal of the apparent rivalry between brothers and sisters in fairy tales is in actuality an Oedipal conflict, since the usual number of brothers or sisters is three. In the stories of two brothers or sisters, Bettelheim suggests that the story is about the divided self, which must be integrated before maturity can be attained. Although both of these explanations make sense, I do not think we can avoid the most obvious meaning of the stories, which is that among children who grow up together in a family there run depths of feeling that will permeate their souls for both good and ill as long as they live.

I was the middle child of five, swivel position, the youngest of the three older children and the oldest of the three younger. Although I can remember distinctly occasions when I determined that someday I would show my older brother and sister a thing or two, and I have no recollection that my two younger sisters were plotting to do me in, still the stories in which the younger by meanness or magic or heavenly intervention bested the elder always bothered me. They simply weren't fair. The divine powers, whether the Hebrew God or the European fairy, always weighted the contest. And although the civilized Calvinist part of my nature spoke in quiet tones about the mystery of divine election, there was a primitive, beastly part, a Calaban, that roared out against such monstrous injustice. Novels, I have learned, tend to come out of the struggle with the untamed beast.

It was the fall of 1977. *The Great Gilly Hopkins* (Crowell) was at the printers, the hoopla following the National Book Award for *The Master Puppeteer* (Crowell) was over, and I had finished the curriculum unit on the Shang and Chou Dynasties of ancient

China. I could no longer put it off. I must face the beast in its den or, what was worse, that stack of blank paper beside my typewriter.

How do you begin a book? People always want to know how you begin. If only I knew. Think of all the agonizing days and weeks I could have spared myself, not to mention my long-suffering family. They know better than to ask me about my work when I'm trying to start all over again. My replies are never gracious. There must be a better way. My way is to write whatever I can, hoping against hope that with all the priming the pump will begin to flow once more.

Here is a sample from those dry, dry days in the fall of 1977:

> Her name is Rachel Ellison but I don't know yet where she lives. It might be in the city or in the country. It might even be Japan. It seems important to know what her parents do. How does religion come into the story? Will Rachel be burdened by guilt as well as everything else? Will her relationship to God play counterpoint to her relationship to her brother? I said brother, but perhaps after all it has to be a sister. I'm avoiding sister because it comes too close to home. Am I contemplating a book I can't write? The feelings start boiling up everytime I begin to think about it. All raw feeling. No story. There has to be a story. There has to be a setting. There has to be something more than boiling anger. Why am I angry? . . . Where is the key that turns this into a book? Jacob and Esau. Cain and Abel. Rachel and Leah. Prodigal and elder brother. Joseph and his brothers. The sons of David. Lord, make my brother give me the portion of the inheritance that comes to me. Maybe Rachel's brother is an adopted South Asian war orphan. Sister.
>
> Excitement to pity to rage to hatred to some kind of accommodation. Step one: Go to the library and find out everything possible about Southeast Asian orphans. . . .

And I was off on a wild-goose chase that lasted for days.

All November and December were spent in pursuit of similar geese. How long this would have gone on I have no way of knowing, but Christmas came and with it a gift of grace. It was not even intended as a gift for me. My sister Helen gave our son John a copy of William Warner's *Beautiful Swimmers: Watermen, Crabs, and the Chesapeake Bay* (Atlantic-Little). I began reading it during those low after-Christmas days, and by the time the new year dawned I had a place to set my story, the Chesapeake Bay, less than an hour from my front door.

In the Bay there are many islands, most of which are not inhabited. Two of these islands, Smith and Tangier, are separated by miles of water from the rest of America. Even now, with television, telephones, and—in the case of Tangier—an airstrip, they seem a world apart. My story was going to be chiefly about a young adolescent who felt terribly isolated. Of course, all fourteen-year-olds who are not social clones feel isolated, but what better way to show this isolation than an island? Rass—the name for my island squirted up from my subconscious and has yet to reveal its source or meaning—Rass would be none of the actual islands, but something like all of them.

Now I began going to the library as well as to the Bay to find out everything I could about the Chesapeake. At the same time I began setting down on scraps of paper and three-by-five cards ideas as they would occur, things that might happen in the story.

What about a grandmother or other live-in relative who spouts pietisms? She may be one who brings up "Jacob have I love. . . ." theme.

Old man gets off ferry. He left thirty years before and has come back. Takes shack at farthest end of island to live as recluse.

Make the kid sentimental—moons over tombstone—tries to convert friend who is boy to sentimentality.

These are bound with the same sturdy rubber band that holds notes taken from reading and observation.

> pain of being stung in the eye by jellyfish
> how peelers are separated
>   2 wks. to go—snots, greens, white sign crabs
>   1 wk.—pink sign
>   hrs to go before busting—rank, red sign
> reactions to thunderstorms
>   chopped down mast
>   climbing up it swinging hatchet at the almighty-
>   daring God to meet him halfway—
> cats around garbage dump scavenging. Big cats.
> wintering birds on Smith
> "Oh, my blessed, what a noise."

There is another large pack of four-by-six cards, but I think all those notes were collected much later. I think so, not that I ever seem capable of dating, but the cards are ones I remember buying at Gray's Pharmacy in Norfolk. So between the first batch of cards and the second, there came the January 1978 announcement of a Newbery Medal, the acceptance, the knowledge that after thirteen years in Takoma Park we would be moving, the discovery of my mother's terminal cancer, the choice of *Gilly* as the Newbery Honor Book, the move to Norfolk, Mother's death, and a National Book Award. That is not everything that happened in our lives between the fall of 1977 and the spring of 1979, but it may give you some idea why poor *Jacob* was languishing.

But even as I present to you these impeccable excuses, I know in my heart that the reason I nearly despaired of finishing this book was more the internal storms it stirred up than those that came from without. I was trying to write a story that made my stomach churn every time I sat down at the typewriter. "Love is strong as death," says the writer of the Song of Songs, "jealousy is as cruel as the grave." I did not want ever again to walk the dark path into that cruelty.

Yet even while I was having trouble going back into my young self, I was being drawn more and more into the world of the book. I knew that in Rass I was trying to create a facsimile of the Bay islands, but my feeling as I worked was not so much that of a creator as that of an explorer. Here was a hidden world that it was my task to discover. If I failed, this world would remain forever unknown.

I do not mean by this that I thought I had a monopoly on the Chesapeake Bay. Not long after I had begun work on my book, James Michener's massive *Chesapeake* (Random) was published. I read it with dread, fearing that he might have preempted me, might have discovered my world. But he hadn't. He couldn't have. The Chesapeake world I was exploring was mine alone. No other living soul had access to it unless I could somehow reveal it in *Jacob*. I think I have finally learned that no one can steal your novel from you. No matter how closely his material may come to yours, he can only write his story, and you, yours—the intricate design of an individual life upon some portion of the outside world. I knew, for better or worse, that if I did not write *Jacob,* it would never be written.

I say my world, my story, but it hardly ever felt like mine. For one thing, it refused to obey my rules. I have always sworn that I would never write a book in the first person. It is too limiting, too egotistical. And yet, the book refused any voice but Louise's. "Oh, well," I said to myself, "I'd better get it down any way I can in the first draft. In the next draft I can write it properly."

At some point I wrote a very peculiar note to myself. Not content with writing a book in first person, I apparently was thinking of writing it as three first-person stories—one for Louise, one for Caroline, and one for Call. "Perhaps," I added, "end with a fourth section which goes back to Sara Louise and ties the story together."

Heavens above. I think the only reason this book ever got written is that I would regularly lose all my notes. I must remember that next time. Take all the notes you wish, but do not fail to lose them once you start.

By now it was the fall of 1979. I was piling page upon page, revision upon revision, until finally my husband made a strong suggestion that it was time to get the manuscript out of the house and to Virginia Buckley. I think he felt that if drastic steps were not taken soon, he would be living with *Jacob* in an eternal triangle. He was right. I had become so entangled in the story that I did not know if it was worth further effort, if it would ever be a publishable book. So I sent it.

Virginia got it on Friday and called me on Sunday. "I love it," she said. I knew that she did not mean it was perfect. I knew there were months of intensive rewriting ahead, but you cannot imagine the joy with which I heard those words. I know very well that I am capable of writing a bad book, but I have never, in my right mind, believed that Virginia would publish one. She loved *Jacob,* and, as I began the painstaking revisions, I came to love it, too— until, though I never managed to bring it to perfection, I felt that it was the best that I could do. My child had grown up and must, at long last, be let go.

An earnest young reporter asked me: "What are you trying to do when you write for children?" "I'm trying to write as well as I possibly can," I answered. He thought I hadn't understood his question. "No, no," he said. "What I mean is, what is your philosophy of writing for children? Isn't there some moral you want to get across to them? Aren't there some values you wish to instill in your young readers?" "I'm trying," I said, "to write for my readers the best story, the truest story of which I am capable." He gave up on me and changed the subject, frustrated and annoyed. He seemed to share the view of many intelligent, well-educated, well-meaning people that while adult literature may aim to be art, the object of children's books is to whip the little rascals into shape.

But you and I know better. We know that those of us who write for children are called, not to do something to a child, but be someone for a child. "Art," in Frances Clarke Sayers's wonderfully passionate definition, is "a controlled fury of desire to share one's private revelation of life." And she the librarian summons us who are writers to the service of art—to give the best that is in us to "the audience that lives by what it feeds upon."

Among my notes I found this one written while I was stalled one day during August of 1979. I can date it because it is written on Gene Namovicz's electric typewriter and is full of stray *l*'s and *k*'s.

There is another sibling rivalry in the story of Jacob. It is, of course, the story of Leah and Rachel. "Jacob have I loved—" Poor Leah, the homely elder sister. Married in trickery to the man passionately in love with her younger sister. She goes to his bed and must lie there and bear his seeing who she is. Watch his face as the truth of his father-in-law's treachery dawns. His disappointment. How does he react? What does he say? Even if, and it is hard to believe he might have been, even if in his own disappointment he remembers her pain and tries to be tactful and kind, that very kindness would be next to unbearable, if Leah loves him at all. Esau's grief is nothing compared to Leah's. She must watch her husband go joyfully to her sister and joylessly come to her. But God does give her many sons. That would be a comfort if we did not know that Rachel, who only has two sons, is the mother of Joseph—that younger brother of all younger brothers. This puts a new dimension into the phrase, "Jacob have I loved...." It is a woman speaking now, a wronged and grieving woman, not God. The loving is not here a matter of divine election but of the eternal weight of women who have neither the beauty of Rachel nor the cleverness of Rebekkah. What shall we do for the Leahs?

The only thing I can do for the Leahs, the Esaus, and the Louises is to give them now, while they are young, the best, the truest story of which I am capable. I have learned, for all my failings and limitations, that when I am willing to give myself away in a book, readers will respond by giving themselves away as well, and the book that I labored over so long becomes in our mutual giving something far richer and more powerful than I could have ever imagined. I thank you, and I thank God that I have been allowed to take part in this miracle once again.

And now, if you will excuse me, I have this book I want to write.

BIOGRAPHICAL NOTE

Jill Paton Walsh

Katherine Paterson
by Gene Inyart Namovicz

Katherine Paterson has had seven prestigious books published since 1973. Their overlapping honors include four ALA Notable Children's Books, one Newbery Honor Book, one Edgar Allan Poe Special Award nomination, one Christopher Award, one Lewis Carroll Shelf Award, two National Book Awards, the United States nomination for the Hans Christian Andersen Award, two William Allen White Award nominations, and now—two Newbery Medals. Why Katherine? How has this happened?

Perhaps her very first book, which few people know, offers a clue. *Who Am I?* was published in 1966 by the Covenant Life Curriculum Press in Richmond, Virginia. In it Katherine quotes the following anecdote told by one of her teachers at Union Theological Seminary—Earl Loomis, author of *The Self in Pilgrimage* (Harper):

You may have heard the story of a small boy who was taken by his mother and a much older sister to a restaurant for dinner. The waitress came out and took the orders of the two ladies and then turned to the child. "And what will you have, young man?"

"I'll order for him," said his mother.

The waitress repeated her question. "What will you have, young man?"

His sister got impatient. "I'll order for him."

"What will you have, young man?" the waitress asked again.

"A hamburger!" His eyes were shining.

"With or without onions?"

"With!"

"Toasted or plain?'"

"Toasted!"

The waitress went to fill the orders and the happy little boy turned to his mother. "Mother!" he exclaimed. "She thinks I'm real!"

To my mind, nothing better illustrates Katherine Paterson's attitude toward her readers of all ages. This respect for others is but one facet of her open-hearted approach to life—a trait which her editor Virginia Buckley, in the August 1978 *Horn Book* at the time of Katherine's first Newbery, called her "ability to relate instantly to others."

When Katherine's *The Sign of the Chrysanthemum* (Crowell) was published in 1973, two librarians from different nearby libraries said to me, "You two must meet! You both write children's books, and each of you has four children. Besides, both of you read so much. You'll love each other!" In a pig's eye, I thought!—already too busy with my own four children and the children's book I was trying to write. Anyway, I'm shy. I don't telephone perfect strangers to introduce myself. But Katherine does. She called to say that her daughter Lin had brought home a paperback copy of *Jenny* (Archway). "I see from the back cover that you live in Takoma Park, too!" she said happily. "We've got to talk!"

We did talk, and we've talked ever since. In those days, because our children were young, it was exciting for each of us to find a friend within the natural boundaries of our busy lives. Thirstily, we engaged in a continuing dialogue—at each other's houses, on the telephone, and in supermarkets, auto repair shops, pediatricians' waiting rooms, shoe stores, and pharmacies as well as at PTA meetings and Boy Scout dinners. We tumbled all our concerns, like unsorted laundry, into the same conversation— whether about books, children, or the dogs' fleas.

Katherine once said to me that in *The Great Gilly Hopkins*

(Crowell) she had drawn both Maime Trotter and Gilly larger than life deliberately in order to make her point. Katherine Paterson, by virtue of her talent and integrity and joyousness, seems somewhat larger than life, so that it is hard to describe her without sounding extravagant.

I must say first that Katherine is fun to have around. She is also funny, warm, and generous. She and her husband, John Barstow Paterson, complement each other. They argue freely, but they sustain and restore each other in adversity and even in good fortune, which is sometimes more exhausting.

Katherine continues to change and grow in her writing but the amount of mail to be dealt with has grown as well, as has the number of requests for speaking engagements. Fortunately, she is a person of considerable vitality. She sings herself hoarse at choir practice, talks herself hoarse at lectures, meetings, and parties, and has the loudest, most genuine and unladylike horselaugh ever sounded in this hemisphere—altogether a magnificent blend of Christian involvement and irreverent glee.

She works hard at her writing, typing on her old manual typewriter—in winter wearing a pair of old slacks and a bulky sweater in front of a portable heater on the jalousied sun porch of their house in Norfolk and in summer wearing shorts and a T-shirt in their converted barn at Lake George.

She will not say a word about a book while she's working on it, and once she's completed it, she is certain that she will never be able to write another. (I've told her repeatedly that this is as unlikely as the thought of her never talking again—which provokes the horselaugh.) But if she can't speak of a work in progress, she cannot help living it. The day that she sent the manuscript of *Jacob Have I Loved* to her editor, she wrote a long and delightful letter, in every way typical except for the last paragraph, which is not her usual brand of humor: "The snake was missing when John (Jr.) got home from school yesterday. He was eventually located in the piano, missing some scales. Get it? The snake, not the piano. Brup. How low can one sink?" Louise Bradshaw was still very much with her, even though the manuscript was in the mail.

In ordinary conversation, as in her letters and books, Katherine is an irrepressible storyteller. She has a feel for the dramatic value of an episode, and her speech is larded with anecdotes. "Didn't I tell you about the time Blossom ate the light bulb?" "No," I answer, settling back as happily expectant as Jess was, waiting for Leslie to tell him the story of *Hamlet*.

Katherine knows her own worth, but this awareness is tempered by a fiendish sense of humor, which she turns on herself like a laser beam, telling jokes on herself at every opportunity. When she was enrolling the children in new schools after the family moved to Norfolk, the clerk filling out the necessary forms asked Katherine her occupation. "I'm a writer," Katherine explained. "What do you write?" the clerk inquired doubtfully. "Children's books." Katherine says that at that point the clerk smiled very sweetly and said, "Why don't we just put down *housewife*?"

Katherine is a housewife and a good cook who sometimes bakes her own bread and makes her own doughnuts (which Blossom, her springer spaniel, consumes by the warm dozen unless a Paterson guards them until they're cool enough for the family to eat). She enjoys good food but eats almost nothing before a speech and sleeps poorly in hotel rooms. Whenever possible she takes one or more of the children with her when she must travel to keep her speaking engagements, but sometimes the demands are too frequent or infringe on the needs and claims of her family. Then pressure builds up, and she becomes exhausted. When she is very tired, she seeks respite in music, which nourishes her—and always in books.

For Katherine is a passionate reader. Her talks about her own writing, formal or otherwise, are filled with glowing references to Joseph Conrad, Jane Austen, Tolstoy, and C. S. Lewis, together with newer favorites like Flannery O'Connor, Anne Tyler, and Mary Lee Settle. Whenever an opportunity presents itself, she urges teachers and parents to read aloud to their children of all ages and gives spontaneous and enthusiastic book talks calling attention to those many children's books which delight her—from Peter Spier's *Noah's Ark* (Doubleday) to Fritz Mühlenweg's *Big Tiger and Christian* (Pantheon).

Whether she is speaking of books or of Oriental food, Katherine is the magnetic center of a roomful of people. Her autographing sessions last twice as long as scheduled because she becomes involved in an animated conversation with every person in the line. Moving her through a crowd of well-wishers after a Library of Congress lecture or a Book Guild luncheon takes as long as it does to get bubble gum out of a child's hair.

The thirteen years that Katherine lived in Takoma Park, Maryland, was the longest time she had ever spent in one place. She was born in China of missionary parents and moved more than fifteen times before she reached the age of eighteen. She attended King College in Bristol, Tennessee, graduated summa cum laude, taught a year in Lovettsville, Virginia, and then moved on to Richmond to get her master's degree in English Bible. For the next four years she served as a missionary in Japan, an experience she feels had a powerful influence on her and one that certainly influenced her writing. In 1961 she returned to this country to accept a fellowship at Union Theological Seminary in New York, where she met and married John—thus beginning a new career as wife and mother that soon brought her to Takoma Park.

To understand Katherine, you must know her family. Her husband is her first editor (after each manuscript is completed) and her staunchest champion. A dedicated Presbyterian minister, John has a special knack for recognizing and encouraging talent. The walls of each consecutive Paterson home are covered with the many original art works that he has purchased from aspiring painters and skillfully framed to their best advantage. It was John who initiated the custom of having Katherine write a special Christmas story each year—which he read aloud as part of the Christmas service at the Takoma Park Presbyterian Church—a tradition eventually resulting in *Angels and Other Strangers* (Crowell). It was John, too, who suggested that she revisit Japan to research the background for what became *The Master Puppeteer* (Crowell), set in the puppet theater of eighteenth-century Osaka.

Since that first Newbery Medal in 1978, John accepted a call to become pastor of the Lafayette Presbyterian Church in Norfolk, Virginia. The move from Takoma Park was a wrenching one because it occurred when Katherine's mother became suddenly ill and it was learned that her death from cancer was imminent. In their new house the boxes were not unpacked, the children were uneasy in their new schools, and John needed her. In Winchester her mother grew weaker. For several harrowing months in the dead of winter Katherine drove back and forth between Norfolk and Winchester, learning to maneuver her small car on Virginia's icy roads as she had once mastered riding a motorcycle on the muddy roads of rural Japan.

Now, two years later, the Patersons are settled in Norfolk. The striking and exuberant Lin, their oldest daughter, attends Earlham College in Indiana. John Jr., of scuba diving, tennis, and rappelling fame, cleans their new house as expertly as he did their smaller home in Maryland. David Paterson, cross-country runner and thespian, received rave reviews for his role as Stephen in the Riverview Playhouse production of *The Shadow Box;* and Mary, at age thirteen, already displays considerable writing talent and plays first flute in the school band.

C. C., the cat (with his Charlie Chaplin mustache), found as a starved and wormy kitten in a shoe box in Maryland, has grown into a sleek Virginia cat. Blossom, the springer spaniel, now has a canine companion named Princess. This tiny white mixed-breed belongs to David and goes for walks holding the end of big Blossom's leash in her mouth.

In a talk she gave at Simmons College earlier this year, Katherine spoke of three dominant influences in her own development, which amount to a triptych of experiences embodying the critical times in China and Japan, her youth and adolescence in the American South, and her strong Biblical heritage. To quote from that speech:

The way a writer shapes human experience depends to a great extent on her history—all those forces, most of which she had nothing to do with, that made her what she is. In speaking of those forces, we are speaking of our human heritage, our particular family history, and our individual past experience. These are the memories which we call up, consciously or unconsciously, as we write.

Certainly the child who twice fled China because of imminent wars and who felt herself an outsider and a misfit in a succession of American schools is very much alive in the adult Katherine Paterson. She remembers how it feels to be uncertain of acceptance, to fear ridicule, to be dependent on the moods and will of those in authority who may be—or seem to be (which is the same for a child)—uncaring or even malevolent. Her deep respect for the individual, as evidenced in her writing and in her personal relationships, is based on her belief in God and on her hope for man. Like one of her favorite writers, Flannery O'Connor, Katherine sees God as "the object of ultimate concern" and never forgets that "life . . . for all its horror, has been found by God to be worth dying for."

Katherine often tells of the time, after she won the first National Book Award and was beginning to speak at a great many schools, when a child asked her earnestly: "Do you know any *real* writers?"

I do. I know a real writer and a real human being—Katherine Womeldorf Paterson. To borrow the ending of her 1978 Newbery Acceptance speech—*"Banzai!"*

Hurray! May she live forever!

The Newbery Medal 1982

A VISIT TO WILLIAM BLAKE'S INN: POEMS FOR INNOCENT AND EXPERIENCED TRAVELERS

written by NANCY WILLARD

illustrated by ALICE AND MARTIN PROVENSEN

published by HARCOURT BRACE JOVANOVICH 1981

BOOK NOTE

In her introduction Nancy Willard tells the "innocent and experienced travelers" for whom she has written the poems how she made the acquaintance of William Blake and his poetry: When she was ill with measles at the age of seven, her baby sitter recited "Tyger, Tyger, burning bright" and later sent her *Songs of Innocence and Songs of Experience* inscribed with William Blake's best wishes for a speedy recovery and the dictum, "Poetry is the best medicine." The sixteen poems that follow the introduction constitute the structure and ambiance of the inn and the adventures it inspires.

The poems bring the visitor, via " 'Blake's Celestial Limousine,' " to the inn, where a rabbit is the bellhop and a bear is the bed. The guest, made wakeful by the twirling moon and dancing sun, is reassured by the rabbit, only to be wakened later by the man in the marmalade hat, come to "Call out the keepers/And waken the sleepers." The King of Cats eats a breakfast " 'on the house' "; the Wise Cow eats a cloud " 'raw/on freshly buttered bread.' " Two sunflowers " 'weary of weather' " request a room with a view; and the Wise Cow makes *"Way"* and *"Room"* for all. Blake leads rabbit, cat, tiger, rat, and visitor on a walk through the Milky Way and on their return lets them rest at the hearth before the marmalade man leads them, with other animals, in a dance. The King of Cats sends a postcard with messages to his wife and friends; and the tiger, who feels ill, asks Blake for a story. Blake tells "The Tale of the Tailor." The visitor advises travelers who reach "a lovely inn" where a rabbit makes the bed and the bread is baked by two dragons to "rest a little for my sake,/and give my love to William Blake."

Newbery Medal Acceptance
by Nancy Willard

The Provensens and I would like to thank the members of the Newbery and Caldecott Committees for honoring our book and to thank everyone at Harcourt Brace Jovanovich with whom we worked. And we are especially glad for an opportunity to honor the remarkable woman who brought us together and who has seen me through ten books: Barbara Lucas.

When I was a child, I often heard it said that "little pitchers have big ears," and I knew in my heart that if I turned into a pitcher, no other pitcher in this world or out of it would have bigger ears than mine. I was luckier than many eavesdroppers. I spent part of my childhood in a house that had a party line. There were seven people on the line, and each household had its own ring. Ours was four short and one long. My mother made it clear to my sister and me that only very ill-bred people lifted up the receiver, when the telephone rang for somebody else, and listened in on other people's conversations.

One afternoon I was alone in the house, and the telephone rang: three short rings. The bell did not toll for us. A terrible curiosity overcame me. I lifted the receiver and heard a concert of clicks, like claws scampering over a bare floor: the sound of five other ill-bred people lifting up their receivers to listen in. I held my breath. Now I would find out how the world conducted itself when children were not keeping watch over it. A voice that sounded as far away as Australia exclaimed:

"And they had cloth napkins, with Briarcroft Inn printed in the corner."

"You don't mean it," purred the voice of Mrs. Johnson, who lived three houses down from ours.

"I could only get five of them in my purse," said the voice from Australia.

And then, with a flourish of chimes, the Good Humor man turned into our street, and both speakers and listeners hung up and ran out to meet him.

I did not know exactly what an inn was and supposed it was a place that had to take people in. If there was no room at the inn, you got the stable, which was guaranteed to hold a mother, a father, a child, shepherds, three kings, a company of angels, and a lot of animals. An inn was a place of great mercy and variety, where no one was ever put out.

That evening I asked my mother, "What is an inn?"

"It's a resting place for travelers," she said, "like a hotel, only friendlier. Your father and I stayed in a wonderful inn on our honeymoon in a very small town in Germany. I remember when we got off the steamer, the porter met us and put all our luggage on his bicycle."

I felt a flood of sympathy for the porter.

"Were you the only people at the inn?" I asked.

"No, indeed. A great many interesting people stayed there. And the rooms were over a hundred years old."

"How did you know they were over a hundred years old?"

"Because our guide said so," answered my mother, "and because there were so many cracks in the plaster."

A resting place for interesting people, cracks in the plaster—if this was an inn, then all my life I had lived in one without knowing it. Surely no other inn had cracks in the plaster to match ours. Finding pictures in them was like looking for creatures in the shifting shapes of clouds. Whenever a new crack appeared, I fetched my box of paints, and my mother and I discussed the possibilities.

"What do you think it looks like? A whale?" I suggest.

"Yes, but do we really need a whale in the guest room?" asks Mother. "Couldn't you turn it into an angel, like the one you painted over the crack in the bathroom?"

And so in guest room and bathroom and crumbling hall, the patient angels went about their bright business, and the cracks went unobserved, for who looks at plaster in the presence of angels?

As for guests, nobody could ask for a greater variety than ours. On the third floor lived my grandfather, whose room held his clothes, his chewing tobacco, and the books he counted among his special friends: the Bible, *Pilgrim's Progress,* treatises on beekeeping and osteopathy, and the works of Edgar Allan Poe. When I came home from school, I could hear his voice rolling through the house, breathing life into the raven, Annabel Lee, and the tintinnabulation of the bells. The room opposite his stood empty until one evening my cousin, a sophomore at the local teacher's college, dropped by and told us he'd had a fight with his mother; could he please spend the night with us? He stayed six months.

A week after my cousin moved in, his best friend had a fight with *his* mother and moved in also. Unlike the rest of us, who enjoyed our creature comforts, they converted their beds to pallets on the floor and atoned for their sins with loud prayers, which started at six in the morning and stopped when the two penitents left for their eight o'clock class. Scarcely had the door closed behind them when my grandmother began humming and stirring in the room below theirs. From morning till evening she talked to herself, to the quick, and to the dead.

"Get the ladders ready, I got five men coming to pick cherries," she would call to the hired man, who had died fifty years before, but who once sowed and slaughtered on her father's farm in Iowa. At night her English slipped away, and she recited prayers in German and dreamed herself back in that country church where the women sat on the left side and the men on the right and heard about the wages of sin, while an occasional wise cow waited outside like a visitor from a more peaceable kingdom.

Reading, drawing, doing my homework, I listened and noted in the margins of my books and math papers and class schedules whatever seemed worth the saving: a fragment of speech, a line of poetry. Years later, I was reading the poetry of William Carlos Williams and suddenly felt that he was speaking directly to me. "What do I do?" wrote Williams. "I listen.... This is my entire occupation."

And I would add: The poet writes poems for people to listen to, poems to be heard as well as read. Skipping rope or trading taunts on the jungle gym, children know the importance of hearing and saying poetry. But do we ever really outgrow that wish to hear a story, to say a poem? The babysitters and teachers who read to me have gone the way of all flesh, and I have had to make do with recordings of poems and stories played on a small portable phonograph, which I move from room to room while doing my housework. Scrubbing a floor is child's play if you can listen to Ralph Richardson reading William Blake.

One night, after laundry was folded away and the floors swept, I stacked half a dozen grocery cartons in the living room and started to build a house in which wishing did the washing and magic did the mending. Here nobody kept house. The only thing anyone kept was the secret.

I knew my handmade house was going to be an inn when it started attracting guests. Every afternoon our plump cat climbed into the cardboard dining room and quite literally brought down the house. A friend who earned his living building real houses witnessed this awful spectacle and said, "Let me copy the house for you in wood." He took the measurements and a month later appeared with a tall wooden structure on his truck.

"Now paint it," he said.

Was it this habit of mixing poetry with homework that made me take the inn for a subject when Barbara Lucas asked me to write a collection of poems for children? Although I had been listening to Blake's poetry, I knew two editions of his poems from my childhood: *Songs of Innocence and Songs of Experience,* with Blake's pictures, and a selection of those songs called *The Land of Dreams* (Macmillan), illustrated by Pamela Bianco. What interested me as much as her drawings was her letter to Blake, which opens the book:

Dear Mr. Blake,

When I was first asked to make these drawings, it made me very happy because I had known and liked your poems for a long while.... yet when the opportunity at last presented itself, I began to get scared.... For, since you had made your drawings so well, I knew that nobody had any business to attempt to make different ones. And then I consoled myself by thinking that if I wrote and explained the whole thing to you, you would understand, and perhaps, after all, you wouldn't mind so very much.

Since Pamela Bianco had written a letter to Blake, then surely somewhere, somehow, Blake was alive and could read it. Many years after I'd laid her book aside, I was attending a panel discussion at Princeton on the state of the arts and was startled to hear one of the panelists, Allen Ginsberg, quietly remark, "The last time I talked with William Blake . . ."

And now I find myself making the same statement. The last time I talked with William Blake, I was wrestling with the problem of how to move the inn to Philadelphia for this conference, and I had just lost my glasses.

"You can get a new pair of glasses," said my son.

"No, I can't. Those frames belonged to my father before he died. They're irreplaceable."

That night I dreamed myself on a country road, driving a horse hitched to an open wagon. On the wagon rode my homemade house, William Blake's Inn. All at once the heavens opened, and the rains came, and when the air cleared and the sun returned, I discovered to my horror that the inn had vanished. And who was this small man on a bicycle, gliding toward me? He was, I was sure, none other than William Blake. In my dream I burst into tears.

"Oh, Mr. Blake," I wailed, "I've lost your inn."

He pedaled more slowly, but he did not dismount.

"You haven't lost it," he assured me. "You've just lost sight of it. Be good to my guests. They're irreplaceable. Birds, beasts, air, water, flowers, grass. Me. You."

BIOGRAPHICAL NOTE

Michael Metz

Nancy Willard
by Barbara Lucas

"Would you like to meet Father Beasley?" she asked with a laugh. Before I could answer she added, almost shyly, *"You know, in The Highest Hit"* (Harcourt). She needn't have identified him. The characters from Nancy Willard's books are old friends. They are so real that I often find myself wondering what one of them might be doing at that moment.

"Does he know he is Father Beasley?" I asked after exchanging pleasantries with the priest who looked remarkably like Emily McCully's illustration. "I think people enjoy seeing how other people might see them," she answered abstractly. "Don't you?"

I had met Uncle Terrible a year earlier, when visiting Nancy, at the Aurora Cafe. (Both the man and the place figure in the last book of her "Anatole" trilogy—*Uncle Terrible,* to be published by Harcourt this fall.) "Don't mention the manuscript," she had whispered then. "He doesn't know he is in it."

It is remarkable to me that I cannot remember my first meeting with Nancy. It was at Putnam's, of course, and I do recall Rita Scott's phoning to tell me about this young client who was so tremendously talented—who had published adult books of short stories, poetry, and critical essays; was teaching at Vassar; conducted workshops at the Breadloaf Writer's conferences; and had been a visiting poet at Oberlin. The author had never published a book for children but had some ideas. I bought the first of these ideas rather quickly but left for Harcourt shortly afterward, and Margaret Frith brought out Nancy's inaugural children's book, *The Merry History of a Christmas Pie* (Putnam).

At Harcourt we had set about finding the right artist for *Sailing to Cythera: And Other Anatole Stories*. It turned out to be David McPhail, who was immediately captured by the magic of Nancy's storytelling and, adding sorcery of his own, created the final dimensions for those shimmering supernatural worlds in which the stories take place. Anatole is the Hero and, like those in myths and legends, he receives the call to adventure; survives the initiation of trials, temptations, and the forces of nature; realizes his quest; and returns at last to the threshold of his simple home, triumphant but humble. Nancy, like Grandma in these stories, never throws anything away, and her writing bursts with artifices skillfully wrought from bits and pieces of the classics, folk tales, the Gospels, and whatever events might be taking place in her own life.

James Anatole, her son, was four when the trilogy was begun and was, of course, the model for the Hero. Nancy wrote:

... what wonderful drawings. I like the pictures of Anatole on the horse and Anatole with the soldier. And, curiously enough, the drawings do look like James, which pleases and rather astonishes him, I think; they made him forget the loss of a ball which his papa threw so high 'the sun got it.' The sun has a toy chest, I'm told, where he *keeps* all such lost objects; unfortunately, he never throws anything away.

A sudden spate of picture books was delivered before *The Island of the Grass King: The Further Adventures of Anatole* was to arrive. This seemed appropriate for a poet, but it also had something to do with the limited time left to Nancy after the demands of being mother, housewife, teacher, guest lecturer, and reader. Induced, however, by our enthusiastic pleas to "write about your own childhood," *The Highest Hit* found its way into publication with anticipated applause. It was a witty, warm novel in which the protagonist Kate, among other things, developed a deep friendship with an elderly neighbor. This relationship and her family's concern for a mentally ill relative are treated with gentle sensitivity, humor, and genuine love—long before such subjects became popular. During the writing of the book my staff and I were to receive photos of the beauty shop and the mysterious magic shop in the story, taken in the small Michigan town where Nancy's family has had a summer cottage for years. Scenes and characters from these summer reunions with her mother, her sister, and her sister's family have taken root in much of her work.

Dominating her work are descriptions of her childhood home, where her mother (Grandma) still lives and where the stars that glow in the dark on the ceiling of her room (and Kate's) still exist. "The painter came, and all the animals which had decorated the walls were being painted over. I remember thinking with alarm, 'but I'll never see those animals again!' " It was then that her father pasted up the stars. "It was a real night sky. With the dippers and everything."

This was in Ann Arbor, Michigan, where Nancy was born. She had a World War II childhood and recalls the things a child would remember: the blackouts, rations, but—most of all—the time "we made Kool-Aid, *once,* a great event. It nearly wiped out our sugar rations."

After high school graduation she studied at the University of Michigan, where she received a B.A. degree. Her father had taught there; he was internationally known for his work on fluorine and for his textbooks. Her M.A. in medieval literature was earned at Stanford University, and her Ph.D. from Michigan in modern literature. Nancy's dissertation on the poetry of Rainer Maria Rilke and William Carlos Williams was later expanded and published by the University of Missouri Press as *Testimony of the Invisible Man.* While an undergraduate, Nancy won five Hopwood Awards for poetry and essays. Other books of poetry followed as well as adult fiction. Her latest book of poetry—for adults—*Household Tales of Moon and Water* is due this fall from Harcourt. She has received the Creative Artists' Public Service Award and a National Endowment for the Arts Award—both for poetry. It was like pulling teeth to get this information from Nancy, much of which I had been unaware of despite the fact that I had worked with her for a decade.

There's more. Nancy is also an artist. She studied art in Oslo and Paris and recently illustrated two small books for Seabury

Press. She began creating little books (as her son does now) when she was a child. As a teenager Nancy discovered crow-quill pens and India ink. Becoming enamored of illuminated manuscripts, she began to illustrate her books with elaborate borders "made of thousands of figures and flowers, on real parchment" and almost went blind trying to imitate the crosshatching in the illustrations she found in the classics in the family library. "I didn't know that the drawings had been reduced. I thought artists simply drew things that small."

When asked about her working habits, she smiled.

> Eric [her photographer-husband] says I'm always working. I *do* have bits of things in progress in the corners: crafts, things like that, which I can work on in the evenings when there is noise—you know, people and records playing. But I usually write in the mornings when James is in school and I'm not teaching. When I needed the quiet to do the drawings for the Seabury books, I worked from nine in the evening until two in the morning.

Nancy's magic with the sewing machine produces most of her own clothes as well as stuffed toys and Halloween costumes for James. Ilse Vogel, the children's author and a good friend of hers, said about another of her talents, "I admire Nancy's way of cooking, the imaginative variety of her vegetable dishes. Especially so because when I had known her only casually, I was convinced that a creature like her would be living only on nightingale's tongues and moonlight dew."

Other things in progress in the corners range from life-size soft sculptures and painted ceramics to just about anything else she gets her hands on. Most of these creations find their way as gifts to Nancy's friends and colleagues. Those that remain fascinate me, for they are usually somehow connected to the book she is currently writing. Until recently, I had never been able to judge which came first—the artifacts or the story in which they played a role. The truth was revealed when I heard her speaking to several groups of elementary school children in Scarsdale. In each school she introduced first herself and then a six-foot-long soft sculpture which reclined in a most ungainly way on a chair beside her. The sculpture looked pleasant enough, but it certainly did not resemble anything yet discovered on this planet. Its head had ears and antlers, and its torso had plainly been a twenty-pound sugar bag.

Otherwise, it seemed fairly human in appearance. She had brought this creation in a large suitcase (with its head protruding) from Poughkeepsie that morning on a commuter train. As she spoke to the children, I could not help but visualize the possible reactions of the stunned early morning passengers headed for their offices in the city.

"If this creature came into school one morning and sat down beside you, what would you do?" she asked the children. There were always varying responses. A few youngsters seemed horrified by the idea; most were intrigued and said they would try to make friends with the stranger and find out who he was and where he had come from. They would also try not to be afraid of him just because he was different. It was then that she revealed that the creature was a character in *The Marzipan Moon* (Harcourt). "In the story 'he' is very real, as real as you are in your life. When you stop to think about it, why can't 'he' be just as real in his world as you are in yours?" she asked. She admitted that the artifacts she made usually came before the stories they were later to figure in. "Winnie the Pooh was a real teddy bear," she pointed out to the children. "He existed before the stories about him did. Remember? I like to have these characters around me for a while before I set anything down. They help me to create the story because they become so real to me."

I remember very well a lopsided four-room dollhouse which Nancy had made from bits and ends and furnished in a most intriguing way. It sat in her living room and was Uncle Terrible's domain (when he had become the appropriate size). Months later many of the furnishings were moved into a startling seven-room house, sturdily built of wood by a friend, Ralph Gabriner. This grand edifice became the inn of William Blake. Its rooms were papered with Blake's engravings, Kate Greenaway's illustrations, and Lewis Carroll's photographs of Alice. New inhabitants included two green rabbits; a staff of Dutch girls with silver shoes and cooks with silver spoons monogrammed with moons; a Wise Cow; a dragon; and other assorted animals.

I cannot list the hundreds of objects which reside in this inn, but I do have some favorites. For example, there is a prophet with gold hands and a silver star-moon pendant around his neck. His wings are made from the tail-bone of a fish brought home from a dinner party. ("The cat used to steal the prophet and run around the house with him in his jaws.")

The warmth and restive creativity of the entire family is striking. Eric's arresting black-and-white photographs have appeared in several New York shows. James, an avid reader, is also drawing now—small books of clever cartoons.

When Nancy was seven, her first work, a poem, was published on the children's page of a Unitarian church magazine. An aunt had sent it in. Her first miniature book was published when she was a high school senior. It was an illustrated story called *A Child's Star,* and it appeared in *The Horn Book Magazine.* She later received a letter from Bertha Mahony Miller saying that Mr. Miller was so taken with one of her drawings that they wanted to use it for their Christmas card that year. "Would ten dollars be a fair fee for this?" wrote Mrs. Miller. *"Would it!"* thought the young artist.

While Nancy was in college, another of her little illustrated books was published—this time in the University of Michigan literary magazine. Shortly afterward, Nancy received a letter from the poet Marianne Moore asking if she could have a second copy. "Someone had given her a copy during her visit to the Michigan campus. She enclosed five dollars in a pink Kleenex. I am sure I saved the Kleenex." Eric discourages her from saving *everything*—I don't know how successfully. It is not that Nancy is a hoarder, but as she once confided, "I think to myself, 'Don't throw this away because you could make something with it. *It could belong to something.*' "

Working with this sort of creative spirit over the years has been a joy and a rare privilege for me. I have been struck again and again by her generous nature; her lack of demands; her willingness to accept suggestions and her gentle firmness in explaining why, if she could not. When the extraordinary art for *A Visit to William Blake's Inn* was being prepared by Alice and Martin Provensen, she sent me a card with a single statement. "Can you ask them, please, to make Blake look like the real Blake? That's my only request regarding the pictures."

A few weeks ago, watching his mother autograph books, James remarked, "If somewhere Blake is watching all this, he must be pleased to see all this fuss being made about him."

Well, *I* am pleased to see all this fuss being made about Nancy Willard. She has long deserved it.

The Newbery Medal 1983

DICEY'S SONG

written by CYNTHIA VOIGT

published by ATHENEUM PUBLISHERS 1982

BOOK NOTE

Dicey Tillerman thinks that her hard work is done after she has managed to bring her younger brothers James and Sammy and her younger sister Maybeth safely through their journey from a beach shack at Provincetown on Massachusetts Bay to Gram's old house on Chesapeake Bay. Gram is their mother's mother, and once she learns of her daughter's breakdown and thirteen-year-old Dicey's determination to keep the children together, she agrees to give them a home. Dicey hopes at last for time to spend on herself and her plan to fix up an abandoned boat and sail it. But she is immediately faced with more realities: She launches the boat and it sinks; Gram's budget and garden provide food but not clothing; Maybeth is slow at school; Gram is apparently known as an eccentric loner. And underlying everything is the realization that Momma may never recover to take care of her children. Although Gram is willing to adopt them legally, the process of doing so and filling out Welfare forms rankles her independent spirit. Dicey knows she still can't escape her responsibilities.

Dicey persuades the owner of a small grocery to hire her after school; she worries about Maybeth's learning difficulties and about the strained docility that Sammy, usually an angry fighter, shows in school; she rebuffs attempts to be friendly by a vivacious black girl, Mina, and by Jeff, a boy who sings and plays the guitar; her only time for herself is spent in scraping and sanding the hull of the recovered boat.

When Maybeth's music teacher, Mr. Lingerle, reports she is talented and should have special piano lessons, Dicey takes on more work at the store. Even James, who prefers spending his time reading and researching things that interest him, takes on a paper route. Dicey knows Gram receives letters from the hospital in Boston where Momma is and that she is collecting the papers necessary for their adoption. The girl also senses it is hard for Gram, long widowed and long distanced from her daughter and a son who has moved away, to share her reclusive routines with four children; nor does Gram want to share family history. What little Dicey learns about her comes from the grocery owner, Millie Tydings.

As the weeks go by, Dicey's challenges are in scraping the boat; calming Gram about accepting Welfare; taking over more work at the store; making a hated apron in Home Ec; and writing a paper for English class which has to be a character sketch showing conflict in the life of a real person she knows. Changing her mother's name to Mrs. Liza, Dicey writes about Momma and her conflicts with reality. Gradually she finds pleasure in getting James to research Maybeth's problem with reading and in hearing Maybeth's talent for piano developed by Mr. Lingerle, the fat, lonely man who becomes a family friend. Little by little she allows herself to be more friendly with Mina and Jeff. When the English teacher reads Dicey's paper in class and accuses her of plagiarism, Mina defends her, and the teacher apologizes.

By November Sammy feels secure enough to get into a fight at school and Dicey is ready for Jeff to come and hear Maybeth sing and play the piano; Gram talks more about family, and Mr. Lingerle is invited to share Thanksgiving dinner. James makes a friend, Toby, who shares his interests; Mina comes to add her voice to an evening's music. The adoption becomes legal, and Dicey knows, from Gram's willingness to take them in and let them bring friends home, that they have developed into a family unit—except for one thing: the never forgotten shadow of Momma's illness.

When Gram receives an urgent message from the hospital, she and Dicey go to Boston where Momma is dying. Dicey experiences the grief of letting go—not only of Momma, but of having to feel so responsible for Maybeth and her brothers. Finally she can take leave of the driven, determined girl she has been and look forward to finding herself and her own voice.

Newbery Medal Acceptance
by Cynthia Voigt

When I first heard that *Dicey's Song* had been awarded the Newbery Medal—which was, by the way, several minutes after Peggy Coughlan had actually told me the news, several minutes and a couple of glasses of champagne—I entered into a state of massive incoherence. I have not yet completely emerged from that state and suspect now I may never, but one of my first sensible thoughts during the time was: "I did not know good news could pack such a wallop." I didn't know good news could keep you awake into the night, distract you so effectively from all appointed tasks, make it difficult—when you confronted it head on—to breathe properly. One of my second thoughts was: "I guess it's time to learn how to spell Newbery." For years, on reading lists and curriculum suggestions, in letters recommending books to friends, I have misspelled it, known I was misspelling it, and never remembered what the particular error was that I tended to make.

I know how to spell it now, N-E-W-B-E-R-Y, savoring every letter; and I thank you—privately, for my confidence in myself as a strong speller, publicly, for the honor. But primarily as a writer: first, quite humbly for the high compliment, and then with a sense of rejoicing because you have given to the Tillermans (people of whom I am terrifically fond) a chance for the kind of immortality only characters in books can possess. The pleasures of the Newbery Medal are many, are various and deep, are all intensely satisfying. The terrors of the Newbery Medal are, I find, while not so numerous and in a perverse way equally satisfying, very real. Large among them has loomed the very occasion which finds us here this evening. Natural vanity aside, whatever is there for me to say to you? Thank you, thank you, of course, and I would be quite happy to repeat those words for several minutes; but I was given to understand that if I could think of something else, something perhaps more substantial, it would be preferable. Obediently, I examined the possibilities. I thought of simply telling the string of anecdotes which I label Newbery Stories, as a show-and-tell of the pleasure you have given. I thought of conducting an analytical review of past Newbery books, by way of ostensive definition that I know what an honor it is. Since it is the book, not the author, which receives the award—although the author bears the brunt of it—I considered reading aloud to you my favorite passages from *Dicey's Song*. I even thought that this might be the occasion for my famous fall-back position: Should all else fail, I've always thought I could deliver a brilliant lecture on Shakespeare's sonnet 87, "Farewell! thou art too dear for my possessing."

In short, I boggled. A friend suggested I was having difficulty assuming the role of cultural spokeswoman. I agreed, which got me no further but clarified much. I at least understood that this was yet another of the ambiguities of being a writer.

Perhaps these are not really ambiguities, but merely oddities. The most basic oddity is that curious time-lag between the writing and the reading. When I signed the contract for my first book, I looked at the time schedule with some surprise, realizing that in those same months I could produce two babies. Later, the time-lag established itself into the position of being held responsible—for good or ill—for a work I had finished long ago, which was not the work I was presently wrestling down, not what I was presently fully engrossed by, not what I presently referred to when I spoke of "my writing." The second oddity has to do with the question of an appropriate attitude toward my own work. I have discovered that I do not want to be the best critical reader of my own books. I do not even think I should aspire to that, any more than I should aspire to holding the most accurate objective attitude toward my own children. When I submitted *Dicey's Song* to my editor, it was with the firm conviction that they would probably not want to publish it. My cover letter read something like: I don't know that you will want this, but I think you will love reading it.

The third oddity is the most interesting, the most engaging. This one crops up when people—readers, editors, friends, reviewers—tell me about my work, because often I am enlightened by what I hear. The first time this happened, I was asked quite casually, about *Homecoming* (Atheneum), "Isn't that every mother's dream? Just to walk away from it all?" Well, I thought to myself, recognizing the validity of the observation; and then, thinking on, I understood how reassuring the story was to me as a parent. Since that time I have understood more clearly that while a book may be out, that doesn't mean necessarily that I am finished with it, or it with me; and perhaps that is why I have never had the impulse to type *the end* at the conclusion of a story. Moreover, I have begun to see that when one writes a book, one is in the rare position of being responded to on a level which for most of us, most of the time, goes unremarked. One bases one's life on certain essential ideas about the nature and purpose of the entire endeavor and the participants thereof—but seldom do these essential ideas, which in fact govern choices and actions, receive direct attention. Seldom, in the course of daily living, do people have the opportunity or the inclination to tell us about ourselves, how they see us, what they think of what we do.

It is this third oddity which has led me to my topic. I would like, if I may, to tell you how I see you, what I think of what you do. In the back of my mind my remarks tonight are entitled "The Argument for Excellence: An Appreciation."

In the field of children's literature it seems to me the word *excellence* can be applied with unusual frequency. I will not repeat it often, lest I sound too much like one of my own characters, but I would like to start out with a couple of interesting points about the word as defined in the *OED*. Its Latin root *excellere* means "to rise above others" and itself comes from the word *cellere* (to rise high, to tower), which—and I like the implications of this—occurs only in compound forms. The first definition of the English root *excel* is: "To be superior or preeminent in the possession of some quality, or in the performance of some action, usually in good sense." The idea that "good sense" is closely associated with preeminence, is a necessary attribute of superiority, rings in even more implications. It removes from excellence the stigma of otherworldliness, or ivory-towerhood, and places the word squarely where it belongs—in the realm of the possible and desirable.

In thinking over this subject, I have broken children's literature down into three large areas: first, the end results, the things themselves—books; second, the enablers—publishing houses and their editorial staffs; and third, those which make available—libraries and librarians. These three aspects exist in some symbiotic relationship to create what I call the field of children's literature.

First, the books. Any field that can regularly produce four or five stunning books a year has to have an eye on excellence. A stunning book engages the imagination, sets to work the intelligence, fills the spirit. The reliability with which such books appear in children's literature is wonderful, satisfying, and too marked to be accidental.

The works that appear in children's literature easily bear the analytical approach. In a classroom I teach that the elements of fiction are plot, character, and theme, with the unspoken understanding that a writer's style will be good. In plot, children's books are characterized by boldness and amibition, by unhedged bets. Without apology or excuse four children walk through the back of a wardrobe into a magical land. A boy is shanghaied into service on a slave ship, and the grim experience marks his entire life, as it must. A wind-up mouse and his wind-up son make a journey through servitude, the arts, philosophy, war and peace, love, despair, and spiritual rebirth—all this in a world observed by a powerful being who occasionally utters not entirely coherent phrases of challenge and benediction. A good story declares its own terms; excellent books are those which work within those terms without compromise.

The range of characters in children's literature is not so remarkable as is the consistent validity: a thoroughly unexceptional pig grown to understanding of how to value what he has and what he has lost, able to recognize that a good friend who is also a good writer is a rare spider; a homosexual teacher whose face has been horribly burned, who still suffers, still honors the justice of it, still can give love; a child-spy who scouts the streets of New York, her originality more clear to the reader than to herself; a clear-headed doll whose hundred years of existence broaden her mind without dissipating her sense of values.

In excellent books, plot and character exist in appropriate symmetry under idea, or they emerge out of idea in a synthesis that can lead the reader who is ready back to the governing idea. Those Minnipins who win the Gammage Cup have earned it by reaching beyond themselves. They value their achievement and the changes it has brought. Moreover, they recognize that they may never again reach so far; and further, that they will, in need, be able to do so again. The idea leads on and out, backward and forward through the book, informing plot and illuminating character. The quality of having been thought through is characteristic of children's literature.

Effectively, what this excellence means is a range of books I can recommend with confidence to a variety of readers as well as several books which year after year I can take into the classroom; they do not fail to engage the students, and they do not fail to evoke from me my own best work, year after year.

In a lecture given at St. John's College, Joe Sachs speaks of the purposes of reading, declining to accept the categories of amusement and instruction as exhaustive. He says: "Stories that affect us set our imaginations to work. That activity can disclose ourselves to us, what we care about, what we fear, what we long for. The combination of disclosure and stimulation may, as it does with Don Quixote, inspire action. Even when it doesn't, it may enrich the interior realm from which thought and action can be nourished." He speaks, of course, of fiction at its best. I add only that children's literature tends, with exhilarating frequency, to be at its best.

These children's books do not appear upon the shelves *ex nihilo*. They are brought forth by the publishers and editors whose governance enables excellence. Publishers are structural enablers—they establish and maintain the business which produces the books; they work with the hard edges of necessity. When my first book appeared, it was at two thirds of its original volume, and even so, it set new horizons of price. The publisher both required and permitted this, made and enacted the decision. He worked his work, which enables me to work mine.

And editors. I have a long, rhapsodic speech about editors in me, to which I will not subject you. The editor works upon, works over, the manuscript, to enable it to be the best it can. An editor must be, more than anything else, dexterous, able to cover the territory between the publisher and the writer as well as the territory between the writer and the reader. An editor must be able to sit in all three of those chairs, without losing her grip on her own sense of what is good in literature. An editor deals critically with the writer and in so doing sees both the overall effect of the work and the functioning of each contributing part. The editor sees not only the work accomplished but also the work to come, which means seeing more of the writer than the writer does. The job involves appreciating what is and eliciting what might be. This has become clear to me in hindsight, which is itself appropriate; it is not a sign of being managed well if you notice at the time that you are being well managed. During our shaking-down period, when my editor was writing me letters that instructed me to do some severe cutting back and I was answering with letters that began, "I have no theory of art, but . . . ," I suspect she knew that it was just that, a shaking-down period. I suspect that she knew we would, one way or another, move past it. I suspect, further, that she hoped—as much as I would have done had I known just what was going on—that we would move well beyond it. I feel myself extremely fortunate in my editor. More significant, I know that my experience is not unique: Other writers in the field feel and speak just so of their editors.

There is dexterity implied in this. The same dexterity is clear before you if you look at the variety and quality of books that have come out from under the hands of editors, even so narrow a list as that of this year's Newbery Honor Books: one, an adventure-fantasy built around a full-blooded character, which it is perhaps needless to point out is Tolkien's essential strength; one, a picture-storybook marked in illustration and diction by delicate wit; one, an autobiography that makes real and comprehensible a foreign land and people as well as—not incidentally—underlining the sense of one's own land and people; one, a modern ghost story written in the kind of virile and poetic style any writer must envy, which also points out the possibility of breaking the restrictive patterns of the past; one, three short tales, each wrought with a sense of irony. The list has great variety and consistent quality; the books themselves argue the kind of editorial work that has gone into them and give evidence to its excellence.

Once out in print, these children's books become the concern of libraries and librarians. Libraries house, safeguard, give place to; librarians are stewards who care for, supply, and maintain. In my mind's eye, the words *library* and *librarian* evoke three images. First is the library at Alexandria built by kings of Egypt upon Aristotle's personal library. The collection contained many thousands of papyrus manuscripts; several thousand scribes and scholars worked and studied there. There Euclid wrote *Elements;* there the water-clock was invented. I see it as sun-drenched buildings, its halls worn gently by the passage of sandaled feet. The second image is that of the monasteries, where monks copied and illlustrated manuscripts, making them beautiful and preserving what would otherwise have been irretrievably lost. The third is more personal, a memory of a library in Connecticut, a building with thick stone walls, where dust motes moved through the light; rooms filled with the kind of silence peculiar to temples of all religions, as if the air itself were enriched with the ideas contained therein. Granted, these images are some ideal vision; granted the overwhelmingly mundane quality of daily life; still, the ideal informs the real—shapes and guides it—justifies it, in both the concrete and abstract meanings of that word. So I allow myself the image of what a library essentially is.

What a library actually is, what librarians actually do, may be less idealized but is no less designed for excellence. They make available the books, display them, put them into the hands of readers. They maintain the dialogue with the community they serve. This dialogue involves not only knowing what books there are and where to find them but also knowing how to recommend to individual readers those books that will suit. Like teachers, librarians gauge ability, maturity, interest; they note not only present achievement but probable direction of growth. Librarians go into schools to do storytelling, give book talks, perform puppet shows. They encourage responses and give room to them. Any free wall space of the children's library in Annapolis is covered with drawings and comments from its readers. In Prince George's County a panel of children has for years published *CRABS*, a small magazine of reviews and recommendations, under the aegis of the library system with the guidance of the librarian. Libraries and librarians make available books covering a broad range— picture books, science fiction, books of poetry and history, cookbooks, books on dinosaurs, books on drugs; the complete list exceeds Polonian abilities. They also make available movies, pictures, and tapes and records of music, stories, and song. They not only make available but also give space and forms to responses. So that libraries can be seen, and rightly, as cultural storehouses. Moreover, so viewed, the ideal is not that distant from the real. The architecture changes, and the habit, but the purpose remains.

Finally, the field of children's literature is controlled by two factors which operate in its favor, making it somehow more possible to achieve excellence.

The first of these is money. It is all right to talk about money. In *Moby Dick* Melville recognizes and addresses the question of commerce; in an emblematic, mystical work which may be about the confrontation of good and evil or may be about the unity that binds polarities into place, commerce has its role. Commercially speaking, it can be said that children's literature is not a greedy industry. To this, everyone—writers, publishers, editors, library systems, and librarians—can attest. The commercial modesty of children's literature, I suspect, enables the field to continue its steady emphasis on quality. So that, far from being a dismal fact, it is a situation of which the soul approves and common sense argues the wisdom. An adequate but not seductive financial base insures that the main motive of all concerned in the field can be the overall quality of the field. In other words, the limit works for excellence.

The second controlling factor is the audience. Children. I recognize without being able to define it that the audience of children's literature does establish limits. Most vivid is the most extreme example—the notion of writing books for those who cannot read. This model can be expanded along a chronological and emotional path to express the controls the audience places upon the field. The model expresses also the unique nature of those controls. It is in the nature of children to be creatures in process. Perhaps because they are so aware of that, it is in the nature of children also to know what we have foolishly forgotten, or improperly subordinated—that the possible is a viable and functioning part of the real. This insight of theirs marks the field of children's literature, encouraging excellence.

To answer my own questions then: How do I see you? I see you as I see myself, a part of something in which we can all take pride. What do I think of what you do? I think it is important, I think you work hard and well, and I think you are—as I am—lucky to be involved in children's literature.

As you probably realize by now, I have been craftily following my first plan for these remarks—to say thank you. As reader and teacher I thank you for the excellence. As writer I want to say thank you again, to the Newbery Committee, to the ALA and its members. I want also to say thank you to publishers in general, to Atheneum in particular, and to Gail Paris most particularly. And lastly, I would like to acknowledge some private debts of gratitude. To my parents, who taught me about family love and gave me the space to make mistakes. To my husband for, among many other things, both his good readings and his good influence. To Jessica, who from the first draft of the first chapter has followed the Tillermans and asked to hear more about them. And to Duffle, too. What can a five-year-old imp of unreason contribute? Oddly enough, what nobody else so consistently can. I will give you an example from life. Forty-eight hours after the Famous Phone Call, during which hours the house had been reverberating with the words Newbery and Los Angeles, we went out for a family celebration dinner. Duffle leaned forward to announce to his grandmother the big news: "We are going to Chicago, because Mommy won the Blueberry Award." So to Duffle, who keeps my feet on the ground, and to the rest of you, who have put my head in the clouds, thank you very much.

BIOGRAPHICAL NOTE

Cynthia Voigt
by ELISE K. IRVING

When Cynthia called that Monday night, she asked if I was sitting down before she told me that she had won the Newbery. And she was right. It is an overwhelming honor. Having had a bookstore for a few years, I think she knew that I would be especially aware of that fact and appreciative of the magnitude of the achievement. And it is that duality that makes it so gratifying—the quality of her effort and the quality of the accolades rarely come into such a happy balance. She has worked long, hard, and lovingly and encountered more than her share of rejection slips. There is something, too, of a Cinderella syndrome since Atheneum did pluck from their mailbag, read, and accept her unsolicited manuscript and first book, *Homecoming*. She has been blessed with luck and talent and enhanced them both with discipline and perseverance.

Cindy is the second of five children; she had two sisters, and then when she was thirteen, suddenly twin brothers. She was a straight-haired, plump little bookworm, who felt that she lived in the shadow of her slender, curly-haired older sister. She puts it most succinctly: "In nursery school—she was Miss Muffet, and I was the Spider. When we got to dancing school—she was a Sweet Pea, and I was a Head of Cabbage."

Whether her thirst for books was a by-product of this notion or a natural reflection of her intellect, I don't know. But the library has always been her haven and her joy.

Most of her childhood was spent in southern Connecticut. She attended Dana Hall School in Wellesley, Massachusetts, from which she graduated "with distinction," president of her senior class and a member of the Cum Laude Society. After her graduation from Smith College and a haphazard tour of Europe with a college friend, she settled into an apartment in Greenwich Village and a job at the J. Walter Thompson Advertising Agency.

A couple of years later she married a young man who was a student at St. John's College in Santa Fe, New Mexico. There she worked briefly at odd jobs until she enrolled in St. Michael's College to obtain a teaching certificate and found her other vocation —or avocation. It is difficult to draw a distinction between the two as she is devoted to both pursuits and each one enriches the other.

For personal reasons the young couple found it necessary to move East and finish the husband's education at St. John's in Annapolis, and Cynthia found her home. The marriage foundered and dissolved after the birth of her daughter Jessica, but her love for Annapolis, the Eastern Shore, and Maryland never has.

In 1974 she was happily remarried to Walter Voigt, a teacher of Latin and Greek at the Key School in Annapolis, where she teaches senior English and directs the English department. Their son Peter (Duffle) was born in 1977.

She lives a busy life with two children and an active teaching career but preserves her mornings for her typewriter. Cynthia is unswervingly loyal and attentive to family and friends but equally devoted to privacy. They now have an island in the Chesapeake which is devoid of any amenities, save a small generator to run her typewriter—not even running water. Here she and her small family cheerfully vegetate through the hot Bay summers and gorge on crabs which they catch themselves.

And she has a delicious sense of humor. She needs it to scramble through her days. When *Homecoming* was nominated for an American Book Award, she and her husband drove to New York for a festive weekend at the Plaza—in their cluttered, battered, and rusted little green heap. She gleefully reported that the doorman "whisked it right away!" And on the morning of their departure, having ordered their treasure from the garage, her husband—looking handsome, Nordic, and urbane in his trench coat—approached the doorman to inquire how long it would take for the car to arrive. Would there be time for a little window-shopping? To their mutual chagrin he turned without hesitation but with some disdain and asked:

"Is it the green one?"

If you are her friend, she has a tireless ear and an inexhaustible coffee pot. Should you be ailing, she will be the first one there with comic books or *Moby Dick,* a flower, a loaf of homemade bread or a Scrabble board—whatever is needed to amuse you and to advise you that she knows and cares about you.

If you are her child she will be your constant shadow in your early years. You will live some part of every week in a playpen at the rear of her classroom, lest she lose a minute of your day while she pursues her teaching. She'll feed you richly, hug you often, and restrain you little.

If you are her student, while you may delight in the charmer at the back of her classroom, I suspect you will know her to be both a demanding and a rigid disciplinarian, whose total pleasure is in helping you to realize your potential. Her love of books will infect you.

She regards cooking as a treat and housekeeping as a consummate bore only to be undertaken when there is an impending visit from her mother. And if you *are* her mother, you will know her to be a modest, witty, joyous, and loving friend. And you will think how fine it is to see her talent and diligence accepted and rewarded by such a distinguished body and to know that so many children will enjoy her gifts.

Cynthia Voigt

by Jessica Voigt

My mother is not perfect, but then, whose mother is? She is medium height, with dull black hair and eyes that laugh naturally. Even so, she can be very serious. She has wrinkles, but she doesn't try to hide them because they are part of her. She only wears make-up for special occasions.

My mom is always quoting Shakespeare at me. She always understands me and what I want, but she doesn't always do it. She can be grouchy, but she can also be the most fun person you have ever been with. She is *trés intelligente,* but she doesn't force it on you. She loves to laugh; she is laughing almost all the time. When I ask her a question, she hardly ever just tells me the answer. She asks me questions so I can figure it out myself.

My mom loves water. She loves the silent ripples in the morning, and she loves the thunder waves during a big storm. She loves the way you can see clear to the bottom in the winter.

Her favorite animal is the Great Blue Heron. It is a grouchy bird which reigns over the Eastern Shore marshes. It is also a solitary animal, and it emits a loud squawking noise when disturbed.

My mom hates housework, and she loves creative writing. She doesn't like the word *creative* though, because of the way people use it. She loves to read other people's writing notebooks. She can always do with a good "nosegay" by D. E. Stevenson or Elizabeth Cadell. She is working constantly, not always on her books, but molding her children and reaching out to touch the world.

The Newbery Medal 1984

DEAR MR. HENSHAW

written by BEVERLY CLEARY

illustrated by PAUL O. ZELINSKY

published by WILLIAM MORROW AND COMPANY 1983

BOOK NOTE

"Leigh Botts (boy)" writes to Mr. Henshaw, author, after Leigh's second-grade teacher reads *Ways to Amuse a Dog* to the class. In third grade Leigh writes to the author again, reporting that he has now read the book himself and telling about his dog, Bandit. As a fourth-grader, Leigh asks Mr. Henshaw to reply "in his own handwriting" and signs himself, "Your best reader." *Ways to Amuse a Dog* is Leigh's basic book; in fifth grade he gets an A— for a report on it. This leads Mr. Henshaw, in a reply to Leigh which is revealed through Leigh's next letter, to suggest that the boy try reading another book of his, *Moose on Toast*. Leigh, now Mr. Henshaw's "number 1 fan," does. A letter from Leigh, now in sixth grade, to "Dear Mr. Henshaw" reveals that he has moved to a new town, and he includes a class assignment—a long list of questions to the author. Some of Mr. Henshaw's less-than-serious answers are shown in Leigh's next letter as well as the boy's reaction to the author's sending him a long list of questions. Leigh replies that he won't answer them, but his mother finds the list and tells him that he should.

    Reluctantly, the boy does, and his situation becomes clear; his mother, Bonnie, has divorced Bill, his father, who is a trucker. Leigh knows a lot about rigs and cross-country hauling. He misses Bandit, who rides with Bill, and wishes his father would keep in touch. He is lonely because his mother works for a catering service days and studies nights to become a Licensed Vocational Nurse. Leigh doesn't have friends at his new school except for Mr. Fridley, the custodian. By the time he answers the tenth question, "What do you wish?" Leigh has dropped the "Dear" and writes curtly to "Mr. Henshaw." But he admits to two wishes—that somebody would stop stealing the catered goodies out of his lunch bag and that Dad and Bandit would come in the rig to take him for a ride.

Mr. Henshaw acknowledges Leigh's answers with a postcard and suggests the boy keep a diary. Leigh tries but finds he can only do this if he writes his entries as letters—still to Mr. Henshaw, but unsent. He cheers up a little at Christmas when his father has a down jacket delivered to him by a trucker friend, but after vacation he is really plagued by the lunch-bag thief and by his father's forgotten promise to phone. Meanwhile, his teacher urges him to write something for the Young Writers' Yearbook. Besides seeing his piece in mimeograph, he could win lunch with a "Famous Author." During the following weeks Leigh's diary shows how frustrated he is—he can't think of a story to write; his father doesn't call. Finally the boy calls Bill and hears the bad news that his father lost Bandit when he was stopped by a snowstorm in the Sierra Mountains and also discovers that Bill is about to take a boy and his mom out for pizza. Leigh now sees more about his father and the way his father's life as a trucker disrupted his parents' marriage. He feels less bitter about his mother divorcing his father.

Leigh thinks up a way to foil the lunch-bag thief—a metal lunch box with a burglar alarm—and he also thinks up a title for a story: *The Ten-Foot Wax Man.* His father sends him twenty dollars to make up for losing Bandit. When Leigh is stuck on his story, he mails a letter to Mr. Henshaw and asks for help, and the author sends him some tips. He buys an old lunch box, batteries, and wire and makes a burglar alarm. But by lunch hour no one has tried to open the box, and Leigh knows that he can't get his lunch without setting off the alarm—which works just fine. The principal is impressed, and several kids want alarms. He ends up making friends with a boy named Barry. Bill phones and says he's always asking other truckers over the CB if anyone has seen Bandit; he asks if Leigh misses him.

At the last minute Leigh writes a description of a trip he took once in his father's truck—"A Day on Dad's Rig" by Leigh M. Botts. His piece only wins an Honorable Mention, but his teacher manages to get him to lunch with the prize winners and the Famous Author—a Mrs. Angela Badger, who is, according to Leigh, a plump nice lady with wild hair. To his surprise she has read his piece, and she calls him an author and says he did splendidly for a boy his age: He didn't try to imitate anyone. She tells him to "keep it up." Leigh asks if she has ever met an author named Boyd Henshaw. She has and says that " 'he's a very nice young man with a wicked twinkle in his eye.' " Leigh writes to tell Mr. Henshaw about his Honorable Mention.

Leigh comes home to find his dad and the huge rig by the house. Bill has found Bandit and brought him to Leigh. When his father comes in for coffee and asks Bonnie if there's still a chance to work things out, she says no. Leigh is sad, but he understands, and as his father leaves, the boy tells him to take Bandit again to keep him company.

Newbery Medal Acceptance

by Beverly Cleary

After the excitement and pleasure of receiving the telephone call telling me that *Dear Mr. Henshaw* was the winner of the 1984 Newbery Medal, my first thought was: I have to give a speech. Over sixty acceptance speeches have preceded mine; for over thirty years I have spoken about my life and works until I feel the subject is frayed beyond repair. So I begin, trying to feel undaunted, by saying thank you to the members of the American Library Association who have wished me well over the years and to the Newbery Committee for honoring a book that can be read by eight-, nine-, and ten-year-old children. These early years, I believe, are the years in which children's imaginations may be captured by the printed word. If books evade young readers during these years, the joys of reading may be lost forever. Although children are not present this evening, I should also like to thank—pass it on!—the thousands who have written to me in the past thirty-four years and who are the inspiration for *Dear Mr. Henshaw*.

I might not be standing here this evening if it were not for a succession of aloof, exacting English teachers in Portland, Oregon, to whom I am indebted for their teaching and for their comments, "Very funny" and "You show talent," on my stories. Such lavish praise was rare and precious, for praise was meager in those days. Hand out an overdose, and the youth of Oregon would be spoiled forever. The most important teacher of all, however, was my mother, whose praise was almost nonexistent. Because I was an only child, she felt I was in dire danger of being spoiled, perhaps even spoiled rotten.

My mother was an independent, determined, vivacious, intense woman, ambivalent about the life she led. She had unshakable faith in the importance of books, reading, and libraries, and in many ways her thinking was ahead of her time. She had both a sense of humor and a sense of drama—and a way of describing, with lively eyes and animated hands, any event exciting to her. I regret that she did not live to experience the eruption of nearby Mount St. Helens.

Around the turn of the century my mother and two of her cousins, armed with classic, liberal high school diplomas and letters of recommendation from a year or two of teaching, boarded a train in Michigan and came out West to teach in the sagebrush country of eastern Washington where they had, as she often said, a high old time. Single women were scarce; single men were plentiful. My mother loved teaching, but marriage ended her career, for at that time married women who lived in small towns were usually prohibited from teaching. Years later, my mother was still able to help neighborhood students with Latin and mathematics. When she was in her seventies, worn down by life and by years of caring for her own mother, she admitted that those years of teaching in one-room schoolhouses were the happiest of her life.

My mother had, however, one pupil—me. She taught me constantly. Her words still play through my mind: "Always sift cake flour before measuring"; "Windows washed when the sun is shining will streak"—advice followed by all excellent housekeepers when I was growing up. Otherwise, what would the neighbors think?

In addition to her homely directions, my mother had more important wisdom to impart to her pupil: "Reading is to the mind as exercise is to the body." (Every time a jogger thumps by our house, I wonder whether he goes home and spends equal time reading.) I was constantly directed to use my imagination and my ingenuity and to stand on my own two feet. One of her assignments was "Go ahead and be somebody." During the Great Depression her text was "Every woman should have an income of her own." Another assignment was "Always try to make the world a better place." Cleaning up my room was the way to begin.

When a teacher required a composition, my mother said, "Always remember, the best writing is simple writing" and produced her own high school rhetoric book to prove it. Unless I was assigned an essay on William Gorgas clearing the Isthmus of Panama of rats and mosquitoes, or that topic I resented most of all, "Could Beowulf Make the Team?" she added, "Write something funny. People always enjoy reading something that makes them laugh." Her final and mysterious advice, followed by laughter, was "Don't forget you are related to Ring Lardner by divorce." I know this unrelationship is remote but true, for my mother mentioned names. But we can't remember everything our mothers tell us, can we?

When teachers began to inspire me with their comments, my mother encouraged me to become a writer but cautioned me that writing was an unreliable livelihood. "Every woman must be able to support herself and, if necessary, her children," was one of her favorite precepts.

And so, with some hardship to my parents, I was sent off to college, not to catch a husband, as was the custom for young women of that time and place, but to become independent. I became a children's librarian, the next best thing to a writer, married the man I had met in college, and when the right moment came thirty-five years ago, I wrote simply a funny book about a boy named Henry Huggins and set it in the neighborhood in which I had lived when I was his age. The children's editor at Morrow, the first to whom I submitted my manuscript, accepted it. My mother's teaching was sound.

This brings me, as my English teachers would have said, to the body of my talk: *children,* that beautiful word so often today replaced by *kids.* We talk about excellence in children's books and of their place in the mainstream of literature but say little about readers. There are those who feel that children need not be considered when evaluating their books. I am not one of them. Neither do I believe that children have natural good taste and that any book they are willing to read is therefore worthwhile.

Soon after the publication of *Henry Huggins* in 1950, children began to write to me, many for school assignments, letters carefully or carelessly written, almost all conforming to a teacher's instructions because my books are read at the age children are taught letter-writing. I now receive thousands of letters every year, more than I can answer. I am haunted by disappointed children. Most letters say the writer has read and enjoyed my books. Some say they have read them over and over. A few express resentment at being required to write—I am on their side! Many children manage an original sentence or two. One girl interrupted her proper school letter with the words "Growl growl growl SHUT UP TUMMY!" Another closed with "Well, this is one thing in the mailbox that is not a bill." Last sentences often reveal what is on the child's mind; and rare children write long, spontaneous letters that are a joy to read.

The diversity of the lives of children amazes me: a crop-duster's son in South Dakota; children who dislike living in mobile homes; a lonely little girl whose father is stationed in the Philippines and who has brought her friends with her in books; a child whose family built a log cabin in the woods and who lives without electricity; children of all races—I know from the pictures they enclose—who write as children, with no mention of color; blind children whose teachers translate their braille letters; brain-damaged children whose brave letters are barely intelligible; wealthy children who write of horses, swimming pools, and the latest video equipment; poor children—one girl wrote a happy letter listing her Christmas presents: pajamas, a sweater, and a toothbrush; inner-city children who wish they could live in Henry Huggins's neighborhood; boys and girls who live in children's homes—one girl wrote, "I used to have a father. My grandma says he loved to read so naturally I take after him"; farm children, who almost always write interesting letters; a girl who wrote that she read my books in cars, trucks, and jeeps; refugee children, who write meticulous letters and whose teachers enclosed notes describing the terrors the children have survived to reach the United States or Canada; children who live on streets named Bunny Run, Sodom, or Enchanted Freeway; children who hate reading; children who say they can't get enough of reading; happy children, grieving children, exuberant children, sick children. The saddest letter I have received came from a boy with a Spanish name who wrote, "I am a cancer victim. Life is as short as the wind."

Adults often ask me whether, over the years of receiving letters from young readers, I have noticed changes in children. Yes and no. Their deepest feelings remain the same. Letters reveal that children want to love and to be loved by two parents in a united family. Many children describe their families and say, I love them all. Children want pets and if they have them, often list them ahead of brothers and sisters. They want to get along with their siblings but express a need for improvement, especially in their brothers. An amazing number have little brothers or sisters exactly like Ramona. They want teachers who like them. Some want many friends, while others are comfortable with one or two best friends. Most appear to be resilient and, like the girl who was happy to receive the toothbrush for Christmas, accept without complaint whatever circumstances life hands them. They want books they can understand, books in which they do not "get lost in the first chapter and can't tell what the author is talking about."

In the past seven or eight years, however, letters have begun to reflect changes in society that affect children. As parents grow critical of public education, an increasing number of children write from private schools—expensive private schools in New York, country day schools, religious schools, and academies. Some children now ask whether I have been saved.

The most noticeable change is the increase in the demands that children feel free, and are even encouraged, to make on authors. Has the "me" generation, I wonder, produced a "gimme" generation? Today every mail brings demands for books, something unheard of a few years ago, when a child might wish he had a book but never asked outright for it. Children demand answers in an author's own handwriting by a certain date and say they get extra credit for an answer. They expect authors to participate in a variety of school projects; one project requires children to ask for something from my wastebasket, along with an explanation as to how the discarded item relates to my life.

Hundreds of children now begin by saying, "I am in a Gifted and Talented Program. We are studying authors. Please answer the following questions. . . ." Their lists of five to thirty questions sometimes include "What are your books about?" and almost always end with "Give me some tips on writing." The ghost of my mother whispers over my shoulder, "Stand on your own two feet. Go to the library. Read," while I wonder what would happen if I sent long lists of questions for children to answer. The temptation is great. I compose a few questions.

Children have grown more sophisticated, as least on the surface. Letters written on computers are beginning to arrive. A boy inquires about my stock portfolio. A girl asks, "Could you tell me about your love life, if it is not a secret?" Several boys have expressed a love of guns. Mothers who stay home to care for their families are dismissed with "My mother just stays home and works around the house," even though that mother may have a family of six.

Recently, children have begun to refer to writing as a business and want to know whether I make a lot of money and get a lot of publicity. They have no idea of the meaning of plagiarism. They tell me they plan to write books about my characters when they grow up. A new and frequent question is "Don't you just take parts of different books and sort of mix them around?" They ask whether I get my ideas from TV shows or movies. Boys tell me they want to be comedians, cartoonists, or professional athletes; many girls, influenced by the Olympics on television, are working at gymnastics and ice skating. Others tell me they want to be stars or they want to be famous "and get a lot of publicity"—but for doing what, they do not say. Many children seem to feel that anything that requires effort to master, including reading, is a bore and not worthwhile. A sixth-grade girl tells me, "I am one of those people who don't think a lot."

The last sentences of letters are often a revelation of the dark and lonely side of childhood, as if the writer is reaching out for help but has no one to turn to. A ten-year-old girl writes, "My hobbies are collecting stickers, riding boys' ten-speed bikes, doing nothing in school and having no friends, listening to the radio all day long. That's my whole life." A boy confesses, "Everyone at school thinks I'm a clutz! [sic] It can really get on your nerves afterwhile." Another child tells me, "My parents are devvorst. My dad is the kind of person who never wants to be around kids." Many children say they remain with their mother, but their pets live with their father. A girl confides, "I wish I could sue my parents for malpractice but I know I can't so I just try to forget what they do." A boy refuses to capitalize the name of his school because he doesn't like it. My book *Runaway Ralph* brings forth the comment "I had a father named Ralph once, but he ran away." Another boy writes, "Ralph wants to run away. This is how I feel about my father. My father gets me mad. I want to get custody of my mother but I am not sure. My mother is better." The letters from almost every child in one class contained such statements as "Mr. Quimby should have kicked Mrs. Quimby in the butt" or "Mr. Quimby should have given Mrs. Quimby a bloody nose." Many children tell me Ramona should be spanked. Recently, two boys from different parts of the United States wrote asking why I live in this country. I wonder if this is the start of a new trend.

On the positive side, an increasing number of children write of turning to books for comfort. A girl with four brothers goes to her room and reads whenever she "gets mad." Children write of reading when they are lonely, sad, or afraid. Many read after bedtime by a flashlight hidden underneath the blankets, as I did when I was their age. The past few months have made me think books may be gaining on the temptations of television. One girl wrote, "There are five people in my family so you know how hard it is to get the TV set. I just go to my room and read." Another said that reading was better than television because the pictures were in her head, and still another, "Reading is like having your own little television set in your head." A New York City child tells me, "My father says the library is my best friend." The library was my best friend, too, and still is.

Readers often suggest books for me to write about Henry or Ramona or books featuring themselves as central characters. The suggestion that stayed with me came in 1982 from several boys unknown to one another: "Please write a book about a boy whose parents are divorced."

For some time I had been thinking about writing a different sort of book because I find change refreshing and because I had noticed that, although I have written a variety of books, I was being stereotyped as always writing a certain kind of book. The new one would be about a boy. Girls, it appeared to me, had taken over children's literature. A story began to fall into place. Leigh Botts, child of divorce, living with his mother, longing for his father. Those thoughts that are jumbled in an author's mind began to separate themselves and cling to this nucleus. An overheard sentence spoken in grief by a strange woman: "It's so terrible when his father promises to call and doesn't." A remark by a teacher: "This kid in my class rigged up a burglar alarm for his lunch box. It made a terrible racket." These were joined by boys' pride in fathers who drive tractor-trailer rigs, grief at the loss of a pet, loneliness in a new school. My own idle thoughts about sending children lists of questions were no longer idle. Letters to an author who sends questions and demands answers followed by a diary seemed right; let the boy reveal his own feelings, for I believe children who want to write should look within themselves, not within the books of others.

One problem was the author Leigh was to write to. He must be a young foot-loose male whose books did not resemble mine. Creating Mr. Henshaw, from a name plucked from an obituary column (I read names anyplace I can find them!) was great fun, for he writes the books I have wanted to write but could not. His *Ways to Amuse a Dog* goes back to the 1940s, when I first heard that booksellers' legend of a woman who misunderstood the title of a book called *Forty Days of Musa Dagh* and asked for *Forty Ways to Amuse a Dog*. This struck me as a splendid idea for a book because most of the dogs I knew were bored. *Moose on Toast* came out of a visit to Alaska, where a librarian asked, with a touch of desperation in her voice, whether I would like to take home some moose sausage. Her husband had shot a moose, and the family of three was faced with eating a thousand pounds of moose meat from their freezer. When I mentioned this to other librarians as having humorous possibilities for a story, no one was amused. All had a moose or part of a moose in their freezers. This discouraged me but would not discourage Mr. Henshaw, who would spend his time in Alaska climbing mountains instead of speaking at banquets and would be hungry enough to eat moose, even though I was told it is dry and stringy. Mr. Henshaw's third and more serious book *Beggar Bears,* about bear cubs in Yellowstone National Park, who are taught to beg instead of forage and whose mothers die from eating plastic bags, is another book I could not write because I lack a naturalist's knowledge. Footloose Mr. Henshaw was free to travel and research bears.

When *Dear Mr. Henshaw* was published, almost every note on the Christmas cards we received asked, "How come *you* know so much about trucks?" Fortunately, our son had been able to answer my questions. When he was in college, he worked summers in produce warehouses and packing sheds, where he came to know the ways of truckers. I also visited a truck repair yard in Salinas—not an easy experience, for the dusty truckers found my asking questions amusing and I had to be wary of having my leg pulled. Our son also rigged for me a lunch box with an alarm that does indeed go off with a racket. I was tempted to bring it along tonight, but was deterred by the thought of the panic that wires and a battery would incite at the airport.

Dear Mr. Henshaw was a most satisfying book to write. It seemed almost to write itself. Because I find life humorous, sorrowful, and filled with problems that have no solutions, my intent was to write about the feelings of a lonely boy and to avoid the genre of the problem novel. David Reuther, my third-generation editor, understood and was enthusiastic. As soon as the book was published, more letters—the first, from adults—arrived. Some said it was the best book I had ever written; others expressed disappointment, even indignation, that I had not written a book as funny as the *Ramona* books. This surprised me. Writers of humor for children often hear that they "just write funny stories" and are made aware, even though they know it is wrong, that serious books are considered superior. A couple of people said they liked the book themselves but expressed doubts about giving it to children because it wasn't funny and because Leigh's parents were not reconciled at the end—a conclusion that I felt would be sentimental, dishonest, and a source of false hope to many children. Teachers wrote that the book would be valuable for classroom discussion because so many pupils came from single-parent homes. Mothers struggling to rear sons without help from fathers wrote moving letters of appreciation.

Then letters from children began to arrive. The first came from a boy with two parents, whose father owns a gas station in Leigh's town. He said he read *Dear Mr. Henshaw* straight through the day he bought it and five times the next week. Others said it was my best book. Children found more of the humor in the story than adults and expressed interest in Leigh's lunch-box alarm, although one girl wrote a wistful letter saying she never had anything good in *her* lunch. Another girl said she was *so* glad Leigh's parents didn't get together at the end. Many told me how hard life is in a new school, that their lives were very much like Leigh's, or that there were "lots of kids like Leigh" in their school. Several letters ended "Please don't send *me* a list of questions." One boy wrote, "I was really moved by the book. I felt as though I was gona [going to] wake up from a dream state and find myself in Leigh's body."

Other children wrote that they liked Leigh, but they liked Ramona better. And why shouldn't they? The rallying cry of my library training was "the right book for the right child." In a world in which children's lives vary so widely, there is no reason why every child should like every book, even Newbery books. I recall my own sixth-grade teacher, who held her forty restless pupils engrossed by reading *Smoky* (Scribner), the Newbery winner of 1927. Here at last was a book about the West which used dialect familiar to young Oregonians and was not a pioneer story. We read every word written by Will James, played cowboy, and tried to learn to lasso with clothesline rope. In 1928, however, none of us cared to read a Newbery winner about a pigeon in India.

No, when I wrote *Dear Mr. Henshaw,* I did not expect every reader to like Leigh as much as Ramona. Although I am deeply touched that my books have reached two generations of children, popularity has never been my goal. If it had been, I would have written *Ramona Solves the Mystery of the Haunted House and Finds a Baby Brother* or followed trends and written something like *Henry and Beezus Play Doctor,* instead of a book about the feelings of a lonely child of divorce.

"Who is Leigh Botts?" adults now ask. "Is there really a Leigh Botts?" children want to know. "Is he a friend of yours?" There is not one Leigh Botts; there are many. Leigh Botts is all the brave and lonely children I have ever known who have found books and libraries to be their best friends.

BIOGRAPHICAL NOTE

Sandra Hansen

Beverly Cleary
by David Reuther

"It is a rare thing to be hailed by audience and critics alike," wrote Natalie Babbitt in *The New York Times Book Review.* "In our field, children do occasionally take up a writer critics have spurned.... More often, children spurn writers that critics have taken up. But in Mrs. Cleary's case, everyone seems delighted."

For two generations, Beverly Cleary has captivated children and their parents with her unique ability to re-create the everyday joys and sorrows of childhood. Where does this gift come from? The author herself provides a clue: "I write books for children to read for pleasure," she says. "Reading meant so much to me when I was growing up. It made all the difference in the quality of my childhood."

Like her characters Henry Huggins, Ellen Tebbits, Otis Spofford, and the remarkable Quimby family, Beverly Cleary grew up in Oregon. Born in McMinnville, she spent her first six years in Yamhill, a tiny farming community in the Willamette Valley. "I loved living on the farm," she says. "I didn't have any brothers or sisters, so I had to amuse myself. I rarely played with other children until I was six and we moved to Portland. That was the most traumatic year of my life."

Her first-grade classroom with forty pupils seemed dark, crowded, and stuffy after her life in Yamhill. And her teacher was a terrifying woman who whipped the pupils' hands with a metal-tipped bamboo pointer as punishment for minor transgressions. "I became a very quiet child," recalls Beverly, "and I think observant, because I didn't want to do anything wrong in school." Second grade was easier, but it wasn't until the following year that Beverly made the miraculous discovery that reading could be fun. "From then on I was the library's best customer."

In the 1920s, however, Beverly found that most American children's books were pioneer stories or moralistic tales about boys and girls who lived in foreign countries. She says, "I wanted to read stories about ordinary children who lived in a medium-sized town and had to walk to school, just like me. I didn't want them to solve mysteries or have adventures that would never happen to anyone I knew. Most of all, I wanted the stories to be funny."

Such books were scarce, and a sympathetic teacher-librarian suggested that when Beverly grew up, she ought to write the kind of books she wanted most to read when she was a girl. The idea appealed to Beverly, but her mother, a practical woman, suggested she should also have a way of earning a living. So, after graduating from college Beverly entered the library school of the University of Washington, where she specialized in work with children. Later, she became a children's librarian and storyteller in Yakima, Washington, until she married Clarence T. Cleary and moved to California.

During the fall of 1948 Beverly worked in the children's book department of a store in Berkeley. Surrounded by books, she was sure she could write a better book than some she saw there, and after the Christmas rush was over, she says, "I decided if I was ever going to write, I'd better get started." She expected to produce the usual novel about the maturing of a sensitive female who wanted to write. What came out instead was a story of an ordinary little boy named Henry Huggins.

When I was in Yakima, I worked with a group of little boys. They weren't exactly poor readers—they just didn't care about reading. I soon discovered that they had the same problem I'd had as a child. There weren't any books in the library they wanted to read. They wanted to read books about "kids like us." I really wrote *Henry Huggins* for them.

Beverly sent her manuscript off to William Morrow and Company because of Morrow's reputation in the field and, she confesses, because she had heard Elisabeth Hamilton, the editor in chief, speak at a conference and she wanted to know what the person who would read her manuscript looked like. Six weeks later, there came a letter from the publisher saying, "Several of us here have read your story, *Spareribs and Henry,* and we are very much interested in it as a possibility for the Morrow list." The letter also asked if the author would be willing to make minor revisions in the last chapter of the manuscript. These were gladly agreed to; *Henry Huggins* was published in September 1950 and immediately became a bestseller. Children were delighted to find a book about ordinary boys and girls, and reviewers said such things as, "We defy anyone under seventy not to chuckle over it.... It is hard to decide which of these incidents is the funniest."

The next year saw the publication of *Ellen Tebbits,* and since then there have been over two dozen wonderfully funny books for children, each of them filled with a warmth and a humor which are Beverly's hallmarks. And over the years, Beverly Cleary has been honored with an impressive number of awards (starting at age ten with a two-dollar prize for an essay about the beaver, "because no one else entered the contest"), including the prestigious Laura Ingalls Wilder Award in 1975 for her "substantial and lasting contribution to literature for children" as well as the 1980 Regina Medal, the 1982 University of Southern Mississippi Medallion, and two Newbery Honor Books—*Ramona and Her Father* and *Ramona Quimby, Age 8.* In addition, she was the United States nominee for the 1984 Hans Christian Andersen Award presented biennially by the International Board on Books for Young People. But perhaps the finest tributes to Beverly Cleary are the more than two dozen awards she has won, based on the votes of her enthusiastic readers.

Beverly begins work on most of her books on the second of January, the date she started *Henry Huggins.* She works in a cozy book-lined study off the living room of her comfortably elegant house in Carmel. When she is working on a manuscript, she spends each weekday morning writing in longhand on a legal pad. After the first draft is complete, she types it herself and then revises the manuscript until she feels it is exactly right. It then goes to a professional typist before being sent to the publisher.

A book usually takes Beverly about six months to a year to

write, but often she will think about a story for several years before putting pencil to paper. "I thought about Ramona for fifteen years before I started writing a book about her," she says. Her books are inspired by memories of her own childhood and by events in the lives of her own two children—the twins Malcolm and Marianne—or by the world around her; or they are simply plucked from her imagination. She hardly ever uses a story line, preferring to begin with a character and several incidents and then working out whatever her character did before or afterward. "Part of the fun of writing," she says, "is discovering how the story is going to turn out."

Beverly Cleary has been writing for more than three decades, and her books are just as popular today as they were in the fifties and sixties.

Fundamentally, I don't think children have changed through the years. Maybe they have acquired a certain sophistication from watching television, but it's only on the surface. Childhood is universal, and I write about childhood feelings as I knew them growing up in Portland, Oregon.

A modest, soft-spoken woman, Beverly Cleary masks a delicious wit. I always look forward to my frequent conversations with her, and her fine eye for the inevitable absurdities of life often has me roaring with laughter. To work with Beverly is a constant delight, and as I've begun to know her, these last two years have been a special privilege and a pleasure.

What next for Beverly Cleary? This fall will see the publication of the seventh—and perhaps final—novel about the Quimby family, *Ramona Forever*. And recently, Beverly has turned to writing short stories for adults, the first of which, "Papa's Pistol," will be published soon in *Woman's Day*. A surprising tale of premeditated murder, it reveals the same wit and insights into humanity that highlight her work for children.

Asked what she finds most rewarding about her career, Beverly responded,

The number of people who tell me of a child who didn't enjoy reading until my books came along. I remember the great feeling of release I got when I discovered I was reading—and enjoying what I read. And today I receive letters from adults who say my books helped to make their childhoods bearable.

The Newbery Medal 1985

THE HERO AND THE CROWN

written by ROBIN MCKINLEY

published by GREENWILLOW BOOKS 1984

BOOK NOTE

Aerin, daughter of King Arlbeth of Damar by his second wife, has much to learn—of her heritage from her mother who died giving birth to her; of how she can find the strength and courage to save Damar from its enemies. Because Aerin's mother was a witch-woman from the North who was believed to have tricked the king into marriage, Aerin is trusted neither by the court nor the populace. From childhood her friend and protector is her cousin, Tor, who will one day follow Arlbeth as king.

As the story begins, Aerin is only too aware of her inadequacies and of the suspicion that surrounds her. It has taken her two years to recover from an unwise gesture of defiance when, goaded by her malicious cousin Galanna, she ate surka leaves and nearly died. Her recovery is aided by her concern for her father's war horse, Talat, crippled in battle and put out to pasture. She grooms and encourages him until she can ride him. During this time, too, she experiments with a formula found in an old manuscript for making kenet, an ointment that will protect its wearers from dragon fire. She persuades Tor to train her in handling a sword. When she becomes eighteen, Tor realizes he is in love with her, and he presents her with a sword. At last she discovers how to make the dragon-fire ointment successfully.

At a time when King Arlbeth, Tor, and the king's army are busy preparing to defend Damar's Northern border, a messenger comes to beg help in killing a dragon harassing an outlying village. As the king cannot promise immediate help, Aerin slips away with Talat and goes to the village. Protected by the kenet, using her sword and Talat's battle experience, she routs and kills not one, but a pair, of small dragons. When her father learns of her deed, he awards her a sword, making her an official swordbearer, which binds her always to do his bidding. She continues to kill dragons and becomes known as Aerin Dragon-Killer; yet Arlbeth refuses to let her ride out with his army to fight the rebels in the North.

News comes that Maur, last of the great dragons, has awakened and is devastating a village, but the king and his army must put down the rebellion. Aerin, with Talat, goes to combat the dragon. It is a fierce fight in which she is severely wounded. Days pass before she can travel with Talat back to the City, bringing a glittering red stone from the debris of Maur's body. Since the dragon's head has already been brought to the City, Arlbeth and Tor are waiting for news of her. Her father punishes her for taking up her sword without his command, yet because she has done such a brave deed, there is a celebration in her honor. Maur's head is displayed in the great hall. But the head makes mischief, and Aerin feels people see her now as the witch-woman's daughter and that her killing of the dragon was accomplished by magic and luck rather than skill and courage. In feverish dreams she sees a tall blond man who promises to heal and help her and to aid her in saving Damar. She leaves a note for Tor, as she has always adored him, saying she must find someone to help her. She flees the City, taking only Talat and the red dragon stone.

When her journey brings her to the mage, Luthe, Aerin is close to death. Luthe uses all his powers to save her from a tempting figment of death and heal her body. In so doing, he has made her, like himself, more than mortal—a mage. She spends several seasons with Luthe, learning the truth about her mother and that Luthe must, with sorrow, send her on to confront Agsded who holds Damar's future in his hands. Agsded is the figment of death who taunted her in her extreme illness and now haunts her dreams. Aerin knows she must defeat him.

Luthe gives her Gonturan, the blue sword. On her journey with Talat she befriends the folstza, huge catlike animals, and the yerigs, great wild dogs, who then join her. But when she climbs to Agsded's tower, she is alone—with only the dragon stone woven into a wreath of surka leaves, the blue sword Gonturan, and her faith in Luthe to help her. As they fight, she sees that Agsded is wearing the Hero's Crown, Damar's treasure. Since neither of them is quite mortal, his conjured fire cannot kill her; her sword cannot kill him. She throws the surka wreath at him; it encircles him, and, screaming, he disappears in his own fire. The tower falls. All that is left from the battle with Agsded is the charred wreath with the dragon stone and the Hero's Crown, which she must return to Damar. On her way, Luthe intercepts her, and Aerin learns that she loves him for time immortal; that their parting now will not be forever.

Leaving the dragon stone with Luthe, because it would be too tempting for humans desiring power, she and Talat hurry south. They arrive in time to defeat the Northerners and lift the seige off the City. Arlbeth is killed in the battle, but Aerin and Tor reach the castle. With Gonturan's thrust, she knocks Maur's dragon head from the wall of the treasure hall, and they roll it out of the City. The evil is dispelled; the Hero's Crown is safe in the treasure hall; Tor is king, and Aerin agrees to be his queen, for the mortal part of her will love her country and her husband.

Newbery Medal Acceptance
by Robin McKinley

I started this speech one day in the third week of January on a plane flight from Bar Harbor, Maine, to Boston; from Boston I was to go on to New York City, where Greenwillow was waiting to pour champagne over me and shout "huzzah"—and make me sign hundreds of copies of *The Hero and the Crown.* I was looking forward to it, I thought.

The plane was late; the wind was blowing, hard, in the wrong direction. I was reading Tolkien's *Letters* and paying as little attention as possible; the whole purpose of public transportation is that the weather becomes someone else's responsibility. When my flight was finally called, you couldn't see out the windows for the flying snow. Now the terminal at Bar Harbor is about the size of your average living room, and you have to walk outdoors to get to your plane, which will be an eight-to-twelve seater with so little head room that you must crouch down almost double and scuttle along the aisle. If, as I invariably am, you are carrying a knapsack bulging with books and papers, you have very nearly to crawl on your hands and knees.

It was hard to see the plane and harder still to climb its stairs without being blown away. The plane shuddered where it stood as we four passengers strapped ourselves in. The pilot told us casually that it might be a little rough; the propellers spun, and we wobbled off down the runway. Wobbled or veered or staggered. We rambled so badly that we rambled right to the end of the tarmac and turned around and had another go. We did get off the ground this second time—with a violent heave such as I am more accustomed to on horseback, facing off a five-foot wall; but you're expecting it then, and you also know you get to come down again very soon, just over on the other side.

I've traveled on small planes before. I've flown, for example, in a two-seater—one of them the pilot's: an open-cockpit biplane, with my suitcase on my lap, looking down at the cars on the road beneath us making better time than we were. But this last January was probably the worst flight of my life, thus far anyway, and I would be more than happy to let it remain so. About ten minutes of being knocked all over our bit of sky, losing the ground completely in the driving snow, and then having a gap open up just long enough to see that we were now over water with whitecaps from an angry-looking Atlantic just beneath our wings, the spume reaching up like sea serpents to grab for the plane's undercarriage—about ten minutes of this and I was groping frantically for pencil and paper. It was too rough to read; human eyes couldn't focus, and I had to do something before I simply went off into hysterics—and it had occurred to me that I had the opening here for my Newbery acceptance speech. With a yellow legal pad jammed between my knees and my knapsack, trying to keep my eyes averted from the chaos just beyond the small, round window with its thick, distorting plastic pane, I wrote, my pencil flinging itself across the page with every lurch: This is typical. This is just the way my life goes.

It is, too. Some years ago my epitaph occurred to me: "There must have been an easier way." The year that *Beauty,* my first book, came out was probably the most harrowing of my life; this last year at least runs it a close second, and I have thought upon occasion that it has indeed overtaken it. I don't know that fate likes me exactly, but she sure has a good time with me. Shortly before I was due to turn in *The Blue Sword* to Greenwillow, a horse fell on me and broke my hand, thus bringing the book to a brutal halt for about six weeks—first while the bones healed so I could type again, and second while I got over having the fantods because, having had to stop working on it at such a crucial point, I was convinced I'd never be able to finish it. About a month before I was to turn in *The Hero and the Crown,* I fell on myself and broke my ankle. This was actually very good for the book because there was for nine weeks very little I could do but type, but I do now suffer from an interesting new paranoia and am planning to withdraw into a padded room with my typewriter when the next book gets close to its end.

But my life has gone on in heaves and crashes for much longer than I have been bright enough to be looking for patterns. I didn't realize, and a good thing too, that the pattern of an absent-minded, jump-first-and-think-later childhood was going to have quite so far-reaching an effect on all aspects of my later life. I was a military child, and my mother and I followed my naval officer father all over the world. When you're a child, where your parents are is "home": It's not till later that you begin to think about what else home means; and one of the things it seems always to have meant to me is "somewhere else." The nearest I came to being able to hold or define that somewhere else was in books, in rereading my favorites and finding new ones when some character or situation spoke directly about that slowly revealed place. I was a very bookish child, as will surprise no one; people think that the line on several of my book jackets about how I keep track of my life by what books I was reading at a given time is just a humorous way of emphasizing that I've always been bookish. Not so; it's simple fact. One of the most dramatic examples of this occurred just after I turned eleven. I was in bed one morning reading *The Hobbit* for the first time—and finding it much inferior to *The Lord of the Rings*—when my mother came into my room. She was carrying our portable radio and, I think, a hairbrush, and said, "They've shot the president." It was 1963; we were living in Tokyo.

So, two things about the way I grew up: I read a lot and moved around a lot, and the outside world and the inside world blurred somewhere. I played the same sort of wild-horse games—I was always big on anything that involved whinnying and jumping over things—on the rocky shores of Lake Ontario and under palm trees in Japan; I reread Oz and Andrew Lang in California and Rhode Island.

Another central fact about my childhood was that I was clumsy. Perhaps I would have seemed less clumsy—although I doubt it—in a house with more than one child in it; but as it was, even when I wasn't in disgrace for breaking something irreplaceable—irreplaceable because it had been bought several postings ago, somewhere half the world away—I was covered with the bruises resulting from constant battle with intransigent door frames and pieces of furniture.

I'm still clumsy; I'm still bookish; I still travel a lot. I also still have trouble with the real and the unreal, and with door frames and pieces of furniture. I'm merely moody and restless and awkward on a different scale. I can admit to one small breakthrough very recently, however. Most of my adult life I've had the nagging fear that at any moment my life is going to settle down and become boring—even though if that meant I could stop breaking bones, there might be something to it. I think perhaps that fear left forever, winging into the howling wind around our tiny plane on its way to Boston last January, and I wish luck to whatever star-crossed mortal it lands on next.

I've always told myself stories, and as I got old enough to write them down, I wrote them down. My stories happen to me; I bump into them, like pieces of furniture; and they are clear and plain to me—like pieces of furniture; and they are clearer and plainer to me now than when I was a child, for which I am grateful. It seems to me that getting older then is a good thing and not a bad one. The main circumstance of getting older that I'm aware of as Damar's historian is that the connection between the dangerously exhilarating ether where Story is and my fingers around a pencil or on a typewriter keyboard is more directly made. The necessary egotism of a child, or at least of the child I was, could not ever be set aside; and now, years later, and thousands of words later, of practice words and practice stories, the flicker of Story on those cave walls is more easily read because I myself throw fewer distracting shadows.

I am not saying this here and now on this very special occasion so that you can murmur to yourselves that I take my own part too little or that I'm protesting too much. I'm trying—largely because the focus on me as the author of the Newbery book this year unnerves me rather extremely—to tell you how I view my own authorship and my existence as an author. I wrote bad stories before I wrote good ones—I still have a drawer in one of my filing cabinets labeled "Juvenilia." Or, to be exact, it is labeled with a series of upper-case-of-top-row-of-typewriter symbols—what back in the days before one was allowed to swear in print was used for swear words. But I know what it means. It means garbage. This drawer contains such jewels as the novel I wrote when I was eighteen, and the half-finished epic poem about some enchanted rocks that I worked on, off and on, through junior high and high school, with the aid of a well-thumbed rhyming dictionary. I don't know when the line was crossed from drivel to stuff that other people might want to read. I don't know when the shaft of Story streaming in through that crack in my skull grew bright enough for me to see it with my dim eyes; I don't know when I got comfortable enough with the English language to be able to translate Story into the only words I know. I don't know.

I had started working on the Damarian cycle when, terrified by how much of it there seemed to be, I set it aside to write *Beauty*. The first publisher I sent *Beauty* to took it. The line had been crossed.

One of the first questions—after what do I eat for breakfast and what color is my typewriter—that I had seriously to consider as an author speaking to a reader came about at my first public-speaking gig, at my old prep school, Gould Academy, where I had been invited back as a graduate who seemed to be doing something interesting with her life. A sophomore boy, having been compelled to read *Beauty,* said grimly, "They're always talking to us about themes and symbols. Do you *put* that stuff *in?*" The answer is no. I don't put much of anything in consciously, except commas, and my copy-editor takes a lot of those out again. The stories are there; I am only sorry, every time, that I can't do a better job by them. I, like many of the people, young and old, who write me letters, would far rather simply have been born Arlbeth's daughter; I am a historian only because I wasn't given that choice.

But perhaps you can believe that I say conscientiously that I don't know when the line was crossed; and a central reason why I don't know is that my obsessions haven't changed. Those of you who have heard me speak before have been wondering when I was going to get around to talking about Girls Who Do Things; it's about the only thing I do talk about, and it has begun to amuse me that queries about my availability as a speaker refer more and more often to the likelihood of my talking about strong female roles in literature. The subject of Girls Who Do Things has the added benefit that it's one of the few things I feel strongly enough about to be willing (or able) to stand up in front of a lot of people to talk about.

I can't remember a time when the stories I told myself weren't about shy, bumbling girls who turned out to be heroes. They were usually misfits, often orphans, and invariably misunderstood by those around them. Everyone, I think, goes through a period when they first get a glimmering of adulthood and independence from such awful parental rules as brushing one's teeth and doing one's homework, of secretly believing that one is really a princess, a cradle changeling—something invincibly splendid—that there is something in the genes that will reveal itself in some irrevocable way, sooner or later—preferably sooner since there's that math test only next week.

I think I must have held on to that secret belief a little more strongly than most of my peers. It wasn't that I wanted not to belong to my parents; it was that I, as I grew up, so obviously didn't belong anywhere recognizable in the world I had soon to attempt to make mine. Girls were supposed to grow out of being tomboys; they were supposed to stop identifying with the Count of Monte Cristo and start identifying with Haydée; stop wishing to have adventures like Harry Feversham, but be willing to stay at home like Ethne and hear of them; stop feeling that Beau Geste really had the better of it than Isobel, who was already a poor relation and then must resign herself to being a poor relation in a household disgraced by the much admired Beau.

But I didn't. I was too clumsy to imagine myself being idealized effectively, even if the young man in question is marching through the sands of the Sahara; too temperamentally cross-grained to see myself an angel of mercy long enough to find my long-lost lover in a soldiers' hospital somewhere; and not nearly pretty enough to sway Edmond Dantès from brooding endlessly over Mercédès.

When I was a child, there didn't seem to be too many alternatives. I'm glad for my stubbornness and awkwardness now—and for the fact that my family moved around so much, which also protected me a little from peer pressure. It's hard to feel much pressure from people you don't know, even if they are your own age and are supposed to be where you make your friends. But being a self-proclaimed obstinate misfit meant I could hold on to my growing obsession with girls who do things. I was never seduced by proms and parties because I was unsuited for them; I didn't discover boys because they didn't discover me, and because their standards of discovery seemed to be too odd to be aspired to.

Not, it must be admitted, that I tried to make myself accessible. Boys, I had decided, were the enemy. They were the ones who got to have adventures while we got to—well, not have adventures. Poor Mercédès: What was she to do? Her lover imprisoned and herself without prospects—I have long thought the Count is harder on her so-called betrayal than she deserves, just as the nubile Haydée deserves no credit for having had the luck to be sheltered all her short life.

The juvenilia hiding in that blighted drawer features girls who do things. It features pretty much nothing else.

Those of you who have heard me talk about *Sword* have heard me talk about its roots in Kipling and Haggard and P. C. Wren—and, for that matter, in E. M. Hull's *The Sheik*, though I suppose I should blush to admit it. I read *The Sheik* when I was old enough to know better, and around it crystallized several of my hitherto less conscious thoughts about heroines: most specifically, that the purpose of heroinely spirit is that heroes should have a more challenging experience taming them. I couldn't buy that any more than I could help rebelling, many years before, at the idea that poor Caddie Woodlawn was more responsible than her brothers for giving their city-slicker cousin a bad time of it. Damar specifically became Damar around my presently thirty-odd viewings of John Huston's *The Man Who Would Be King*—to give you an idea of the depth of that narrow obsession, by the way, I bought the cassette of the movie almost a year before I could afford to buy the video machine to play it. *The Man Who Would Be King* is a wonderful story of heroism and derring-do; it's also the story of a friendship which surpasses everything, including the loss of sanity and life—certainly surpassing any love of women. There are no women in the movie; there's a female plot device to bring on the final catastrophe. I couldn't help being fascinated by the grand wastefulness of Danny and Peachey's nonsensical idealism and loyalty any more than I could help fooling around with the idea that there's no *real* reason a woman couldn't be motivated by idealism and loyalty as well, perhaps even as grand and as improbable.

But *Sword* as *Sword* was a late addition—even as the name of Damar was—to a series of stories already rattling around in my brain and shouting for space and attention. Perhaps the first real flicker of the tale that would become Damar—and even more particularly the kernel of what would become the story of Aerin—is from my many passionate rereadings of *The Lord of the Rings* in junior high. Tolkien has received much criticism for his inability to portray women—or perhaps better to say his unwillingness to deal with women at all, except as tersely and tangentially as possible, and with teeth visibly clenched. When I was first reading LOTR, it never occurred to me to protest—beyond a mild wistfulness—that there were no girls in it. Even in the makeup of the Fellowship of the Ring, the Nine Walkers, so carefully chosen to represent the races of Elves, Dwarves, and Men—and one Wizard, who is also called "he"—no thought is given to, uh, female persons of each persuasion, creed, or national origin. That's just the way the best books usually are.

But wait. In the middle of all this unmitigated male bonding there's a surprising and highly uncharacteristic scene in *The Return of the King*, at the beginning of the chapter titled "The Battle of the Pelennor Fields." For those of you who haven't committed all of *The Lord of the Rings* to memory, or perhaps haven't even reread it in the last six months or so, this scene takes place before the gates of Gondor, where the forces of Mordor have besieged it. The Riders of Rohan have swept down and engaged the enemy in battle, and the defenders are briefly hopeful, but the Nazgûl, the Black Riders, Sauron's deadliest servants, return, and neither horse nor man can stand against the terror of their coming. The

Rohan king, Théoden, falls beneath his maddened horse, and his Riders are scattered. Or all his Riders but one: Dernhelm, the mysterious, solitary young man who befriended the hobbit Merry, remains at Théoden's side, even when the Lord of the Nazgûl threatens him. The rest of this scene is in Tolkien's own words:

[Dernhelm's] sword rang as it was drawn. "Do what you will; but I will hinder it, if I may."
"Hinder me? Thou fool. No living man may hinder me!"
Then Merry heard of all sounds in that hour the strangest. It seemed that Dernhelm laughed, and the clear voice was like the ring of steel. "But no living man am I! You look upon a woman. Éowyn I am, Éomund's daughter. You stand between me and my lord and kin. Begone, if you be not deathless! For living or dark undead, I will smite you, if you touch him."
The winged creature screamed at her, but the Ringwraith made no answer, and was silent, as if in sudden doubt. Very amazement for a moment conquered Merry's fear. He opened his eyes and the blackness was lifted from them. There some paces from him sat the great beast, and all seemed dark about it, and above it loomed the Nazgûl Lord like a shadow of despair. A little to the left facing them stood she whom he had called Dernhelm. But the helm of her secrecy had fallen from her, and her bright hair, released from its bonds, gleamed with pale gold upon her shoulders. Her eyes grey as the sea were hard and fell, and yet tears were on her cheek. A sword was in her hand, and she raised her shield against the horror of her enemy's eyes.

Well. There you have it. It's not that I am tall and light-skinned myself that has made my subconscious carry around all these years a picture of a tall, pale woman carrying a sword and defying something undefiable; although the large clumsiness of Harry and Aerin is certainly an addition by this author. Éowyn was beautiful and gracious and graceful—but never mind. Tolkien really didn't know much about women; but I will always be grateful for the hard, pure light this one scene shed on my own girls-saving-the-universe fantasies.

But *The Lord of the Rings* was published thirty years ago. I'm glad that so many people respond to my lady heroes, my dam-alur-sol, as good characters to have around; but it bothers me very much that people also still seem to think that they are surprising characters doing surprising things. It bothers me the number of letters I get saying something on the order of, "At last! Girls who do things!"

I know that my stories are not the only ones on bookshelves today that feature female heroes—someday, indeed, I want to write a long, graphic essay or teach an arduous course on Real Heroines in Victorian Literature—but there are still far too few. There are still far too many stories in which the female lead is paid only lip service to her potential usefulness; who proves she is worth the hero's time by being "spirited," as if she were a horse to be broken to saddle, which is, in fact, a dismayingly frequent metaphor; or who is lucky enough to have the traditional, accredited female virtues of sympathy and patience and gets along just fine by being patient and sympathetic with the right people.

Not all girls are patient and sympathetic any more than all boys are going to join the French Foreign Legion when things get sticky at home. I wished desperately for books like *Hero* when I was young: books that didn't require me to be untrue to my gender if I wished to fantasize about having my sort of adventures, not about wearing long, trailing dresses and casting languorous looks into pools with rose petals floating in them as the setting sun glimmers through my translucent white fingers and I think about my lover who is off somewhere having interesting adventures.

Book mail is always pleasant to receive (just so long as the letter-writers tell me in detail how much they like my stories), but the best is from thoughtful readers who speak to me as to another thoughtful reader. Several of my favorite letters have remarked that it is to be hoped that part of the point of stories like *Sword* and *Hero*—and *Beauty* too—is that young readers who identify with Harry and Aerin and the others and wish to be like them will also realize that they are. And this should be true (and at least occasionally is, as my book mail also tells me) of boy readers as well as the girls: both sides of our gender-specific event horizon need to be extended.

Unfortunately, very few of us are kidnapped by kings for the magic in our blood, but even if we're large and clumsy and a dead loss at the usual social systems, we can still grow up to do things and do some of those things by conscious choice.

I'm terribly grateful that the stories that are given to me to write are read and enjoyed by so many people, even if the pinnacle of that gratitude and that enjoyment has required me to give a speech to two thousand people and ruined my digestion. I'm equally grateful to have Susan Hirschman and the other admirable people at Greenwillow to prop me up when I need it, which is often, but please don't ask them to confirm this because I embarrass easily. I'm grateful to *The Lord of the Rings* for giving me not only Éowyn, but almost single-handedly starting the new popularity of fantasy that has given my books an easier entrée into the market where readers who might like them can find them. I'm even grateful to E. M. Hull and the Baroness Orczy and various others who gave me wonderful stories that so urgently needed to be done over, correctly this time. I hope some of my doings-over may inspire more girls, both young and grown-up, to do more things they want to do and haven't been quite sure they dared; and more boys not to think it odd that they should want to do them.

You see, it's finally occurred to me that I'm myself a girl who does things. Scribes are, historically, respectable, but not very interesting. It was a letter from a librarian friend in California who pointed out to me that this gap in my thinking was bad for my own cause; and the *ker-chunk* in my head as her words finally fell into place occurred during that plane flight you've already heard about, probably at about the same time that my fear of boredom detached itself and left looking for a less cynical host. The stories may simply happen to me, but I have chosen to accept the responsibility to write them down as best I can.

And so, finally, thank you all, and especially the members of this year's Newbery Committee, for your extraordinary support of that decision and responsibility. Thank you for helping me stay at the typewriter by insisting that the shadows on the wall of Plato's cave that it is given me to see are worth seeing. Thank you for the strength that your enthusiasm for my work gives me to put into more stories. Thank you very much.

BIOGRAPHICAL NOTE

Helen Marcus

Robin McKinley
by Terri Windling and Mark Alan Arnold

It was necessary, perhaps inevitable, that Robin McKinley would become an important writer of our generation—prominence being one of the few social strata amenable to a woman with so much talent and personality. And *personality* is not used as a euphemism for arrogance or egomania but rather to describe a person who approaches every instant and event with such boisterousness, energy, and vehemence that even the most mundane aspects of her life are infused with vibrancy. This vividness is intrinsically Robin, special and extraordinary.

Her personality combines traits which might be, in someone else, desperately contradictory: Robin is stern and gooney, intensely private and flamboyantly zany, earnest and hilariously ironic. She is a nineteenth-century English literature scholar; and she haunts film revival houses to soak in Hollywood epics, mysteries, sci-fi, and old monster movies. She is devastatingly articulate; and yet her most frequently used expressions are "Rats!" and "Quack-quack!" She is a staunch feminist who reveres Kipling and Conrad. She is an opera fanatic and a classical and Celtic folk music buff; yet her record collection also includes albums by David Bowie, Billy Idol, The Cramps, Siouxsie and the Banshees, and a wealth of Heavy Metal and obscure punk and new wave rock.

She collects imported English toiletries and has a discreetly sober wardrobe of tweeds and L. L. Bean sweaters (fitting for a Gould Academy alumna and *summa cum laude* graduate of Bowdoin College); but she tends to favor a more motley ensemble of leather miniskirts, stud bracelets, a Harley Davidson jacket, gold lamé sneakers, antique silk and lace, furs, fishnets, and feather boas—and looks stylish dressed either way. Her consumption of chocolate, tea, dairy products, and sweets is Rabelaisian (we remember one grocery trip when Robin surveyed a cart laden with pounds of butter, gallons of whole milk and ice cream, quarts of cream, sacks of sugar, and a half-dozen bags of cookies and then added more of each to ensure that she wouldn't run low); but she remains slenderly beautiful by virtue of daily ten-to-twelve mile walks, during which she listens to music on her Walkman and plots her stories. She has a taste for electronic gadgets and video and stereo equipment, but she will not even dream of trading up "Nellie," her long-suffering old Selectric I—which, if typewriters had the equivalent of car odometers, would long since have passed the one-million-mile mark.

Robin is often reticent among people she does not know and will attend parties only at gun point; but she posts thousands of words of personal correspondence a day to friends, colleagues, fans, and strangers. She considers herself aloof and reclusive, but the addresses of her close friends range from England to California. She describes herself as "cranky," "difficult," "intolerant"—but is in fact a generous and affectionate woman, a person who inspires loyalty and love from her friends. And while she claims to be a cynical misanthrope, Robin populates her novels and stories with some of the most civilized, decent, honorable, and well-rounded heroes and villains in modern fiction. She eschews not only helpless heroines and hapless swains but also the one-dimensional, rotten-to-the-core villains of other fantasies. More than adventure, more than romance, more even than her determination to write stories about "girls who do things," her tales are about honor—which is perhaps the key to the "real" Robin McKinley, just as the complexity and vividness of her created worlds resonate from the strength and vibrancy of her own life.

Jennifer Carolyn Robin Turrell McKinley was born in her mother's home town of Warren, Ohio, but grew up all over the world because her father was in the navy. She says she keeps track by remembering which books she was reading at the time: Andrew Lang's *Fairy Books* in California, *The Chronicles of Narnia* in New York, *The Lord of the Rings* in Japan, *The Once and Future King* on an island off the coast of Maine. She went to school briefly in Pennsylvania, spent some time living the Bohemian life and zipping around on a motorcycle in Washington, D.C., and returned to Maine to attend Bowdoin College. It was in Maine that she wrote her first book, *Beauty: A Retelling of the Story of Beauty and the Beast,* which—like all her books—quickly gained a wide readership in its young adult hardcover edition and in its adult fantasy paperback publication. "I don't write 'children's books,' " Robin says; "I write my books for anyone who wants to read them."

When we met Robin, she had moved from Maine to Boston, had squeezed into a three-room Allston apartment with her thousands of books, and was walking miles daily to Beacon Hill—singing the score of *Sweeney Todd* in her head—to her job in the Children's Book Department of Little, Brown, Publishers. It was in Boston that she wrote *The Door in the Hedge,* her wondrous collection of original and retold fairy tales. After that came a stint on a horse farm in eastern Massachusetts—horses have long been a passion of Robin's—where she divided her time between the barn and the typewriter. The final draft of *The Blue Sword,* her first novel set in the land of Damar, was delayed because, as she wrote us, "a horse fell on my hand."

The Hero and the Crown was written while she was living with us in New York City, in a run-down section of Staten Island overlooking the bay and the lights of Manhattan, and she attributes the particular gruesomeness of Aerin's battle with the dragon to the daily stresses and dangers of living in an urban slum. Our keenest memories of life with Robin include early mornings arguing about books or trading publishing gossip over tea, late nights of champagne and music videos; the walls of the apartment covered with political articles and cartoons ripped from the pages of the many magazines she subscribes to. There is a photograph we treasure of tall blonde Robin—wearing an elegant silk robe from the 1940s—squatting on the floor to race Godzilla wind-up toys.

At present she has solved the dilemma of her contradictory love for both country and city living by maintaining an apartment on Manhattan's Upper West Side but spending the bulk of her time in her recently-purchased, idyllic, lilac-covered house in a small town on the northern coast of Maine. The rooms of the two-hundred-year-old cottage are filled to bursting with books and music and video tapes, with polished wood furniture and a baby grand piano, the walls adorned with Pre-Raphaelite prints and original New Romantic artwork by artist friends—interspersed with a classic McKinley collection of *New Yorker* cartoons, rude post cards, and pictures of Heavy Metal bands. In the driveway, next to a roaring stream, is her beloved red MG convertible—an up-scale successor to her motorcycle.

Robin once told us that an odd—but typical—goal of hers is to become, forty or fifty years hence, "one of those cranky, literary old ladies—the kind who absolutely terrifies young writers." A matter of simply refining attitudes into mannerisms? No, Robin's "cranky, literary old lady" must be a person who, by constantly striving to excel and grow in the years and novels to come, earns a steady elevation from prominence to fame. Having known Robin for five years, we can attest that she has the talent, perseverance, and vision to secure a lasting place in literature. Someday she might well be a literary old lady, quite irascibly cranky—but still incandescent; for Robin McKinley possesses, like her characters, the stuff of legends.

Newbery Medal Books 1976-1985
by Zena Sutherland

Since few of us who are involved in the field of children's literature have agreed wholeheartedly with the choices of Newbery Committees of the past, even when we have been serving on those committees, it would be foolish to expect from any of us a stream of blissful encomiums as we evaluate in retrospect the choices of the decade that has just passed. In his essay, "A Decade of Newbery Books in Perspective," which appeared in *Newbery and Caldecott Medal Books 1966-1975,* John Rowe Townsend, always astute and articulate, says, "The most authoritative of all critics is Time, and no committee can tell what picture will emerge in the longer perspective." It might be added that no critic can judge with infallibility even in retrospect.

It must also be added that no Newbery Medal Committee has an easy time in arriving at a decision. First, it is incumbent on the committee to choose a book even though it is difficult to agree on what the most distinguished book of the year is—or even that there *is* a distinguished book. The Newbery Committee does not have the prerogative of the jury for the Carnegie Medal, who may withhold an award in any year in which they feel no book deserves it. Second, it is both difficult and frustrating to pit one genre against another—fiction versus poetry, for example—or a book for younger readers against a more complex book for older readers. Third, the voting system with weighted balloting does indeed offer safeguards against hasty or capricious judgments, but the system also makes it possible for a "safe" third choice to move up when ardent partisans are in a deadlock over two favorites. Then there is the "hidden agenda" as it was called by an irate member of the committee in the year I served as chair. This is a controversial area.

The remarks that follow, however, are based on off-the-record comments by many members of the joint Newbery-Caldecott Committees of the past and by men and women who served on the Newbery Committee after 1980, the year when it first functioned as a separate committee. What my colleague meant by "hidden agenda" was the factors that are not supposed to be considered—yet often are: Has the author repeatedly had Honor Books but never made it to the top? Or, on the other hand, is it not wise to vote for someone who has already proved worthy by having already won the award? And what about the nagging worry that the book will have little popular appeal? Popularity is not supposed to be a criterion, but it would be nice to have the approbation of the ultimate audience—the readers. I have served on many book juries and have listened with great interest to the wonderfully devious ways people find to insinuate, without being specific, some of that hidden agenda. This is not meant as criticism, for we all have our own agendas (sometimes we hide them from ourselves) but to point out that such factors influence voting just as do standards for the stylistic idiosyncrasies that may or may not add up to distinguished writing.

Last, there is the grab-bag factor: What books are available each year; what won the year before (we don't want to seem to be in a rut); who is on the committee, and how assertive, persuasive, and articulate are the individual members. Given that all of these aspects do obtain, the wonder is that one finds a retrospective evaluation so impressive. Perhaps one cannot overestimate the discretionary powers of those who nominate and elect the committees and serve so diligently when they are elected. Like the authors whose books reflect the society from which they emanate, the people who select books to be honored may be governed by a conviction that literary quality is of paramount importance or by a conviction that social message is of supreme importance or by a passionate interest in a cause or a subject. As well as a Newbery winner, what emerges is a group integrity, a vindication of the democratic process.

Less discernible in a retrospective evaluation of the Newbery books considered here is any pattern. Although it is possible to say that most of the ten winners are realistic fiction, one must wonder, for example, if this is significant given the thousands of titles published each year. Even when one also considers the Honor Books, they add up to a very small sample. Yet some perspective may be gained by discussing the contents and quality of the books and then placing them within the matrix of general trends and developments of the decade.

The books are discussed in the chronological order of the year in which the award was conferred, with occasional comments on the Honor Books of that year. A complete list of the Honor Books of the decade we are considering will be found at the end of this section. Among the Medal books are one historical novel, one poetry book, five books of realistic fiction, one story that strains credulity but remains within the bounds of the possible, and two fantasy novels, interestingly placed as the first and last winners of the decade.

The Grey King, winner of the 1976 Newbery Medal, was fourth in a series of five books by Susan Cooper; the second book, *The Dark Is Rising,* had been the only Honor Book in the year that Paula Fox's *The Slave Dancer* had won the medal. It is not unusual for this choice of a later book in a cycle to become a winner when the first book has won critical acclaim. It is true of Lloyd Alexander's *The High King* (the final volume in the Prydain cycle) and of *The Hero and the Crown,* Robin McKinley's book that rounds off our present ten winners. It may be due in part to the judges' growing familiarity with the series, to the competition in individual years, or to the developing strength within the cycle. The latter, I think, is true of *The Grey King.*

Susan Cooper writes in the tradition of high fantasy, creating a magic, wholly conceived world in which there is a sustained and cosmic struggle between the forces of good and evil. While *The Grey King* can be read profitably on its own, it gains stature when read in sequence, and it is masterful in the meshing of the fantastic elements and their realistic matrix. It moves from the Cornish setting of the earlier books to Wales, where Will, a boy of eleven, carries the burden of responsibility as last of the Old Ones, the timeless defenders of the Light, battling against the evil encroachment of the rising Dark. Will makes a new friend in Bran, who, in proving to be King Arthur's son, exemplifies one of the many ways in which Cooper introduces elements of Arthurian legend and British folklore. Read again ten years later, I found the book no less compelling. It has the classic form of the quest, and its intricate yet cohesive plot is developed with a high sense of drama—and even a bit of the inevitability of a Greek tragedy. It is no small thing to make a character believable both as a mortal child and as an immortal and a powerful magician. Cooper is not only one of the most intense writers in this group of authors, but also holds her position as a writer of fiction whose narrative sense is as strong in fantasy as in realism.

In the following year the Newbery Medal was awarded to Mildred Taylor for *Roll of Thunder, Hear My Cry,* the story of a Black family set in Mississippi during the Depression era. It is both a bitter indictment of the prejudice and persecution of Blacks in the rural South and a testament to their pride and resilience. There is no doubt that this book remains today as effective dramatically and as important sociologically as it was when it appeared. It is one of several books in this decade of Medal winners to be written in the first person, and in that respect, it now seems disappointing: The nine-year-old protagonist, Cassie Logan, is the narrator, and although her observations have the usual advantages of intimacy and immediacy and reflect the period and the setting, they are not evenly effective, sounding too often an adult or authorial tone in the exposition that is in conflict with the childlike tone of the dialogue. It is also noticeable that the children's speech does not reflect their mother's speech patterns.

The trenchant picture of bias in Taylor's book, however, is devastating and believable; alleviated only slightly by a few sympathetic white characters and one amoral Black adolescent, the story pictures a Black society oppressed by its sneering, malevolent white neighbors. The Logan family is admirable in its interfamilial love, its idealism and tolerance, and its courage in the face of white persecution that is all the more bitter because the Logans, as landowners, cannot be controlled as can the Black families who are sharecroppers. This is not an unflawed book, but it is a memorable one. It is memorable in large part because of Taylor's strong identification with her characters and because of the message that Cassie gets from her parents: " 'There are things you can't back down on, things you gotta take a stand on . . . How you carry yourself, what you stand for—that's how you gain respect. But, little one, ain't nobody's respect worth more than your own.'"

When Katherine Paterson's *Bridge to Terabithia* was given the 1978 Newbery Medal, the taboo on the subject of death which was maintained in the first part of the twentieth century had already been broken, even in books for younger readers. These books, especially fiction, were patently purposive, so that the reader's reaction was apt to be that this was a good, or not good, story by an author who wanted to inform the audience about the processes of grief. Paterson is both more open and more subtle: She is open in the candor and pain she reveals; she is subtle in making the death of a friend and the sorrow of the child who mourns that death inextricably linked to other relationships and secondary effects.

The "bridge" of the title is a rope on which Jesse and his friend Leslie swing over a ravine to the secret place where they have created a land of sustained imaginative play, Terabithia. Leslie and her parents have brought new insights to the boy's life, theretofore culturally impoverished. The author's depiction of disparate cultural patterns is notable because she does not disparage the intellectual aridity of Jesse's parents. They retain their identity and their dignity, and when Jesse is desolate, these two habitually undemonstrative people show their love and sensitivity. The poignant story is all the more effective because Paterson lets Jesse express his grief and guilt rather than telling readers that he feels them. There is no glossing-over; nor is there a reaching for dramatic effect. This is the essence of Katherine Paterson's durability as a writer and of her literary integrity. In her books—of which this is one of her best—there are never extraneous characters, and those who are there are wholly drawn and believably motivated; their relationships are conceived with insight and drawn in depth. She is adroit at putting the elements of a story together.

Ellen Raskin's *The Westing Game* is the maverick of this retrospective: It is a realistic novel in the sense that events are within the bounds of possibility, but it is a realistic novel that is not in the least believable. Raskin wrote it as a humorous mystery with a large cast of zany characters, and its humor, minimal suspense, and the intricacies of the puzzle in the book's treasure hunt—almost a game—are the qualities that have made the book appealing to many readers. On rereading, this seems less distinguished a work than its nine companions. The writing style is staccato; the characters are well defined and often comic, but they seem overdrawn; and the story line is labored.

Six carefully selected families are lured, by direct mail advertisement, to become tenants of a newly erected apartment building. They are then told that they may be heirs to a large fortune and are given written clues that must be solved. The instructions are based on a will made by the millionaire who built the apartment house, lives in a mansion next door, and claims (yes, in his will) to have been murdered. There ensues a frantic treasure hunt—in which there are almost slapstick encounters among the various hunters—and a plethora of subplots. Still a popular book with the group of readers who are mystery or puzzle fans, in retrospect this seems more entertaining than distinguished. Its choice as a Medal book underscores the problematic question: Can a distinguished book also be a popular book?

One wonders whether it is not possible that an individual Newbery Committee is swayed by a feeling, part of that hidden agenda, that it is time for a change or that a genre had been too long ignored. It is interesting to observe that when, in 1980, the award was given to Joan Blos for her historical novel in journal form, *A Gathering of Days: A New England Girl's Journal, 1830-32*, the sole Honor Book was the biographical *The Road from Home: The Story of an Armenian Girl* by David Kherdian. Perhaps this was in some measure a reaction to the levity of the previous winner. At any rate, the journal kept by Blos's thirteen-year-old Catherine Hall proves well worth a return reading.

In an article in the November 1985 issue of *School Library Journal,* "The Overstuffed Sentence and Other Means for Assessing Historical Fiction for Children," Blos expounds on the criteria that pertain to the genre. Her theses are well exemplified in her own book, for she maintains a mode of speech that is appropriate (and especially important in a first-person account) for the period, the place, and the age of the diarist. Blos does not depend on great personages or famous events to give flavor and validity to her story. Instead, she shows how people live and react to changes and developments in their culture. Catherine's journal shows her reflection of diverse viewpoints about runaway slaves, and it makes reference to recorded history; but the details that indicate historical research on the author's part are never obtrusive, and they do not dominate the story by clogging the narrative flow. In sum, this is a book set in a historical period, but it is not a book about nineteenth-century New Hampshire: It is a book about a human being.

It is quite probable that any critic asked to comment on a ten-year span of Newbery books would differ in the reactions to each re-evaluated book; in fact, we might totally disagree. For me, the book that gained most in stature was Katherine Paterson's *Jacob Have I Loved*. The comments made above, in the discussion of her first Newbery book, apply here: the candor, the percipience, the motivation and interreactions between characters, and the knitting of literary elements to produce a smooth narrative in which there are only as many characters as the story needs and only as much structure as the story line requires.

The title is from the Bible—God's pronouncement, "Jacob have I loved, but Esau have I hated"—and the girl who feels that she is Esau, the hated elder twin, is Louise, the narrator. Her twin, Caroline, is beautiful and talented. It is Caroline who is admired, who is sent away from their bleak Chesapeake Bay island to study music, and who is courted and wed by the one young man Louise loves. Of all the books in this group that are in the first person, *Jacob Have I Loved* is the one in which the protagonist's voice is most clear; it is, with the 1983 winner, *Dicey's Song*, the strongest in establishment of setting, and it has one of the most devastating portrayals of an older person crabbed with age in children's literature. The story has a logical, but rather speeded, happy ending, but this minor flaw does not keep *Jacob Have I Loved* from being an unforgettable book.

And now for something completely different—for the very first time in its sixty-three-year history, a Newbery Medal has been given to a book of poetry. Why, one wonders, did this happen after so many years and after not naming even one of the many volumes of poems by distinguished writers for children as an Honor Book? This query is not meant in a derogatory sense, for Nancy Willard's *A Visit to William Blake's Inn: Poems for Inno-*

cent and Experienced Travelers is original in concept, handsome as a piece of bookmaking, and delightfully illustrated by Alice and Martin Provensen. Perhaps this long overdue recognition of the genre is in part because the establishment of a prize for children's poetry (not for a book but for a body of work) by the National Council of Teachers of English has increased our awareness. Perhaps the paintings by the Provensens so imaginatively interpret the poems. Whatever the reason, the choice is a happy deviation from the norm.

Willard's setting and her binding theme is an imaginary inn run by William Blake; it is staffed by angels, dragons, and a rabbit in addition to the host. The guests are equally diverse, and there is magic everywhere. The poems, sometimes playful or even humorous, are just as often thoughtful, and they have fresh, felicitous phrasing to bring vision as a complementary component to writing that shows good control of rhyme, rhythm, and form.

To add to Cynthia Voigt's pleasure in winning the 1983 Newbery Medal for *Dicey's Song*, there must have been a special satisfaction in knowing that the authors of five Honor Books that year included such stellar names as Jean Fritz, Virginia Hamilton, and William Steig as well as two outstanding newcomers, Paul Fleischman and Robin McKinley. The book is a sequel to *Homecoming*, the story of four children who, led by Dicey, the eldest, make their way from New England, where they have been abandoned by their mentally ill mother, to the eastern shore of Maryland where their grandmother lives. In the sequel thirteen-year-old Dicey and her siblings learn how resourceful and compassionate their seemingly crusty grandmother is, and Dicey is able to relinquish the heavy burden of responsibility she has borne and share it with Gram. The first book had more dramatic action, but *Dicey's Song* is much more cohesive, a beautifully balanced and developed story of individual growth and interpersonal support. The characterization is consistent and perceptive, the setting solidly established, and the plot elements are firmly knit by a writing style smooth enough to compensate for the occasional lag in pace that comes with iteration. It undoubtedly surprised few of Voigt's readers that her novel *A Solitary Blue* was an Honor Book in the following year.

Although Beverly Cleary has written—and very capably—fantasy for younger readers and realistic fiction for adolescents, her forte has always been the cozily humorous and simply written novel for the primary or middle grades, usually focusing on some familiar facet of common problems in everyday life, most often, in recent years, in the life of her widely beloved character Ramona. Cleary has been a tremendously popular writer, winning both a wide devoted audience and critical commendation that includes Newbery Honor Books in the past.

Cleary won the 1984 Newbery Medal for *Dear Mr. Henshaw*, however, a book written in a form she had not hitherto used and which does impose strictures on the writer. Despite the limitations imposed by using a combination of letters and diary entries to tell a story that has tenderness, humor, change, and growth, she succeeds brilliantly in *Dear Mr. Henshaw*. To convey so much through the voice of a sophisticated adolescent would be comparatively easy, but to begin with Leigh's letters when he is in second grade (writing to an author) and to conclude with a journal (suggested by the same author) in the sixth grade is inspired. Through the boy's comments readers feel his pain in being separated from the father who has left home, and eventually, through the journal, readers can witness the process of adjustment to loss, acceptance of its permanence, and a realization that although they no longer live together, Leigh has not lost his father's love. Perhaps because Cleary so deftly shows her protagonist changing there seems no need for alternate voices or viewpoints to give breadth to the story. Its immediacy never becomes too intense; its humor never makes light of the seriousness of the theme. A gem in 1983, the year of its publication, it is still a gem as the years pass.

Robin McKinley's *The Blue Sword*, when it was published in 1982, was the first book in a projected trilogy. The second book, *The Hero and the Crown*, which was published two years later and won the 1985 Newbery Medal, is—in her word—a prequel, set in an earlier time than the first book but in the same mythical land of Damar. Unlike the one other fantasy in this group of Medal books, *The Grey King*, which blends a contemporary setting and legendary characters, the story of the hero who wins—or retrieves—the crown is painted on a romantic canvas that shows an imaginary land filled with magic and dragons and psychic powers and love and battles in which animal warriors fight.

Too rich? No. Perhaps a bit overwritten, but McKinley orchestrates the myriad elements of the fantasy deftly. In Aerin, the rejected daughter of a witch-woman, the warrior-maiden who slays a ravaging dragon and saves her country, and the one who wields the sword and wins a throne, McKinley has created a sympathetic and courageous savior of her country. Long and intermittently intricate, the story impresses by its scope and sweep and by its narrative power rather than by the depth of its characterization; it has many familiar folkloric elements, but they are put together with considerable industry and some panache.

What, then, does this brief retrospective assessment show, particularly in the way that the Newbery winners and Honor Books reflect the trends that were established or that began during the decade 1976-1985? Let's look first at the background. As the second half of the century progressed, the domino action of a chain of fallen taboos brought a steady stream of stories, especially contemporary realistic fiction (usually set in the United States), that dealt candidly with all of the issues faced in real life, both in the sense of domestic or personal problems and in the sense of philosophic or moral dilemmas that concerned children as well as adults. The treatment of adult weaknesses was frequent and more forthcoming; the evidence of an imperfect world more frequently incorporated. There were reflections of new lifestyles and frank language: And there was a growing swell of concern and controversy about whether or not these books were harmful to children. There was a marked improvement in the quality and quantity of indigenous fantasy writing and an equally evident improvement in the writing style, authoritativeness, and accuracy of nonfiction. There was a noticeable trend toward making the subjects of biographies human beings rather than idealized stick figures. There were many books about minority group members, some of them written by people from those minority groups. In the last ten years the paperback market grew and grew, and such lucrative, if hackneyed, specialities as choose-your-own-adventure tales and the formulaic adolescent love story took over the racks. And, with every change, there has been some corresponding recognition in award books, although the comparatively few out of the many hundreds published can be only a faint and not always dependable echo of trends.

There are also some recent developments that appear to be mirrored in the books seen as a group from the decade. There has been far less ethnic literature and an observable attrition of minority authors. Books about Black characters, for example: There are less than half as many in the Medal and Honor Book categories as there were in the comparable books of the previous decade. Despite the widespread condemnation of problem books, particularly from conservative groups and individuals objecting to stories concerned with fractured families, imperfect parents, and social ills, half of the books are realistic novels, and they incorporate many of the facets cited above.

One Newbery Medal does not make a trend, but poetry lovers have hailed the fact that a poetry book did win. Perhaps some day a nonfiction book will be chosen. In our decade there were three biographical or autobiographical Honor Books (those by David Kherdian, Jean Fritz, and Aranka Siegel) and only one informational book, Kathryn Lasky's *Sugaring Time.* All Medal winners were women, only one of them from a minority group. Four of the ten books were written in the first person, two in the form of journal entries or letters. And the subjects, ranging from death and glory and the fate of the world to sibling rivalry and a treasure hunt, seem to be indicative of nothing save that there is variety in every decade; that the treatments are fairly conservative whatever the subject; and that the ten committees have chosen, as have their predecessors, to make good literary quality their highest criterion.

A perennial, if not vociferous, complaint about the Newbery Medal books has been that they are most often for older children, even for adolescents. Looking at the appropriate audiences for the last ten years of winners, we find that only two books were assigned reading levels (I use those established by the *Bulletin of the Center for Children's Books* for consistency) in a range that dipped below fifth grade: *A Visit to William Blake's Inn* (grades K–5) and *The Westing Game* (grades 4–6). Five ranged from fifth grade up, one from sixth, and two from seventh. To some degree this does reflect a trend, for children's books have been increasingly sophisticated in their format, their style, and the subject matter with which they deal. Some books are clearly written for young children; some are clearly written for older children, but at the top of the range—in both cases—there is a blurring: books for children that are also appropriate for young adolescents, books for adolescents that are enjoyed by adults. Indeed, some of the latter are frequently found in the adult departments of public libraries. In 1972 a group of Ohio libraries requested the then Newbery-Caldecott Committee to consider for that year's award "only those books intended primarily for children of elementary school age." There is no question that the terms of the award, especially the phrase "most distinguished," have militated against the selection of a book for the primary grades. One unfortunate effect of the tendency to select books for older children has been to label them as "children's books," thereby reducing the number of adolescents who might enjoy reading such a swashbuckler as *The Hero and the Crown* or such a percipient exploration of problems common to all adolescents as *Jacob Have I Loved.*

As the composition and procedures of Newbery Committees have changed, there has been broader participation and a more democratic base to committee membership, with a diligent effort to bring in new members of the Association for Library Service to Children, to include ALSC members who may not be librarians but who are qualified to serve, and to elect men and women from different parts of the country. All of these changes have influenced the caliber of the committees and therefore of the choices they have made. Another influencing factor has been a change in procedure when voting on a book whose author has already been a winner: The requirement that an author's book must have a unanimous vote if she or he is to win a second—or a third—time is now eliminated.

There are some ways in which Newbery selections, whether of the decade past or those to come, have been and will be the same. As a small sample of all the books published, they will never reflect all of the trends or innovations of their decade; nor are they apt to include those trends that reflect the popular culture, like the etiolated adolescent romance that is written to formula and is, alas, so appealing to pre-teen readers. It is unlikely that future winners will have language or concepts that adults, or some adults, find offensive even if the contemporary realistic novel continues to dominate the lists of selections. Despite the improvement in the quality of most nonfiction books it would be a surprise if one were selected for the Newbery Medal. Two changes that are more likely to take place are the selection of books, at least some, for younger readers, and, given the steady improvement in the quality of fanciful writing in the United States, the inclusion of more fantasy titles as winners or Honor Books.

There are some perennial truths that probably would occur to anyone pondering Newbery history, procedures, choices, and changes. One is that there really is no such thing as *the* best book of any year, even though each year each of us has a favorite. (Well, most years.) Another is that the winnowing process is not apt to produce a bad book, but there are always years in which individuals feel the wrong choice was made. There are certainly years in which, looking backward, many of us feel a modern classic was overlooked, with the books of E. B. White and Laura Ingalls Wilder usually leading that list.

It seems a conservative prognosis to say that the emphasis on literary quality will be pre-eminent, as it was in the past decade. And it is certain that, just as this decade's books have reflected concerns and lifestyles and mores and taboos of their time, so will books of the future: so have books of the past. However much each of us may quibble about individual titles each year, a retrospective look at the past decade reaffirms what we must acknowledge in looking back at all of the Newbery choices. They have fulfilled the purpose for which Frederic Melcher established the award: They encourage authors to produce and editors to publish the best in books for children and young people. They gain publicity that makes the public as well as professionals aware of the importance of children's literature. They are a source of pleasure and prestige.

The Caldecott Medal Books
1976-1985

The Caldecott Medal 1976

WHY MOSQUITOES BUZZ IN PEOPLE'S EARS

illustrated by LEO AND DIANE DILLON

retold by VERNA AARDEMA

published by THE DIAL PRESS 1975

BOOK NOTE

In this West African folk tale a mosquito exaggerates a bit of news to an iguana. The iguana can't be bothered to listen to such nonsense and puts sticks in his ears. A python greets the iguana, who doesn't hear him, which upsets the snake. The python hides in a rabbit's burrow, which frightens the rabbit, who runs away. A crow sees the rabbit running and gives the alarm. A monkey, hearing the crow, leaps off to spread the alarm and falls on an owl's nest, killing an owlet. When Mother Owl finds one of her children dead, she is too sad to hoot, as she always does, to wake the sun. The night is so long that all the animals are worried. King Lion calls a meeting and asks Mother Owl why she has not woken the sun, and the owl blames the monkey, who killed her child. In turn and with cumulative effect in the telling, the monkey blames the crow; the crow blames the rabbit; the rabbit blames the python; the python blames the iguana; and the iguana blames the mosquito. When the animals all cry, " 'Punish the mosquito!' " Mother Owl is satisfied and wakes the sun. The mosquito, who was listening, has hidden and is never punished. But even today the mosquito has a guilty conscience and buzzes in people's ears, asking, "Is everyone still angry at me?"

Bold pictures present the animals in flat, stylized shapes that splash over double-page spreads in a lively, decorative manner. In preparing the full-color art, the artists used India ink, water colors applied with an airbrush in both fine spray and spatter techniques, and pastels rubbed on by hand. To achieve the cut-out effect, they cut shapes out of vellum and frisket masks.

Caldecott Medal Acceptance
by Leo and Diane Dillon

Usually when a book is completed, we are on to the next, and behind-the-scenes details are forgotten. But this time is different. It's the first time in our lives we've talked more about a book after its completion than while we were working on it. It all started when Phyllis Fogelman, editor-in-chief of The Dial Press, called us and asked if we would like to illustrate a tale about animals based on a style we had used on the jacket for *Behind the Back of the Mountain* (Dial). We were excited by the possibility of working on a kind of book we'd never done before, and Phyllis began looking for a good manuscript for us. A few months later she sent us Verna Aardema's retelling of the West African folk tale, "Why Mosquitoes Buzz in People's Ears." When we first read the manuscript, we were both amazed that in just a few pages there was such a wealth of material. Each paragraph was packed with action, each scene flowed into the next. The cast of characters was varied, and there was a wide range of emotion. There was humor, tragedy, seriousness, and silliness. Needless to say, we were delighted with the visual possibilities.

For the first time, we were about to illustrate a book that was truly for young children, a story that was perfect for reading aloud and one that young children would become intensely involved in. *Mosquitoes* wasn't our usual problem book. Over the years editors have called us when they've had a manuscript that would be difficult to illustrate. And in working on those books, we have, of course, had to spend a great deal of time in the conceptual stages, thinking and rethinking the solution. For *Mosquitoes* the conceptual stage was very easy; this book, we knew from the start, would be fun to illustrate. We have had a few heated discussions in our twenty years of working together about whether or not art is fun, but on this book we agreed.

To us every book we accept is different, and each provides us with a chance to do things we haven't done before, a chance to grow and expand as artists. Every manuscript presents a new challenge. We have looked for new solutions to different challenges, tried out new styles, experimented with different approaches—not without failures, but also never without excitement and growth. One of the things we have avoided over the years is specialization. We have fought against limiting our styles ever since we began working together. When we first started freelancing and took our portfolio around, we were frequently told by art directors that we had too many styles—they'd never remember us, and so, of course, they'd never have any work for us. Because of that we called ourselves *Studio 2* for a while instead of Leo and Diane Dillon. Somehow, art directors were able to deal with a variety of styles when they thought we were a whole studio full of artists.

We never hesitate to try a new technique on a job. In fact, we feel it is the only way to learn its possibilities and limitations. If you make a mistake on a trial piece, you can toss it out; but on a real assignment, you have to find a solution. For *Mosquitoes* the new technique we tried was airbrush, and we had to find solutions to the inevitable problems.

We believe that the role of the illustrator is *not* simply to duplicate the text, but to enlarge on it, to restate the words in our own graphic terms. That's why we enjoy working on children's books so much. In some fields, such as advertising and textbooks, illustrators are not expected to think and are sometimes given specific instructions on what to draw. But in children's trade books the artists have a great deal of creative freedom. We illustrate the text, of course, but we are also free to go beyond it or to pick out certain aspects and play them up.

Take, for example, a couple of the characters in *Mosquitoes:* the antelope and the little red bird. The antelope has a very minor part in the story—he is simply sent to bring Mother Owl and later the iguana before the council. We decided he really wanted a more important part—he wanted to be a star. So he began trying to get attention, peering out and grinning, hamming it up, until finally on one spread he is seen up front in the center, with a great toothy smile. You may have noticed he reaches the peak of his career on the cover of the Newbery-Caldecott program. The little red bird never appears in the text at all. We put her in one spread and became rather fond of her. We began to think of her as the observer or reader and added her to the other spreads. Thus on each page you will find her watching, witnessing the events as they unfold. On the last page, when the story is over, she flies away. For us she is like the storyteller, gathering information, then passing it on to the next generation. We were asked recently if the attention we gave the antelope reflected any feelings we might have of being unnoticed. We'd like to answer that tonight that certainly is not the case.

We were also fascinated by the filmlike quality of the story. So much happens within the space of two or three paragraphs, we felt that to leave any of the scenes out of the pictures would create a jumpy effect. We wanted the pictures to flow the way the story flowed. To accomplish this, we showed the same animal doing more than one thing on a page. We imagined that if we placed each page of the book side by side, the total effect would be that of a long scroll. The story would unfold with total continuity in picture form, and there would be no gaps. In drawing the animals, one of our first concerns was to show the expressions on their faces. We wanted to indicate human emotions that children could identify with yet retain each animal's distinct features. This was challenge enough, but the most difficult part was trying to put expressions onto a mosquito's face.

One important element of the text from our point of view is the repetition. In the beginning the series of events is laid before the reader as each one happens. Later, at the council, each character retells one of those events from his or her own point of view. We didn't want to show the same scenes twice—though we might have met our deadline if we had!—so we decided to focus on each character's perspective. In the pictures we tried to exaggerate each one's story, just as the animal might have done in retelling it. This approach seemed particularly appropriate to us, since at the time of the retelling, the animals are all trying to exonerate themselves. They're trying to put the blame on someone else: It wasn't *my* fault—it was the crow's; it wasn't *my* fault—it was the rabbit's! Hence, when Mother Owl stands before King Lion recalling the events as she thinks they occurred, the pictures show the monkey viciously attacking the helpless baby owlet. The reader, of course, knows that this is *not* the way it happened, and we have enjoyed hearing that children, with their keen sense of justice, protest, "NO! NO! It didn't happen that way!"

Since January we have had the opportunity to speak to a number of audiences about *Why Mosquitoes Buzz in People's Ears.* Invariably the reaction has been, "That's all fascinating, but how do you work *together?*"

We worked on *Mosquitoes* in the same way we work on all our books. After we read a manuscript we discuss it, tossing back and forth ideas about possible styles and techniques until we agree on what will work best. At this critical stage of concept, it is a great advantage having two minds working together—the ideas come twice as fast. Then we proceed to the next step. The drawings are done in pencil, then refined, and finally the finishes are done in color. On *Mosquitoes,* the color was done in airbrush with frisket, which is a form of stencil. One area is done and then masked out, or covered, and the next area is done. The black areas are painted in last, then glazed with blue or purple. But as for who does what—sometimes even *we* aren't sure. Each illustration is passed back and forth between us several times before it is completed, and since we both work on every piece of art, the finished painting looks as if one artist has done it. Actually, with this method of working, we create a third artist. Together we are able to create art we would not be able to do individually. By joining our talents in various combinations, we have several different styles available to us. As individuals we have our own styles and approaches, and we continue to work separately for gallery showings. Most people who are familiar with our individual work and our work together see a resemblance but agree that the third artist is, indeed, a separate person.

There is one more thing we would like to talk about, but we haven't been able to find a logical place for it in this speech—even though we've written several drafts since January. Now that we have a captive audience, and such a large one at that, we're going to talk about it anyway. We feel very strongly about craftsmanship: the tool that gives us the freedom to say what we want to say in our art. It is our vocabulary. An artist *must* know how to use and have control over media in order to express his or her ideas. When we first started teaching in the 1960s we were distressed to see the emphasis shifting from technique and craft to theatrics. Students were being given projects like drawing on a long sheet of brown paper and then wrapping themselves in it or going to the park and experiencing each other. Conceptual experience was emphasized, and although concept *is* important, it is useless without technique. Art is not accidental. Accidents happen; we do not want to rely on them, but rather take advantage of them when they occur. We are happy to see a shift back to an emphasis on craft.

In conclusion, we would like to say that receiving this award has reinforced our faith in what we believe. It has encouraged us to experiment further, to refine and perfect our work. I would like to add here that I was informed that I am the first Black artist to win this award. I felt proud when Tom Feelings previously won honors but never dreamed I would be standing here tonight.

We would like to thank Verna Aardema, whose story was an inspiration; Phyllis Fogelman, whose vision brought the words and pictures together; Atha Tehon and Warren Wallerstein, whose knowledge and perfectionism we relied upon; Ellen Teguis, Regina Hayes, Susan Pearson, Toby Sherry, and everyone else at Dial who worked with us. And to the Newbery-Caldecott Committee, which had the difficult task of making the decision, our very special thanks. We are extremely proud to be here tonight. Thank you.

BIOGRAPHICAL NOTE

Leo and Diane Dillon
by Phyllis J. Fogelman

Diane and Leo Dillon were born just eleven days apart in the month of March and both recall loving to draw for as long as they can remember. Although there are other similarities in their backgrounds, there are also great differences.

Leo was born and brought up in Brooklyn, New York. His parents came from Trinidad to this country as adults, and it was here that they met, married, and had two children. But because their formative years had been spent in the West Indies, they could not perceive the true state of race relations in the United States—a fact that was to be partly an advantage for their son but also an enormous burden. Not knowing they were supposed to stay in the ghetto, Leo's parents made sure that they lived in the best neighborbood they could afford. Mr. Dillon owned his own truck, and Mrs. Dillon was a dressmaker. They rented at first and later bought a house on the same block in the East New York section of Brooklyn where they lived throughout Leo's childhood. This meant that Leo went to better schools than most Black children, for then even more than in the 1970s, ghetto schools got the fewest supplies and the least experienced teachers. His mother and father couldn't understand discrimination, so when the inevitable racial problems arose or when Leo was excluded from things everyone else took part in, they blamed their son, refusing to entertain the possibility of discrimination.

Leo had to cover up his true feelings at school in order to cope. At the same time he was not allowed to discuss his feelings and anxieties at home. So out of necessity the young boy became secretive and something of a loner. Since he could always draw well, he turned wholeheartedly to art which became both a source of pleasure and the main outlet for his feelings. His talent made Leo the center of attention at school and saw him through many painful times. "I could always draw my way out of bad situations," Leo recalls.

His parents encouraged him. They were proud that he was so talented, and they always bought him paints and art supplies. But the thought never occurred to them that their son would pursue art as a career. They, after all, had come to the United States during the Depression, and the few artists they saw were on the dole.

His mother and father had always planned that Leo would study medicine or law, and they knew, of course, that he had to go to high school before college. What they didn't understand and Leo didn't tell them was that the high school Leo had chosen would not prepare him for these professions. Leo went to the School of Industrial Arts in Manhattan which now, in its modern building on East Fifty-seventh Street, is called The High School of Art and Design. It was marvelous for Leo. He loved it, and the four years he spent there were years of bliss. For the first time he belonged. Race was irrelevant in this school; art was important. None of the students felt threatened—they were coming together to do creative work, which was all that mattered.

It was here that Leo met and was taught by Benjamin Clements. "Clements was a great teacher, an excellent draftsman, and a gentle person. He shaped my life." After four happy years Leo made up his mind to join the Navy, a determination which was to serve two purposes: First, it allowed him to put off the decision of what to do with his life, and second, it would make him eligible for the GI bill, providing him with money for college. Leo found the experience boring but bearable. The combination of his physical strength and drawing talent again pulled him through some difficult moments, particularly with white sailors from the Deep

South. After leaving the Navy he worked for a while with his father, building up the business. Then, on the advice of Benjamin Clements, he enrolled in Parsons School of Design.

Diane was born in Glendale, California. She always knew she wanted to be an artist, and therefore she drew all the time. Her father was a high school teacher, and her mother was a pianist and an organist. Although her family always lived in Southern California, they moved thirteen times, so Diane and her older brother attended two elementary schools, three junior high schools, four high schools, and three colleges. The one constant in her life, other than her family, was art.

As a child Diane had no formal art training except during her eleventh year when she took oil painting lessons one hour a week from an octogenarian. Although her parents encouraged her artistic talent, their general attitude was that, while it was nice for her to have this ability, it really wasn't important since she was expected to get married and be taken care of. "I went through a classic period as a proper young girl when I wanted to be a nurse," says Diane. She also fleetingly considered being a stewardess and very briefly went to modeling school, but she really was determined to have some kind of career in art. During her high school years there were a number of discussions about money for college. Diane's parents decided that if there was enough money for only one, her brother would go to college, since it was his work that would matter in later life.

The summer she completed high school, Diane worked at Lake Tahoe and earned enough money to pay for her tuition at Los Angeles City College, which she attended for two years as an art major while her family lived in Hollywood. She started in fashion design but switched to advertising after a year. Then she contracted tuberculosis and spent a year in a sanatorium, reading most of the time. Then Diane went to live in Schenectady, New York, with an aunt and an uncle who sent her to Skidmore College, where she again majored in art. She commuted for a semester, but traveling was a great waste of time, and in her second semester she moved onto the campus. Diane recalls that she didn't fit in at Skidmore and never felt she belonged. After a year her art instructor told her there was nothing more she could learn there in art unless she was interested in weaving or jewelry. She wasn't, so after her third semester she transferred to Parsons.

For the first time she felt at home. She began attending classes in the summer, and one of the first things she noticed was a painting of Leo's. When she saw it, her immediate thought was, "If that's the kind of work that's done here, I'll never be able to compete. I don't belong here." She was intrigued by the enormous talent of the student who could do such work, and she asked about Leo. She was told he was a loner, that he took his lunch and ate it down by the river. Diane, who by all accounts was rather shy and unaggressive, introduced herself. Leo gave her the distinct impression that he wasn't interested. Shortly after this their class had to move to another room, and Diane sat next to Leo. Later she found out he was furious, since he'd hoped to have the drawing board to himself. Leo had always been the best artist in their class at Parsons and had had no serious competition until Diane arrived. He felt Diane was better than he was, and he became very competitive. In the beginning he didn't even want to talk to her. Diane, too, was very competitive, but Leo recalls that she never showed it.

While at Parsons these two highly talented students experienced similar unpleasant incidents that each remembers vividly. One instructor took Leo aside and told him that although he was an excellent artist he wouldn't be able to get work in the art field because of his race. Another instructor told Diane he hated talented females because they always got married and had babies, and all the talent and training were wasted. Despite these discouraging comments, both of them continued to learn as much as they could and planned careers in art.

Diane and Leo both speak of their three years in school together at Parsons as a time of intense competition, anger, and constant fighting. Although after a while they fell in love, their rivalry didn't end, and their different backgrounds caused them a great deal of suffering. Eventually they became so miserable they decided to separate. After college Diane moved to Albany, and they cut off all communication. But they discovered that they were even more miserable apart than they had been together, so Diane returned to New York, and they decided to get married. Both families were against their marriage because of the racial difference, but Leo and Diane were determined; and once they were married their fighting stopped.

At that time Leo was an art director for a magazine, and Diane was the only woman artist in the advertising agency she worked for. Diane soon left her job to be a proper housewife in the accepted 1950s fashion. She concentrated on cooking, specializing in intricate hors d'oeuvres to go with the cocktails she served Leo when he arrived home from work. Every day Leo would ask her what she had done, and she would point to the gourmet food. This nightly exchange continued until one evening Leo became furious with Diane and told her she was wasting her talent. The next night there were no drinks and no hors d'oeuvres. When Leo asked Diane what she had done, Diane pointed instead to a painting.

Now Diane and Leo decided to do freelance work together. They had spent three years in rivalry and competition and were too happily married to risk that again, so they decided to collaborate on everything. They had no money in the bank and no freelance work yet, but Leo, who found his nine-to-five job unbearable, quit. Thus began the Leo-and-Diane-Dillon collaboration which has continued throughout the twenty years they've been married.

The next two years were a time of intense poverty. Often they didn't even have enough money to go on the subway to pick up a job someone had asked them to do. During this time Leo's father fortuitously had a number of deliveries to make in their neighborhood. Once or twice a week he would appear with a bag of groceries, explaining that he had a job on the next block and thought he'd drop in. Diane says it was only after that period had passed, and Mr. Dillon never seemed to have any more trucking jobs in their neighborhood, that they realized what he'd been doing.

On February 28, 1965, their son Lee was born. Soon afterward, they bought their own brownstone house in Brooklyn, fondly called Dillons' Folly, which they have been renovating ever since. Their partnership continued in everything: art work, child care, and running the house.

During their first years the Dillons had worked together on album covers, advertising, magazine illustrations, movie posters, and paperback covers. While continuing their other art work, they now did book illustration, too, and in 1968 my relationship with them began when I called to ask them to illustrate their first picture book, *The Ring in the Prairie: A Shawnee Legend,* which The Dial Press published in 1970. Illustrating children's trade books offered them a kind of freedom they had never before experienced; no one told them what to draw or asked them to repeat a style. And I believe it is this creative freedom which allows these enormously talented artists to capture the essence of a story and to select the style and technique that perfectly complements it.

In 1969 the Dillons began teaching at the School of Visual Arts while continuing their art work. The course is "Materials and Techniques," and at first Leo and Diane taught it together. Later they each had a separate class. Diane left teaching in 1972, but Leo continues.

Although Diane, Leo, and I have worked on only four books together—the fourth, *Ashanti to Zulu: African Traditions* by Margaret Musgrove, is not yet published—not a week goes by without some artist walking over to one of their paintings on my office wall, gazing in admiration, and saying in wonder, "I don't know how they do it."

"Frisket with pastel and water color," I say, if it's the jacket painting for *Behind the Back of the Mountain.*

"No," is the inevitable reply, "I mean I don't know how they work together on the same painting."

"Neither do I," I used to say, "but when I find out I'll let you know."

And now we all know, to some extent, at least. But the more I know, the more I marvel—at their talent as artists who collaborate so completely; at their amazing ability to capture so sensitively such warmth, humor, and feeling in art as stylized as that for *Why Mosquitoes Buzz in People's Ears;* but mainly I marvel at these remarkable human beings who make seemingly impossible things work because of their particular wonderful qualities.

The Caldecott Medal 1977

ASHANTI TO ZULU: AFRICAN TRADITIONS

illustrated by LEO AND DIANE DILLON

written by MARGARET MUSGROVE

published by THE DIAL PRESS 1976

BOOK NOTE

People of twenty-six African tribes, each of whose name begins with a different letter of the alphabet, are depicted with costume, domestic or ceremonial detail, animals, shelters, and a hint of flora and terrain. The text for each picture presents some distinctive aspect of the tribe's life—such as, its way of dancing or drumming; its care of animals; its children; its food, clothing, or artifacts; a ceremony; or a legend.

Each painting is rich in detail and subtle in the use of color. Pastels, water colors, and acrylics were used in preparing the art. The areas of picture and text are outlined on the page by a frame, the corners of which are designed as Kano Knots, symbolizing endless searching.

Caldecott Medal Acceptance
by Leo and Diane Dillon

Last year, after the Caldecott Medal was announced in January, we returned home from Chicago to work on *Ashanti to Zulu: African Traditions*. Our primary concern was to do a book that would show our gratitude for such an honor. We wanted our next book to be the best we had ever done. It would not only be a way of saying thank you, but also a way of proving to *ourselves* that we deserved the award.

For a long time we had been working in isolation. When art left our house, it was out of our hands. We had nothing more to do with the book it became, nor did we hear much about it. We received compliments from time to time, which were appreciated, but we were unprepared for the impact of knowing that people were watching. After the Caldecott we realized something was expected of us; now we had a challenge and a goal—motivation that had dulled over the years. The summer before we had been very depressed at how little we seemed to be moving ahead. Then the award came and with it a feeling of tremendous elation. The sky was the limit! Along with that feeling of elation was a fear that somehow we had reached a peak in our career—would it now be downhill?

Ashanti to Zulu had been in the house and we had been thinking about it on and off for some time. Our first thought had been in terms of a very ornate decorative style, possibly incorporating each letter in the illustration. When we studied the manuscript more carefully, our concepts began to change. Margaret Musgrove's idea of showing the variety of peoples and customs in Africa appealed to us. There was an interesting fact about each of the twenty-six different groups; some we had never heard of before. How different this book about Africa was from the ones we grew up on. We imagined ourselves reading *Ashanti* as children and felt the excitement of wanting to know more. Any single group could merit a book of its own, and it seemed important to expand on the text, to show as much as possible about each people. As we were formulating our thoughts, we asked questions, such as, What do the people look like? What did they wear? What did the country look like? So we decided to show for each group, whenever possible, a man, a woman, and a child in costume, with an example of a dwelling, an artifact, or a type of work, plus an animal from the area.

As we began the first drawing of the Ashanti, we quickly found that the decorative style we had in mind would not be adequate. Because of all the things we wanted to show, the drawings began to take on a more realistic style. To avoid a dry factual statement we wanted to combine realism with the elegance of a fairy tale, that would also be more interesting visually. In dealing with visual images we tend to look at the fairy tale as a vehicle that offers us the most freedom to do whatever comes to our minds. There is no limit to what we can imagine or create, because in fairy tales there are madly ornate costumes, baroque castles, fantasy landscapes, and wonderfully strange creatures to work with. We grew up believing that our ordinary lives were pallid in comparison.

But in *Ashanti to Zulu* the common people were the stars. The text for the most part deals with people in everyday pursuits. We began to appreciate the grandeur in ordinary living, in what actually exists. It is the intelligence in a person's eyes or the nuances of body language—things shared by all people—that make for real beauty. We strove to be accurate with the factual details but especially wanted to stress the things we all have in common—a smile, a touch, our humanity. We took artistic license with particular situations so that they reflected the tenderness that exists among all peoples: It didn't matter if the Ga man would ever be around when his wife was making foufou; the tenderness of his touch, the warmth passing between them is a universal truth. Or with the Quimbande it was irrelevant whether husband, wife, and children would sit down to play a game in the middle of the compound; the love and family closeness were true.

So far things were running smoothly, but not for long. We had no trouble finding information on the Ashanti, but when we got to the Baule we ran into a snag. In all our research material—and we have built up quite a personal research library over the years—we couldn't find an example of the crocodile symbol so prevalent in that area. And when we took stock of the rest of the book, we realized that some one thing was missing for almost every letter. Either we had no costume for the woman, or the type of dwelling was elusive, or the animal was hard to find. We began to doubt the practicality of showing all elements, but we still felt it was right—we didn't want to compromise.

Our usual procedure is to start at the beginning and do each page in sequence. This time we had to skip around according to the research materials we had at hand. So the next two pieces were the Masai and Tuareg, since they were the only ones we had complete information on.

It was about then that we realized this was *not* a simple alphabet book! All our previous books were folktales of a nontechnical nature. They did not require extensive research. We would find photographs of the people of the area, look at their art and patterns as inspiration, something to base our style on. Once we had the basis, we could exaggerate and add our own ideas to that. An example is *Why Mosquitoes Buzz in People's Ears: A West African*

Tale. That art was based on an African batik style with white line but ended up as a flat graphic style. We had occasionally been involved with work that required extensive research—we once illustrated an article about the fourth-century Greek theory of planetary orbits by Eudoxus—but we were provided with the information needed. For *Ashanti to Zulu* we were on our own, and it was a completely new experience in research for us.

After compiling a long list of the specific items we needed, our first attack was on local bookstores for back issues of *National Geographic.* Illustrators' needs are visual rather than verbal. Descriptions help, but words conjure up different pictures for each listener. We could not afford to imagine what something might look like. We had to *see* it. After several days of going through dusty old magazines, we moved on to the picture gallery of The New York Public Library, a valuable collection to many professions but especially to artists. But even they lacked information on a number of things. So while one of us kept working at the drawing board, the other went to the Mid-Manhattan Library, then to the Schomburg Collection, and after that to the library at the Museum of Natural History.

Pages and pages of notes and more possible leads piled up, but we still lacked photographs. The more we read and learned about each group, the more we realized that each was unique. The customs were as varied as the types of peoples. The dwellings were far more varied than we had been aware of. Some were made of mud and wattle, some of stone or mud bricks, some of woven mats. Some were square, others were round. Some roofs were flat, others were conical. The clothing and patterns were specific, from the special blankets of the Sotho with their hats that repeat the shape of the mountains in that area to the ornate embroidered clothing of the Hausa. Even the style of hair had meaning, as did the jewelry. The peoples themselves ranged from warm red tones through yellow ochres to ebony. There was no way of faking it. Like Europe, Africa is comprised of many peoples and customs, even more varied than our own continent.

By now we knew we were in trouble. We had several pieces done, but on most we were being stopped by some missing element. We called on Dial to help. They arranged for us to use the library at the United Nations, and as time got tighter and tighter, they searched for many of the remaining items on our list so that we could stay with the drawings.

Although we had completed the paintings for the jacket and poster and three of the inside pieces, much of the book was still at the sketch stage when we took a week off last July to go to Chicago for a very memorable time, blissfully free of research. But that research was still going on in New York while we were away. The people at Dial had our list of the still-missing items and were in touch with Margaret Musgrove and through her with experts on African culture at Yale. They were calling United Nations embassies, contacting publishers of obscure books, tracking down African experts, and doing further library research.

The last item that continued to elude us was the Lozi barge. We had found one photograph showing the front half from inside the barge, but we couldn't see the black-and-white stripes or the king's shelter that was so clearly described in the text. One of the Dial editors had the misfortune to move into our neighborhood and found herself researching by day and making house calls by night. After much searching she finally located a picture of the barge, for which we are eternally grateful.

Many of the details of all that research have become jumbled and hazy, but one thing we remember clearly is the pleasant and helpful attitude of the librarians who answered hundreds of questions about how to find things and spent hours helping us look them up.

We returned from ALA in Chicago on a Thursday afternoon. Thursday night our house-calling editor delivered the latest batch of research material. And on Friday morning we were sitting at our drawing boards again, finally ready to start the finished illustrations. By now we were months past our deadline. Our usual procedure is to complete all the artwork and deliver it in one package, as it's important for the flow of the book to be able to look back while we are working to see the color, the direction of the action, and the effect one page has next to another. Fortunately, however, this wasn't as crucial in *Ashanti to Zulu* because each page was really a complete story in itself and because each illustration was held together by the border. Everyone was now involved in our hectic schedule, so this time we sent in the finished paintings as we completed them, four or five at a time. First they were checked once again for accuracy at Dial and sent to the separator, who proceeded with the camera work on those pieces while we continued painting the next group of illustrations.

Finally the last piece of art was delivered, the camera work and several provings were completed, and we were ready to go on press. This was the first book on which we were able to experience the printing stage. We had always thought of the actual printing process as mostly a mechanical procedure, but we learned that a great number of creative decisions are made on press. We are more aware now than ever before of the importance of the dedication and cooperation of everyone involved at each step that a book goes through—from editorial to production to promotion.

We would like to thank Phyllis Fogelman for her guidance and understanding, and for the times when she had the vision to encourage our ideas, no matter how abstract they seemed. It is a pleasure working with her. Again we thank Atha Tehon, Warren Wallerstein, Susan Pearson, Regina Hayes, Ellen Teguis, Toby Sherry, and all the others at Dial for their care and talents in producing a beautiful book. We'd also like to express our appreciation to Holyoke Lithograph for their dedication to craftsmanship and accurate reproduction of the artwork. Since so few people ever see the original art, the printed work becomes the original, and to an artist this step is crucial. An African proverb seems appropriate here: Cross the river in a crowd and the crocodile will not eat you.

A thank you seems inadequate to express our appreciation to the Children's Services Division of ALA and to the Newbery-Caldecott Committee. Before we received the Caldecott Medal last year, we felt very discouraged. The award made a substantial change in our attitude and morale. We felt someone was looking at our work. The experience of people waiting twenty minutes in line to show their appreciation was humbling. We found that people knew of work we had done fifteen years ago. Your encouragement and recognition have given us the confidence we needed to go on for the next twenty years. (We hope!)

It has also made us examine who we are and who or what the third artist is. We each have our own distinct styles, but when we work together, as we do on all our children's books, we essentially create a third artist. We've never really allowed ourselves to examine that phenomenon too closely on the chance we might jinx it, but over the years we have blended our thoughts and styles together to produce art we couldn't have produced separately. In the beginning we worked pretty much by trial and error, but later, working together became automatic, the work passing from one drawing board to the other at different stages. When we first sit down to discuss a manuscript, we throw a lot of ideas at each other. Most of them are rejected immediately, as if we're just waiting for a particular idea. And the moment it hits, we both catch the excitement, and the visual images begin to flow. Even though one of us might not have thought at all in a particular direction, as soon as that idea is voiced by the other, it's as though it had always been there—it was just necessary to have it spoken. We've occasionally been able to tap this third awarness at other times in our lives, and there may be a relation between it and the similarity of our tastes. Often we find one or the other of us saying, "That's what I would have done or chosen."

We've always known that in some ways the third artist was quite separate from our personal lives, because in times of anger, when husband and wife aren't speaking, the artist continues to communicate and produce. The fact that we are forced to talk and discuss a job dissipates the anger, and we make up sooner. It's easier to stay angry with your mate than it is with the person you work with, especially when the deadline is the next day!

We've never been able to predict totally what the final product of this third artist will be, since neither of us can actually see what the other is seeing, even though we agree on the words. The surprises have kept us interested. We rely on the advantages that a partnership and collaboration can provide, and we trust each other's judgment and taste. In the early days we worried about the loss of our individual identities, but we have found the third identity is as valid and real and as much *us* as the separate ones.

For illustrators the Caldecott Medal is the most substantial and respected award an artist can receive. The committee this year had difficult decisions to make. Their independence and freedom from extraneous considerations enforces the integrity and meaning of this honor. We are both *very* proud and will try to keep *your* standard of excellence. And a special thanks from the third artist who, after all, really produced the art.

BIOGRAPHICAL NOTE

Diane Dillon
by Leo Dillon

Diane Dillon is one of the finest artists I've ever known, and I realized it even before I met her. I was at Parsons School of Design in New York City when one day I noticed a painting hanging on the wall at a student exhibition. It was a painting of a chair—an Eames chair—and I knew it had to be by a new student because nobody in our class at the time could paint like that. I looked at the painting, and I thought, "I'm in trouble now!" This artist could draw. That was all right—I could draw too. This artist knew perspective, which is one of the most difficult things a beginner has to learn. And most important—this artist had the patience to *render*! This artist was a whole lot better than I. I figured I'd better find out who he was. *He* was Diane.

I hadn't spoken to her yet—in fact, I wasn't sure I was going to—when she came over to me and said, "You are very good." "Hah!" I thought. "Talented Miss Wasp is now going to condescend to tell one of the menials he's good. I know better." I said, "I see that one of your pieces is very nice too." And that pretty much set the tone of our relationship for the next several years.

One of the things about Di's work that's so incredible is her use of color. She can do things with color I can hardly believe—make reds look cool and blues look warm, things like that—because she really understands color. Once, after we were married, we were working on a piece and she mentioned very casually that we should do the color in pink and orange. "If we do it in pink and orange," I said, "that will be the end! I can't live with someone who'd do anything in pink and orange. We'll have to get a divorce!" We did it in pink and orange, of course, and a couple of years later everywhere I turned I was seeing things in pink and orange. It's a common combination now.

People wonder a lot about how we work together. But I don't think people ever realize how hard it was for us to learn how to blend our styles. It was years and years before we could pass a piece of work back and forth between us and not get into a fight. One time we were working on an illustration, and we just couldn't agree about the approach. It was a book jacket, I think, something about medieval knights. I thought the style should be rough and strong; Di thought it should be fine and delicate. We fought about it, but neither of us could convince the other, and neither was willing to compromise. We ended up using both styles—the bottom half showing the horses was done in woodcuts, or anyway, something that was rough and crude, and the top half, which showed the knights, was done finely and delicately. As I recall, it worked out all right, but I know how!

Things are good now, though. It used to be that one of us would do the actual drawing and the other would make comments or draw a change on a tissue overlay. But now one of us can just pass the piece of art to the other, and he or she can erase what's wrong and redraw right on the original. Our egos aren't at stake anymore.

As a matter of fact, everything's going well now. It's really one of the nicest times in my life. The art is good, and our son Lee, now twelve, is old enough to work with. I love working on things with him—like on the house. Once I was putting in a floor and Lee was helping me. I'd measured everything and shown him what to do, and we were both working away. In about ten minutes he came over to me and said, "I think your measurements are wrong." Very quietly. Very modestly. Very correctly. I let him measure the whole floor, and it's a beautiful job. He's wonderful. Having three artist in the house—or maybe it's four, since Di and I do so much work together—is better than anything I ever dreamed of.

Leo Dillon

by Diane Dillon

When I think about Leo, the first thing that comes to mind is his strength. Obviously he's strong physically, but that's not what I mean, although one strength is symbolic of the other. It's more a matter of endurance and remarkable patience—although he's terribly impatient waiting for rubber cement to dry! Leo is really a study in opposites. He's patient with the big things, impatient with the small. He has incredible conviction, and yet he is able to admit mistakes, to change his mind and his direction if he feels he has been wrong.

The most wonderful thing about Leo's strength, though, is his ability to transmit it to other people, to energize them, to act as motivator. He does this to many people, and he certainly does it to me. When we were first married, Leo had a job as an art director at a magazine. I was determined to be the model 1950s housewife, and that didn't include drawing or painting. Leo took this for a while, then he casually began bringing work home, encouraging me to work with him on design problems, easing me back into art. That was really the beginning of our working together as one artist, I think. Finally there was a blowup and I got back to work!

Leo has incredible energy. I don't think he's ever quite understood that I need sleep occasionally; he feels sleep is a form of death—time spent not doing anything. In fact, until a few years ago he slept with his clothes on, so he'd be ready to go at a moment's notice.

Leo is, I think, the kindest man I've ever known—and really that's part of his strength and his ability to motivate people. He doesn't like crowds, big parties—things like that—but he truly loves people, and love radiates from him. He's concerned about how people feel, about what they think—of themselves more than of him—and he'll go out of his way not to hurt someone.

He can be tricky, though: "You're so much better at such-and-such," he'll tell me, implying, "Why don't you do it?" He had me balancing the checkbook for years before he sat down and explained to me a faster way to add! Obviously I wasn't better at it at all—but I'm still balancing the checkbook.

Someone asked us recently who was the perfectionist, and I'd say it was Leo, but sometimes it's hard to tell when you work so closely together. I do know, though, that our real feeling about aiming for perfection began with *Why Mosquitoes Buzz in People's Ears.* Suddenly it seemed that neither of us could tolerate even a tiny flaw, a minute speck on the black night sky, and we strove for artistic perfection on that book more than on any other except *Ashanti to Zulu* (both Dial). In a way, when *Mosquitoes* won the Caldecott Medal, it was as much a reward for us as an award. We had worked harder to achieve perfection—although, of course, we didn't achieve it—than we ever had before, and people somehow knew it.

I don't want to end a biography of Leo without saying something about Lee, for he is so much our pride. Lee has always been a sweet spirit and very much a part of us, never against us in any way. Other babies may have been fussy and colicky, but not Lee—he even seemed to know when we had a deadline to meet. And now that he's growing up, he probably understands us better than anyone, puts up with our quirks, and stands now on his own in a beautiful way.

Leo and Diane Dillon

by Lee Dillon

What I really like about my parents is that I can work with them. I can work with my father on the house, and we can talk a lot of things out without blowing up. I make jewelry, and I really enjoy going to the jewelry district with my mother and talking about jewelry designs with her. And we all have fun teasing back and forth, too.

What I don't like is that they're always working. Since they won the Caldecott Medal the first time, things have been lots happier around here, but there's been a lot more work too, and I don't like that so much. They're really nice people, my parents, and I'd like to have more time with them when they're not working.

My favorite book my parents have done is *Ashanti to Zulu.* I like realism more than abstract designs. I like the way *Ashanti to*

Zulu shows how civilized and advanced the African peoples are, too. Too many people think Africa is primitive and uncivilized, and I hope *Ashanti to Zulu* will show them that this is not true. The research was murder, though, and I'm glad it's over.

Why Mosquitoes Buzz in People's Ears is a nice book, too, but as I said, I'm more into realism. The animals were okay, I thought, but the guy got a little weird.

I've had a lot of hobbies. I've been making jewelry for a couple of months. Before that I was studying Arthur Rackham's illustrations. Before that I collected comic books and original comic-book art. Before that I grew bonsai plants. Before that I collected stamps. And before that I collected coins. I think what I'll be someday, though, is an artist. I haven't decided what kind of art work yet, but I probably will not limit it to just one thing.

Since I'm living with my parents, I learn a lot of things about art, and I can do some specific kinds of things now, but I wouldn't call myself an artist yet. I guess what I mainly want to do is to live nicely, but in the background. I don't think I want to be famous. For instance, at ALA last summer, I liked rolling posters at the Dial booth. It was sort of like a race, to see if I could roll posters as fast as my parents could sign them. And I met a lot of nice people too, which I enjoyed. But once somebody asked me to sign one of the posters, and that really embarrassed me. Maybe I wouldn't have felt embarrassed if I'd *done* something, but I'm not sure. I think I'd just rather be in the background anyway.

The Caldecott Medal 1978

NOAH'S ARK

illustrated by PETER SPIER

published by DOUBLEDAY & COMPANY 1977

BOOK NOTE

For a page of text, Peter Spier has translated from the Dutch a poem, "The Flood," by Jacobus Revius (1586–1658). The poem assures us that "Creatures all,/Large and small,/Good and mean,/Foul and clean,/Fierce and tame,/In they came"—along with Noah and his kin. Then in pictures without accompanying text the artist shows Noah's travails with animals and family and the animals' problems with each other, as the flood carries the ark on its journey to its resting place on a mountain and an unspoiled new life for all.

The black line for the illustrations was done with an F pencil on paper, and further opaqueing and scratching was done on the negatives. In adding the color to blues pulled on paper, the artist used water colors and white pencil as well as drop-out overlays.

Caldecott Medal Acceptance

by Peter Spier

I cannot tell you what a comfort it is tonight to see the faces of so many friends and of those librarians I remember meeting at ALA conventions in years past.

One of my earliest memories has to do with public speaking. I must have been five or six years old when my father took me to the funeral of an acquaintance who lay in state in the offices of the factory of which he had been the president. The minister led the service with practiced ease, a director spoke most eloquently for the board, and the executive vice president of the firm spoke with equal competence. Finally, one of the workers selected to represent the labor force mounted the rostrum next to the open casket. From the beginning it was quite clear that he was very nervous and unequal to the task, even though he must have learned his lines by heart. He began bravely enough with "Ladies and Gentlemen," but in the face of the large audience he forgot everything and just stood there, perspiring profusely, gripping the edge of the lectern with white knuckles, eyes bulging. He started again with "Ladies and Gentlemen" but it was obviously no use. After an embarrassing silence, he suddenly lost his head and bellowed "Ladies and Gentlemen ... HIP HIP HURRAY!" It was, needless to say, an enormous success, and completely changed the mood of the solemn occasion.

Standing here tonight I feel a little like that poor man and know how he must have suffered.

I think I must have come up in the world, though, and I'll tell you why: Some years ago I was asked to give a talk to a group of librarians at a state convention. It was a substantial affair, and the after-dinner speaker was a distinguished former member of the United States government. The following morning it was my turn. I was the breakfast speaker. Not even the after-breakfast speaker but the *before*-breakfast speaker—somewhere between the prune juice and the cold scrambled eggs. So you see, tonight I have arrived!

It seems to be a hallowed tradition to call recipients of both the Newbery and the Caldecott Medals out of bed in the middle of the night or at best in the very early hours of the morning. I suppose this is calculated to add to the dramatic effect, and in my case this was most certainly true: The phone rang at 4:30 Chicago time, and I picked up the receiver with trembling hands and pounding heart. The first thing that came to my mind was: "My parents' house is on fire," or at least someone near and dear had just died. It was therefore an immense relief to hear that *Noah's Ark* had just been given the Caldecott.

Since that memorable morning, I have had five months to figure out that whole early-calling tradition carefully. It may have nothing to do with the dramatic effect after all and may be intended as a loving kindness. A safety measure, if you will. Picture this: Someone hearing that he or she had won during the day might easily suffer cardiac arrest from understandable amazement, joy, and excitement. By cleverly calling in the dark of night, the committee makes sure they catch you where you should be in case something fatal occurs—in your bed!

A few days after being called in January, my wife and I were again called out of a deep sleep. "Aha!" I thought. "Won again! And with what foresight on behalf of the committee: This time they are giving it to me sight unseen for my next book, which is still at the printer's!" I was wrong, of course, for a raw voice asked if he was speaking to the fifth precinct. It is apparent that the whole thing must have gone a little to my head!

In accordance with the instructions I received, my wife and I made our children swear not to tell a soul, and they didn't, although it subsequently became clear that the news had somehow leaked out in other quarters. That same day, on a plane to Chicago, I sat next to an editor I knew. The conversation went as follows:

The editor: "Where are you going?"
Me: "To Chicago."
She: "I see. Why?"
Me, thinking quickly: "Oh, on some Doubleday business."
She: "Is it secret?"
Me: "Yes."
She: "Congratulations!"

My contact with Randolph Caldecott, by the way, is of long standing. My father owned a collection of Caldecott's works, most of them first editions. I do not know whether I was showing early promise, but it seems that I took one of those valuable books—I was three years old—and with a red crayon expertly ruined each and every page of the book. I do not recall the spanking I was given, although my father assures me that it was fairly meted out. The story has a happy ending for me, though, for when I told him that *Noah* had won, he gave me his whole collection of Caldecott books.

Twenty-five years ago I landed my first job as a free-lance illustrator in the United States. It was a book for Doubleday, and since that time I have been singularly fortunate in my relationship with my publisher. I want to thank my many friends at Doubleday for having always left me alone to do "my own thing," without any interference. I want to remember especially the late Blanche van Buren and the late Seth Agnew, with whom I worked closely. I know how lucky I am to be blessed with an editor who also is an old friend, Janet Chenery, whose comments always make sense, even though we do not always agree on everything. At this moment I am also thinking of Ole Risom, a friend of many years, who taught me a great deal about the business I am in. But above all I want to thank my father, the journalist and illustrator Jo Spier, for the help, advice, and friendship he has given me all my life. To no man do I owe more, personally or professionally.

A successful book is not due to the effort of just one man but is the result of teamwork. An author-illustrator can create a most appealing book—but that same book then has to run a long and risky gauntlet before it finally staggers into your libraries! The editor—with the best of intentions—might make changes which could ruin the book. The company that makes the color separations could demolish the artwork. Inferior paper could undo all the considerable expense, time, and effort put into first-class film and outstanding offset plates. The printer in turn could ruin the sheets in countless different ways, and the bookbinder could do the same. And finally, the marketing, publicity, and advertising. These, too, can be done the right way or the wrong way.

With *Noah's Ark* all went well from the beginning, and I do thank all the members of the team for their share in the book! I am aware how much I owe to the printer George Carnegie and the people at Neff Litho. The same is true of the people in Doubleday's production department, especially Virginia Muller and Mary Brandt, her successor. There are so many names that come to mind. Too many to mention, but I do want to thank Bob Banker, Jack O'Leary, and Patty Hinkley, in particular.

One of the questions I am often asked is: "Why did you decide to do *Noah's Ark?*" The answer is simple: Because I have wanted to retell the story for years. The final catalyst was the seventeenth-century Dutch poem by Jacobus Revius, which has the faith and, above all, the childlike simplicity which I found moving and inspiring. It was obviously not an original idea, and I went to our library to look at Bowker's *Books in Print* to find out precisely how unoriginal it actually was. There were over twenty *Noah*'s in print. The library owned seven different versions, and when I tried to have a look at them, I found that they were nearly always taken out on loan. So I bought all the versions I could get hold of to see what other artists had done with Noah. Some were good, others were less so. But I found that virtually all the books had the same slant; the Flood was invariably depicted as a joyous, sun-filled Caribbean cruise: happy flood, happy Noah (wearing a sailor's cap), happy beasts. No drownings, nothing to indicate God's wrath. It was difficult even to recognize the Bible text in any of those books, and it was not what I had in mind at all. A few books were a bit more sombre and followed the Bible closely, without adding any unexpected sidelights or intimate glimpses. None of them showed Noah shoveling manure or even hinted at the stench and the mess inside. It was then that I knew that there was room for one more *Noah's Ark*.

When working on the layout of the book, not in sketches yet but with written notes, I had the ark floating away and the waters rising higher and higher, the animals that remained behind standing knee-deep, then waist-deep, in the water—as I later showed in the book. The next page showed hundreds of drowned animals awash in the waves, some with their heads down, others with their legs sticking up in the air, with small creatures and birds having saved themselves on the floating carcasses. It was certainly dramatic. But it was to be a book for small children, and I decided that it went too far in its grisliness and left that part out.

I always find it difficult to determine where that invisible line, the border between good taste and bad, runs. Between the believable and the unbelievable. Between the acceptable and the unacceptable. Between the grim and the gruesome. Between the necessary and the superfluous. But the pieces fell slowly into their proper places, and today it seems to me as if the book created itself and I was the ever-present and interested observer.

Whenever I finish a new book, I show it to my children to hear their reaction. In *Noah*'s case it was encouraging. They said, "It's all right." That was the highest praise I could expect. This is not always the case. When I showed them my newest book *Oh, Were They Ever Happy* (Doubleday), published last month, they told me that it was "kidstuff" (which of course it is supposed to be!) and, adding insult to injury, asked if it was really necessary to put *our* name on the cover?

Some years ago Lavinia Russ, then with *Publishers Weekly*, and I were asked to be the two judges for the picture book category for Book World's Children's Spring Book Festival Awards. I accepted but later came to regret it, even though it was an education in its own right. It was great fun at first: The mailman delivered batches of new books every day, until I had well over three hundred and fifty on the floor of my study. But that is where the fun ended, and the judging began. At first it was easy, and without doing anyone an injustice, we could quickly discard a goodly proportion of the books. From that point on it became more and more difficult. I believe that it was Winston Churchill who said that there was no book, even the most awful, that did not have something of value in it. And so it was, as we slowly, and not very surely, worked our way through the books, eliminating, weighing, and judging. "Who am I," I asked myself all the time, regretting that I had agreed to do the job, "to judge the work of my peers, of people who take their work just as seriously and work as hard as I do?"

I was also acutely aware that I was holding peoples' hopes, aspirations, and ambitions in my hand, and my personal taste would be the only foundation on which my decision was made. This pile—or that one? It was a painful task, and often Mrs. Russ and I went back to a book we had rejected, shaking our heads, and put it on the other stack. Time and time again. But in the end there were about fifteen books left on the table. Each and every one of them was a beautiful, worthwhile, decent, and distinguished book, each one as worthy as the other fourteen, each one equally deserving to win. My choices were made solely by personal taste and preference. And, curiously enough, while looking at them in all their differences, I realized that they were all books I secretly wished I could have done myself.

When we finally decided on the winner and the runners-up, I was left with a distinct feeling of dissatisfaction and even distress. Not because of the books we had chosen but because of the ones we had to leave behind. Noah must have felt the same way about the animals. And yet, there must be more to serious judging of this nature than only personal taste and experience. For the winner we selected was Brinton Turkle's *Thy Friend Obadiah* (Viking), and the first runner-up, William Steig's *Sylvester and the Magic Pebble* (Windmill/Simon), which a few months later won in reverse order—*Sylvester,* the Caldecott, and *Obadiah,* an Honor Book.

I have, very frankly, always had my doubts about the basis on which book prizes are awarded. I do not for a single moment believe that my *Noah's Ark* is the most distinguished picture book of the year. I believe, with a few memorable exceptions, that such a book does not exist. There are almost always a handful of books worthy of the distinction. Besides, if that book really existed and could be identified on an infallible basis, it would win every prize given that year. Yet that never seems to happen.

In years past—very few, to be sure—awards have been given to books I felt to be unworthy of the honor. And there will no doubt be people who feel that way about this year's choice! When no one really outstanding book is published, I have wondered if in some years awards should not be passed up. The Nobel prize for peace, chemistry, or medicine is not awarded in some years. The most renowned and costly wines have good years and poor ones. And so do picture books. And perhaps in a year in which there appears to be no single one, but several outstanding books, perhaps the prize should be divided among them. I do know that this was not the intention of Mr. Frederic Melcher. The Laura Ingalls Wilder Award, of course, is given to an author or an illustrator for his or her contribution to literature over a period of years.

Although I know it is the fate of some award-winning picture books to languish on library shelves, it is my hope, and the end to which my efforts are really directed, to produce a book that not only pleases me but also will be popular with children. So maybe I really want the impossible: the cake, and to eat it as well, even though I know that distinction and popularity do not automatically go hand in hand. I have by now kept you too long, but I would like to repeat, and this is no false modesty, that I did not for a moment believe *Noah's Ark* stood a ghost of a chance to win. I can hardly tell you how delighted I am with the great honor you have bestowed on me and how happy I am to accept the Caldecott Medal. I'd like to think that it was not given for

Noah only but maybe a little for books I did in the past as well.

I thank you very, very much on behalf of Doubleday and, of course, myself, even if it all makes me feel somewhat melancholy: A slightly different outcome of your vote, and Margot Zemach or David Macaulay would be standing where I stand now—not to mention unnamed other illustrators, who were certainly as deserving as I.

BIOGRAPHICAL NOTE

Bill Sharbutt

Peter Spier
by Janet D. Chenery

Peter Spier was born in Amsterdam in 1927, the eldest of three children. His father was an artist and journalist on *The Telegraaf,* Holland's largest daily paper. Peter went to school in Amsterdam, but the family lived in Broek in Waterland, a small farming village known to Americans as the setting for *Hans Brinker and the Silver Skates.* Drafted into the Royal Dutch Navy after World War II, Peter served at the Admiralty as lieutenant on an aircraft carrier and on a cruiser for some years. When his military service was over, he went to work for *Elsevier's Weekly.*

In 1951 he visited the United States with his father. They drove all over the country and liked what they saw so much that they decided to try living here. Peter's mother and the two younger children came over to join them in Houston, Texas, where Elsevier Publishing Company had a branch office.

After a year, however, the Spiers moved to Port Washington, Long Island, and Peter started to illustrate children's books for a living. His first assignment was to illustrate a book called *Thunder Hill* (Doubleday), a story about a goat farm, and his first real picture book—*The Cow Who Fell in the Canal,* written by Phyllis Krasilovsky—was published by Doubleday in 1957.

Nearly a decade and some one hundred and fifty books later,

Peter decided that it would be fun to do an entire book on his own. He had gone with his wife Kay to her college in Northampton, Massachusetts, in the autumn, and on the way home, driving through the lovely New England countryside, Kay was singing "The Fox Went Out on a Chilly Night." *This* was the setting for the song, Peter exclaimed, and after discussing it with Peggy Lesser, his editor at Doubleday, he spent three weeks driving through the Northeast to Sturbridge and Cooperstown, through New Hampshire and Vermont, and up and down the coast in order to absorb the feel of the land, making hundreds of sketches as he went along—something he does for every book. *The Fox Went Out on a Chilly Night* was published in 1961 and became a Caldecott Honor Book for that year.

"There is something special about books," Peter says. "Most things in history, no matter how ghastly or cruel, are forgotten in the end, but people still talk with special horror about the burning of the Alexandrian Library and about book-burning by dictators or during the Inquisition. Murders are forgotten, but the eradication of ideas, of books, is not."

When working on an idea for a book, Peter does not think about children—"I really do it for myself!"—but feels that only the best is good enough for them. Because he is married to a reading teacher, he has been made especially aware of the importance of books for children and of the enormous influence they can exert. He is always thinking about ideas for books and wonders how he can use this one or that one and what special twist he can give it "to make it work."

He is often asked about his own children, but he never asks them for advice. When they were younger, and both were attending a Friends' school, they said, "Do something nice, with lots of violence in it!"

A good book, he believes, should be childlike. A poor book, on the other hand, too often is childish. Peter chooses to do books for which there seems to be a need—ones that are timely—or books that he simply feels like doing. "To illustrate my own books means that there is no author to tell me that Noah should wear a hat or carry binoculars or that the ark should have portholes; when you come down to it, my own judgment is the only thing that counts," he says. And *Noah's Ark,* which is a moving depiction of an extraordinary journey, is indeed timeless.

Today, Peter counts himself among the very fortunate. "I am lucky to be earning a living at my hobby," he says, "and it is a short commute to the basement," where he has his studio. In his own view he is not an arty artist; rather, he prefers to think of himself as a serious craftsman. "What is art?" he asks, adding, "My father was on the island of Bali and was watching some wood-carvers at work. One artist, a farmer as well as a carver, told him, 'In Balinese, there is no word for art. Skill or craft, yes, but here, everything is art.' " Peter agrees and says that he finds it a great thrill to make something where nothing before existed and loves the total freedom that his work offers.

The Caldecott Medal 1979

THE GIRL WHO LOVED WILD HORSES

written and illustrated by PAUL GOBLE

published by BRADBURY PRESS 1978

BOOK NOTE

A young Indian girl has a special way with horses and spends all her time with them, for her tribe trains its horses for buffalo hunting. In a terrible storm she tries to calm and lead the horses in her care, but they run far away with her. Although she and the horses are lost to her tribe, they are welcomed by a great stallion, leader of the wild horses who run free. A year later hunters from the girl's tribe find her and take her back to her parents. Because she misses her horses, she becomes ill, and only returning to her wild horses will help her. So they let her go, but each year she brings a colt back to her parents—until one year she does not return and never is seen again. The hunters, however, now see a beautiful mare who accompanies the great stallion: Surely the girl has become one of the wild horses.

In vivid colors, the pictures are flat and decorative, with Indian motifs detailed on tipis, blankets, and clothing. The illustrations are full-color pen-and-ink and water-color paintings, the black line separated by the artist from the base plates and reproduced in combined line and halftone.

Caldecott Medal Acceptance
by Paul Goble

I hope being awarded the Caldecott Medal excuses me from clever speech-writing and delivery. I am going to hide behind that hope and will start by trying to answer the question which is most often asked: "How is it that an Englishman comes to write books about American Indians?"

I have been interested in everything Indian since I can remember. The books of Grey Owl and Ernest Thompson Seton are well known in the United States. Before television days my mother read the complete works of these two authors to my brother and me. Many other books too, but I loved best Grey Owl and Ernest Thompson Seton because both wrote about Indians and both were true naturalists. The world they wrote about was so different from the crowded island where I lived. And yet perhaps growing up so far from this country sharpened my need to know more. Over many years I acquired a considerable library of the better books concerning Native Americans, and I really studied those books.

In 1959, after I had finished three years of training in industrial design at the Central School of Art and Design in London, I was fortunate to be given a long summer visit to this country. I accompanied Frithjof Schuon, the eminent Swiss writer on comparative religion. He had contacts among Sioux and Crow Indians, and the summer was spent on reservations in South Dakota and Montana.

Love of Indians and love of nature have always been my priorities, but they never seemed a combination likely to support a family. For the next eighteen years, from 1959 to 1977, I kept it as a serious hobby and put my main energies into industrial design, with the eighteen years about equally divided between practicing and teaching the subject. Nearly two years ago the hobby took over completely when I left England to live in the Black Hills as a painter.

As a teacher in England I had long summer vacations, and in recent years I spent four summers in the United States. My son

Richard came with me on most of those visits. We would bring a small tent, hire a car, and spend the summer with Sioux friends in South Dakota and Crow Indian friends in Montana. During those summers I was privileged to take part in ceremonies, to be present at their sacred Sun Dances. I have taken part in building the Sun Dance lodge and have helped to pitch tipis. Knowing that I loved their ways, my Indian friends have told me much about their folklore and beliefs. They have given me new perspectives, and really all my travels were spiritual journeys.

I do not know what is a valid reason for writing a book. *The Friendly Wolf* (Bradbury) came about because I was distressed at how wolves in Alaska were being hunted to extinction by helicopter. No Indian story I had ever read had anything but fine things to tell of wolves. The Indian understands the language of the birds and animals and seeks to learn their wisdom. He knows they were here long before we were and being older, deserve our respect. We have been subjected to Walt Disney and his many followers. I have a horror of the havoc they have created with literature, art, and the blunting of our attitudes towards nature. Children grow up with the idea that bears are huggable, woodpeckers are destructive, coyotes and tomcats mean; and that whales and dolphins are happiest when being made to clown in a marina. Respect and inspiration are not there at all.

Similarly, in *The Girl Who Loved Wild Horses* I tried to express and paint what I believe to be the Native American rapport with nature. The Indian does not feel afraid or alone in the forests and prairies; he knows many stories about ancestors who turned into the seven stars of the Big Dipper and others who became the Pleiades. Indians tell about a girl who married the Morning Star and of their son who, coming from the Sky but living on Earth, did many wonderful things. Knowledge of this relationship with the universe gives them confidence. They have no thought to reorganize nature in a way other than that in which the Great Spirit made it. Indeed, it would be sacrilegious to do so.

The Girl Who Loved Wild Horses is not a retelling of any one legend but a synthesis of many. Psychological interpretations should not be read into it. Simply, the girl loves horses, and perhaps she becomes one. If we think about something long enough, maybe we will become like that thing. I believe children will easily understand this. By the time we are grown up we might think some thought-doors have been opened, but perhaps others have been closed.

I hope that Native Americans will approve of the book and will feel sympathy for the illustrations. At a recent autographing party in a small South Dakota community, it gave me great joy when an Indian gave me a beautiful feather in a fold of red felt. And there was a sixth-grade Sioux boy who, while having breakfast, heard on the radio that I was to be at the Rapid City library that day. He told his mother he was not going to school, and so it was we met. It gives me a warm feeling when Indians respond to my books. Some will speak no English, and yet the lively discussions amongst themselves which the illustrations provoke tell me they are happy that a white man has admiration for their culture.

I now want to thank my friends at Bradbury Press as well as the printer, Rae Lithographers, who worked to reproduce faithfully the artwork for the book. I am very happy with the result of their work, and we are all truly honored that the book has been awarded the Caldecott Medal. I would also like to thank my several friends at the Macmillan Company of London who encouraged me for many years and published my earlier books. On behalf of Bradbury Press, and for myself, I would like to thank the Newbery-Caldecott Committee and all members of the American Library Association. Thank you.

BIOGRAPHICAL NOTE

Gerry Perrin

Paul Goble
by Joseph Epes Brown

I suspect the ultimate and only biographical sketch that Paul Goble could truly feel at ease with would be one painted on bison hide by a Plains Indian elder in circular pictographic style. Having neither the right nor the skill to do such a depiction, I must rely on the comparative inadequacy of the white man's lineal written word.

I first heard of Paul Goble during the war years through our mutual British friend Marco Pallis, the distinguished Tibetan scholar best known perhaps for his important book *Peaks and Lamas* (Gordon). As Pallis was throughout his life a champion of Tibetan peoples and cultures, he undoubtedly foresaw in the young Paul Goble a potential champion of the American Indians, since their traditional beliefs and cultures were similarly oppressed by peoples of alien beliefs and life-ways. Knowing of my own writings and relationships with American Indians, Pallis asked me to contact Paul to add what I could to the warm encouragement he had always offered this unusual young person. Following a period of correspondence with Paul in the late war years and the shipments to England of Indian books and artifacts, I finally met him and his family at Greatstones, their home outside Oxford. Paul was a sensitive youth with a strong passion and ear for everything relating to North American Indians; with bows and arrows which he had beautifully made, we scouted the English countryside, where lawns became the Dakota plains, British hares became bison, and neighbors' horses were there to be taken with courage and honor. Around our camp fire we talked of the old Lakota sage Black Elk, with whom I had been living and learning, and of the wisdom of his people, which he had been willing to share with the outer world through the two books, *Black Elk Speaks* (Pocket Books) and *The Sacred Pipe* (University of Oklahoma). Indeed, later in life Paul was to write: "It was the books concerning the wisdom of Black Elk which finally determined my life's orientation."

Paul became a student who not only read everything he could find on American Indian history and sacred lore but sought to integrate what he learned into his person; and in keeping with his own art heritage, he applied this learning to his growing understanding of American Indian art forms, examples of which he assiduously sought out in British museums and private collections. At one time Paul was particularly helpful in making for me beautifully executed copies of Plains Indian depictions of animals and birds, a facility now so evident in his numerous books. It is the quality of Paul's understanding of the inner spirit of the Indian, intensified in later years by his travels to America and by direct contacts with Indians, which lends to his writing and painting something of the Indians' own spirit and perspective. At the same time he retains the integrity of his own style and perspective and discipline, which spring from his own background, not the least part of which was his distinguished work in art and design in England.

In becoming an American citizen, in taking up residence in the sacred *Pa Sapa*—Black Hills—of South Dakota, and in placing himself closer to his adopted Indian families, Paul Goble has come home. It is clear that we may now anticipate a continuity resulting from a growing maturity in his writing and illustration, for in his visual and verbal translations of the Native American vision of life, there is a message which speaks to our times and certainly to all ages. *Hechetu welo!*

The Caldecott Medal 1980

OX-CART MAN

illustrated by BARBARA COONEY

written by DONALD HALL

published by THE VIKING PRESS 1979

BOOK NOTE

A New Hampshire farmer becomes a trader when he loads his ox cart with everything he and his family "made or grew all year long that was left over"—from woolen and linen goods, candles, and shingles to maple syrup and goose feathers. He journeys "over hills, through valleys, by streams/ past farms and villages" to Portsmouth. At the market he sells everything, including ox cart, yoke, harness, and ox. He buys an iron kettle, an embroidery needle, a whittling knife, and wintergreen candies and carries them home along with a pocketful of coins. The seasonal cycle starts over, as he splits new shingles, his son whittles brooms, his wife spins and weaves, and his daughter embroiders.

The full-color illustrations often recall an American primitive style of flat figures and panoramic landscape. Yet the artist's seeming simplicity is sophisticated, as is the detail, both of facial expressions and choice of objects depicted. The illustrations were painted in acrylics on gesso-coated board. The art was camera separated and printed in four colors.

Caldecott Medal Acceptance
by Barbara Cooney

Thank you. Thank you, everybody. In particular, I thank the members of the American Library Association for honoring me again with the award of awards, the Caldecott Medal.

A generation has passed since I stood up to accept my first Caldecott Medal. During those twenty-one years I went on living in the same beautiful, drafty old house. The wind still whistled through the light switches. Occasionally, the roof still leaked. Under that roof I went on raising my four children and an uncountable number of cats and dogs. A golden palomino horse was living in the barn, and a Connemara pony. I kept on planting large back-breaking vegetable gardens. I kept on fussing with flowers. Grandchildren began to appear. I kept on illustrating. And my husband kept on coming home for lunch.

Luckily for me, during this time there has been an energetic little Frenchwoman, named Solange, to help me take care of my circus. When Solange came in, the morning after I had heard the news about this year's Caldecott Award, I said, "Solange! Guess what! I have won the Caldecott Medal again!"

"Oh, madame," she said, "your cup runneth over!" And, indeed, it does.

One more biblical quotation, please. "In the beginning was the Word. . . ." Don't let any illustrator forget that! The other time I was given this lovely medal, the author, Geoffrey Chaucer, was unable to be there. Tonight, I am happy to say, the author is here. I would like to thank the poet who made the golden chain upon which I strung my beads, the author of *Ox-Cart Man,* Donald Hall.

I want to thank Linda Zuckerman, my editor at Viking, from whom I received the utmost consideration during the time I was preparing to illustrate *Ox-Cart Man,* while I was doing the actual artwork, and after the illustrations were in her hands. Always she respected my conception of how the pictures should be. Always she had the patience of Penelope, and also, like poor Penelope, she kept on extending the deadline. The pictures for *Ox-Cart*

Man were a long time in the making, but Linda would always say, "I *know* that the pictures will be worth waiting for."

One thing that slowed me up was a house that my son Charlie and I were building in Maine. At least, he was building it, and I was bossing it—although there is some question about who was bossing whom. The house was going to be built in one year. After three years my son said, "We should have built this damn thing upside down. We could have had a sixty-foot schooner by now and been halfway around the world!" Instead, Charlie went off to Patagonia with a seventeen-foot kayak and rowed around Cape Horn. Meanwhile, back at Hermit Wood, I moved into our dream house, which at times had been a nightmare but was now a marvel, to oversee Mark and Leon, the two young carpenters who were to do the finish work. So at last, with the pounding of hammers and the screaming of the radial-arm saw for background music, I knuckled down and illustrated *Ox-Cart Man.* Leon contributed his beautiful red beard to the book. Markie posed for the scene in which the Ox-Cart Man tenderly kisses his ox good-by on the nose. We didn't have an ox, but we used a standing lamp. To keep us all going, I baked lots of Cornell bread, the kind that sustains life indefinitely in laboratory rats. When the pictures were done, Markie made a mahogany box for them, I painted an ox on the cover, and we mailed the box off to Linda. When she got it, Linda said, "I *always* knew that the pictures would be worth waiting for." One of Linda's greatest qualities is faith.

Also at Viking I worked very happily with Barbara Hennessy, the art director. Barbara, I think, is a genius. She solved some of our problems so gracefully that I am envious that it was not I who found the solutions.

I am grateful, too, to the production department at Viking. No illustrator could want finer production than what they gave me. I thank also Capper Rugby Associates, who made the color separations, and Rae Publishing, who printed the book, for their careful, beautiful work.

There are a few standard questions that I am always asked. The most popular is: How come you're an artist?

My great-grandfather was an artist. He was a German immigrant and lived here in Manhattan, down by the old slaughterhouse in an area that would now be under this end of the

Brooklyn Bridge. For a living he made cigar-store Indians. He also painted pictures by the yard. My grandmother, when she was little, sometimes helped him "putting in the skies." In my mind's eye I see that little girl, named Philippina Krippendorf, painting away, making yards and yards of fluffy clouds and sunsets and storms with lightning and rainbows. When the paint was dry, my great-grandfather would go snip, snip and have a dozen or more pictures to sell.

Next in line was my mother. She was an enthusiastic painter of oils and watercolors. She was also very generous. I could mess with her paints and brushes all I wanted. On one condition: that I kept my brushes clean. The only art lesson my mother gave me was how to wash my brushes. Otherwise, she left me alone. I was no more talented, however, than any other child. I started out ruining the wallpaper with crayons, like everybody else, and making eggs with arms and legs. Most children start this way, and most children have the souls of artists. Some of these children stubbornly keep on being children even when they have grown up. Some of these stubborn children get to be artists. So my answer to Question Number One is that I became an artist because I had access to materials and pictures, a minimum of instruction, and a stubborn nature.

Question Number Two then follows: But how come you're an illustrator?

The answer is that I love stories. Lots of artists have loved stories. The sculptures and vase-painters of ancient Greece were forever illustrating Homer. The Byzantine and Romanesque and Gothic artists spent their lives illustrating the Bible. Stories from the Ramayana were the basis for much of the great art in the Orient. Like all these artists, I love illustrating a good story.

"Okay," they say. And then they ask Question Number Three: But how come you decided to make picture books for *children?*

I can answer that quickly. First, in the world of illustration, the picture-book field is far and away the most exciting. And second, I am *not* making picture books for children. I am making them for *people.*

Okay, End of question-and-answer period.

I often go to great lengths to get authentic backgrounds for my illustrations. I climbed Mount Olympus to see how things up there looked to Zeus. I went down into the cave where Hermes was born. I slept in Sleeping Beauty's castle. But to illustrate *Ox-Cart Man,* all I had to do was step outside my back door. (It was a lot cheaper too.)

Ox-Cart Man is the story of a New Hampshire farmer who lived in the last century. The story begins in October, when Ox-Cart Man hitches up his ox, loads up his cart with all the things he and his family have been making and growing all year long, and makes the long trip from the inland hills to Portsmouth Market on the coast. There he sells everything, including the ox, buys a few things, and starts the long trek home. Then the cycle of working and growing begins again.

Even though the story took place, as I said, just outside my back door, I still had to do some preliminary research. First of all, I had to establish *exactly* when the story could have happened. "When" is very important to an illustrator because the sets (the landscape and architecture) must be accurate; so must the costumes, the props, the hairdos, everything.

To begin, I tackled the road that the Ox-Cart Man would have followed. This, I found out, would have been one of the early New Hampshire turnpikes, one which opened to traffic in 1803. This was a toll road. The Ox-Cart Man would have paid one and a half cents a mile for his two-wheeled cart. He paid by the axle, as we still do on the New Hampshire turnpikes. Going to the big markets along the seaboard were great events for New England farmers. Along the road were plenty of wayside inns where they could get hay for their horses and oxen and food for themselves. There were toddy irons in the fire and toddies in the tummy and a good night's sleep for everyone at the end of the day. Every year thousands of carts and wagons passed this way until the railroads arrived in 1847 and commerce took to the rails.

Next, I investigated Portsmouth and Portsmouth Market to ascertain what buildings would have been there between 1803 and 1847. The main difficulty here was that Portsmouth buildings, including the Market, had a bad habit of periodically burning down. It was a puzzle trying to figure out what was where and when.

What finally determined the date was the Ox-Cart Man's beard. I wanted him to have a lovely red beard like Leon's. The story, therefore, had to happen between 1803 and 1847, when the turnpikes were busy, at a time when the brick market building in Portsmouth was standing, and when beards were in fashion. Thus, the date of 1832 was settled upon. After that it was downhill sledding all the way.

Even though we have hard-topped roads and telephone poles and the trappings of the twentieth century, when you get into country up our way, it still looks pretty much like the New England that the Ox-Cart Man knew. In October the leaves are still the colors of fire, and there is a smoky-blue haze over the hills and mountains. After the leaves have fallen, November comes, all tan and gray. The land and the sea lie still, a little sad, waiting for winter. People bank their houses with fir boughs and brace themselves for the cold that is coming. The snow falls. December and January pass, and February. In March the sap begins to run again. People tap their maple trees and put out buckets to catch the sap. Them comes April. Spring arrives slowly in our part of the country. It is a thin spring. The grass takes its time greening up, but the bluets come up in the fields and pastures. The brooks are overflowing from the melted snow and are full of little trout. On a lucky morning people have trout for breakfast along with their coffee and toast. At last comes the lovely month of May. The orchards are in bloom. Every seed you plant, you think, has a good chance of coming up. And, as all of you know, May is much the best month for being in love.

Although *Ox-Cart Man* ends with the beautiful month of May, the month of hope, it starts with October, another beautiful month, the month of fulfillment. In conclusion, I want to read to you a few words from *The New-England Almanack* of 1810. Under the heading "October" it says:

> What pleasure exceeds that of the farmer?
> Now he exultingly beholds the fair fruits
> of his labor. He picks his apples; he gathers his corn;
> he digs his potatoes, and dances round the cider mill
> with a delight that kings and emperors cannot enjoy
> with all their pompous parade and tinsel splendor.

So, thank you very much, everybody. Tomorrow I am going back to New England to dance around my cider mill.

BIOGRAPHICAL NOTE

Phoebe Medina

Barbara Cooney
by Constance Reed McClellan

When Barbara Cooney was awarded the Caldecott Medal in 1959 for *Chanticleer and the Fox* (Crowell), her biographical profile for *The Horn Book* was written by her husband's mother, the wise and kind Anna Newton Porter. Now in 1980, here I am, Barbara's old friend and neighbor, scarcely a peer, attempting to reduce Barbara Cooney to one thousand or so words. It is a challenge for me. I am simply the one who laughs at her jokes, who listens, who nods agreement—a sounding board.

Back in 1959 in her Caldecott acceptance speech Barbara said that winning the award was "the pinnacle" of her career. Twenty-one years later: What has she done in that time besides illustrating another fifty or more children's books? What has happened to her since that pinnacle was reached?

Externally, Barbara Cooney's life has gone on in much the same pattern as it did then. No marital change, no more babies, no corporate transfers. She still lives in the same big, beautiful old house in the same New England town. Her own artist-mother has died, as have Anna Newton Porter and her husband; the children have left home, and there is no longer a horse or a dog.

She does not have to struggle with weight problems; she does not color her hair, which is still blond but now more silvery than golden and usually braided tightly around her head, making her features seem more pointed. Her working clothes are usually of denim; sometimes she wears a tunic and pants or a good new suit for an appointment. She does not worry about growing older and half-jokingly, half-seriously announces that she expects and wants to live to be a hundred. She does seem to be blessed with excellent health; she needs little sleep.

Perhaps because of her wide reputation, her prolificacy, her varied accomplishments, and her success as an illustrator, artist, and winner of Caldecott Medals, many people, even her friends, stand in awe of Barbara Cooney. I am a friend, but I am not awed—I am *amazed*. Amazed at her stamina, her stick-to-it-iveness, her strength, and her ability to tackle something new, again and again.

Barbara Cooney is a many-faceted woman. She is an accomplished gardener; she grows flowers to cut, vegetables to eat, and herbs with which to season. She is a master in her kitchen—from *haute cuisine* to lowly but nourishing whole-wheat bread and white loaves for rolled watercress sandwiches. Year after year, her Christmas tree is a lasting memory for all children who see it, lighted as it is with tiny candles and hung with cookies cut freehand into the shapes of dragons and bicycle-riding bears and of characters from her books, frosted in color. Always there is perfection, flair, and detail.

Barbara has superb self-discipline and understanding of order. Perhaps having a busy doctor-in-general-practice for a husband has allowed her to have her own career, her own independence. She does not leave home to go to a studio but works at her drawing board in a pleasant big room with north and east windows, a fireplace, her store of photographic slides, with reference books at hand.

She has a very good life. Her husband is beloved in the community, dedicated to his patients and to his hospital. The four children, all young in 1959, are now adults. The riding lessons, the car pools, the school and college application forms are all behind her. The Vietnam War years and a son in uniform—all that is over. The children are educated, married—some are divorced—gone away, their varied lives perhaps not exactly what she would have chosen or wanted for them. But she is supportive and encouraging.

In the last two decades Barbara Cooney has moved on in her illustrating, taking broad leaps and jumps from her early scratchboard technique and her drawings of mice and ponies. New assignments have meant new places to be visited, new languages to be studied: a summer in France, a crash course at Berlitz. There were also trips to Ireland, Spain, Greece, Bali, Germany, and Mexico and to India to see a daughter and a first grandchild. She is an inveterate traveler, reader, and student.

And she pursued a new art—photography. Before long came a Nikon camera, photography courses, her own darkroom, and a Cooney book of photographs for the Bicentennial.

The growth continued: illustrating in new formats, mediums, and techniques; a book of games for Colonial Williamsburg; a poster map for Smith College and a cover for the alumnae magazine; illustrations for Homeric legends and for Mother Goose in French and Spanish—along with chalk talks, television appearances, and a long tour of duty as a town library trustee. She did it all. Amazing Barbara.

Sometimes her plans do not go exactly as she has visualized them—unlike the illustrations that she can draw as she likes. She can break, but not for long. She is made of tough, resilient stuff and bounces back quickly from crises and traumas—with some rationalizing, with an inherent sense of humor, and with human resignation.

And there is the balance: time out to lie in the sun on warm rocks on a tidal river in Maine, to share a picnic lunch from a wicker hamper, to play a game of Othello with a visiting grandson, to climb a mountain, to do *The New York Times* crossword puzzle (in ink)—unless her husband has reached for it first! Time for a rubber of bridge, a gin and tonic with friends. Time for a winter vacation with her husband on a sunny island, a trip with a daughter or a daughter-in-law. The balance is there, unusual in a person of genius.

She gave loving attention and care to her own mother in her last years, came to stay with my mother when I was ill and living in the South, and joined her husband in visiting his parents. She has a sense of duty, of right and wrong, and of first things first. She does not dissipate her time or energy. She is dedicated to her work. She deserves her acclaim, her rewards. Amazing Barbara.

Barbara Cooney loves the Maine coast. She spent her childhood summers there and has had the chance to return every summer since then. A few years ago she decided that the time had come to undertake the most ambitious project of all—a house of her own in Maine. She conceived the idea, chose the site, designed and planned the house, watched over and participated in its construction—with most of the work done by her younger son, now skilled and competent. It was an enormous undertaking, with many trips back and forth between Massachusetts and Maine, making extra arrangements and plans for her husband's well-being and comfort while she was away. Even during the building—which went on for more than three years—she continued to work at her drawing board, facing publishers' deadlines, finishing one book, and starting on another. There were problems; there were delays. But the house is now her own—her retreat, her fortress, her castle.

Next came her daughter's wedding, exquisitely staged, a fairytale production performed with inimitable Cooney-Porter style, taste, and understatement. No detail too minute to be overlooked: a stark white meeting house across from fields sweeping down to a cove, guests assigned to box pews bedecked with white ribbons and sea heather, the ring-bearing grandson's sailor suit especially designed and material found of just the right subdued color, a cousin's antique Rolls Royce for the bride's chariot, the August day chosen for the high tide's arrival at precisely the hour of the reception, the backdrop her beloved Maine river and the new house—her castle in Spain.

Barbara has been lucky. Her keen mind combined with inherited and learned talents, a fine liberal arts education, and family stability all provide the most advantageous background; but the success, the fame, and the satisfaction could not have been achieved without her self-discipline, her drive, and her motivation for independence.

As Barbara Cooney goes along in her sexagenarian years—what next? Nothing would surprise me—still another language to be learned, a new art medium, a canoe trip down the Amazon? She does not appear to be slowing down at all but, instead, just looking for another challenge, another pinnacle. She is a very exciting woman, an inspiration to young illustrators and to women everywhere. Amazing Barbara.

The Caldecott Medal 1981

FABLES

written and illustrated by ARNOLD LOBEL

published by HARPER & ROW, PUBLISHERS 1980

BOOK NOTE

In the tradition of Aesop but with contemporary settings and witty detail, Arnold Lobel has created twenty fables, each telling an episode about an animal and each illustrating a trenchant maxim, such as "Advice from friends is like the weather. Some of it is good; some of it is bad."

The illustrations focus on the animals with a minimum of background detail. The artist used gouache and pencil in preparing the artwork for reproduction in the same size, in full color.

Caldecott Medal Acceptance
by Arnold Lobel

It is wonderful to be standing here and to find myself thanking the Caldecott Committee for honoring me with this medal. I do thank you all most gratefully. You have made an old workhorse in the field of children's books sublimely happy.

The creation of most picture books for children is not dramatic. It is a matter of daily, patient, single-minded effort. It is a matter of writing some words on a page in a silent room. It is the soft sound of a pencil or a pen sweeping across a bit of drawing paper. To see a book appearing in front of one's eyes where before there was nothing is a pleasure and a joy. But this elation comes quietly. This was not true, however, in the case of *Fables,* the book that is being honored here this evening. The conception and

FABLES / 221

birth of *Fables* was a fable in itself. A saga with the ups and downs, the climaxes and anticlimaxes, of a real plot.

In March of 1977 I received a phone call from Charlotte Zolotow at Harper and Row. There was an idea for a book that I might be interested in doing. Would I like to come in and talk about it? Well, yes, I certainly would. For a solitary, hermitic artist, the prospect of a business conference in a real office with memo pads and other important things of that nature was indeed an enticement. We quickly agreed on a date for our meeting. The appointed day turned out to be bright and sunny. The midtown skyscrapers of New York gleamed in the light of early spring. Charlotte and Pat Allen were waiting in Charlotte's plant-filled office when I arrived. They were smiling. I smiled back. I remember the occasion as a smiling morning, full of promise.

Their idea was then presented to me. How would I like to write some fresh new adaptations of a selection of Aesop's fables and illustrate them in full color? Immediately, I decided that this sounded like a fine job for me. After all, I thought, were not the *Frog and Toad* stories (Harper) I had written fables of a sort, in their way? Of course they were. A most agreeable advance was mentioned. I heard myself saying, "Yes, I think I would like to do it." Charlotte and Pat were delighted, and our smiling conference came to a happy end.

Outside, on Fifty-third Street in front of the Harper and Row building, I turned the corner of Fifth Avenue, feeling giddy with self-importance at having been summoned and actually commissioned to create a book. But somewhere near the corner of Forty-ninth Street I experienced a sudden sinking spell. I could not—with the exception of that fox and his bunch of sour grapes—I could not bring to mind a single fable of Aesop. Well, never mind, I thought as I made my way toward the subway. Never mind, why spoil the moment? I'll think about it tomorrow. Tomorrows have a way of coming all too soon. Mine did. The hot and humid days of summer found me scavenging in bookstores and slouched in the corners of libraries. I was reading Aesop—a lot of Aesop. I was beginning to feel somewhat uncomfortable, and it was not only the weather.

Children have fallen heir to the fables of Aesop because of the anthropomorphic use of animals therein. I soon realized that these fables were not originally created for children at all. There were no children, as we know them, in Aesop's time. There were only younger and smaller Greeks. I found dogs tearing sheep into pieces. I found snakes strangling ravens. I found deer being chewed to bits by lions. I came upon harsh cruelties and bitter ironies of every sort. The adaptations I was reading were heavily laden with the cautionary moralism of the nineteenth century. Surely it was very interesting, but it was a far cry from *Frog and Toad*. Perhaps this commission was not for me after all?

Summer gave way to autumn. The late afternoons were growing darker, and so was my mood. One morning I stared at myself in the mirror while shaving and said, "No, Lobel, no. Admit it, you do *not* want to do this book." The man in that mirror was giving me such a direct, penetrating look, I could only agree that he was speaking the Truth. I would have to call Charlotte and make an appointment to tell her the bad news.

I am probably being too subjective, but I think the day of this meeting was gray and overcast. I slunk into the office and sadly delivered my message. Naturally, Pat and Charlotte were disappointed, and I was ashamed at having caused them to feel that way. They were both aware of my sense of failure and offered kind words of comfort and encouragement. As I left the office, I turned on the threshold, and, in order to end a gloomy meeting on a note of optimism, I said, "Maybe I can write some fables of my own—who knows?" Pat and Charlotte smiled weakly, and we said good-by. Downstairs, on the corner of Fifty-third and Fifth, I said to myself, "Idiot, why on earth did you say that?" I wondered if it sounded like a promise. I hoped not.

The months went by. Other days, other books. I was busy with several projects. The winter of '78 was a stern one in New York. An abundance of cold and snow. One day in late January our telephone went dead. It happens all the time. Old equipment in Brooklyn. The phone company tells us that the squirrels, driven to desperate measures by the sparseness of the winter food supply, dine hungrily upon our telephone wires, causing broken lines and interruption of service. This proves that even large corporations can invent fables, but I was not amused.

For reasons that I will never understand, I ran coatless into the freezing street and down to the telephone booth at the corner to report the outage. The lady who answered at the telephone repair service was not being cooperative. She was doing her job ever so slowly, carefully taking my name and address and phone number. "What is the problem?" she asked again. "Dead!" I shouted. "The phone is dead!" I jumped up and down to warm myself on that frigid street corner.

I was frozen to the bone. I slammed the receiver down and ran the half-block to my house at top speed. It was as I was just approaching my front stoop that my right foot met the little patch of ice on the sidewalk. There was a snapping sound, a great pain, followed by an ominous numbness. I hobbled into the house, fearing the worst. That evening, after a trip to the emergency ward of our local hospital, all my fears were confirmed. I was crutched and plaster-casted. The diagnosis: a small broken bone below the ankle. The sentence: five weeks of confinement.

Now I must interrupt my story to tell you that I do not particularly love the act of writing. As much as I enjoy drawing, the thought of sitting in a chair with an open notebook on my lap, waiting for nothing to happen, is not my idea of fun. I know that it is my fate to write my own stories and that often, by the grace of the muse, these stories have turned out well; but, in fact, when faced with the prospect of having an hour that could be available for writing the text of a picture book, I have become a master procrastinator. In order to protect myself from the lifeless sharpened pencil, the empty blue lines on the page, I will run, I will escape; any excuse will do. Now there was no excuse. Even if I were to throw all caution to the winter wind and stumble out of the house into the afternoon, the first five-foot snowbank would have stopped me cold. I was trapped. There was nothing to do but face the music and write.

What about those fables that I had so rashly mentioned at Harper? Why not give them a try? I thought of some of my favorite animals that I've always loved but never managed to fit into the scheme of my books. The ostrich, the hippo, the crocodile, and the kangaroo; wonderful, precious creatures all. I put them down on a list.

Day by day, to my great surprise, they told me their stories, and I wrote them. For once the pages of my notebook were not empty. Anita went off to dance class every day. She would return in the early evening and ask in hushed tones, "Did you write another one?" My exuberant answer would almost always be, "Yes I did!" and then I would read her my latest effort. I thank her for her approval and support. I also thank her for her very good nursing. In a month's time I was a movable biped again.

In a great passion, I rushed to do the pictures, for as wary as I am of writing, I do love to draw. I chose to do my first drawings as color paintings instead of the black-and-white pencil sketches that I usually make. The camel wearing a tutu, the pig floating through a dreamlike cosmos, the baboon clutching his ventilated umbrella—these images clicked into being. In no time at all I had a preliminary dummy, stories and pictures all pasted neatly into place. It was ready to be presented to Harper. I thought the book was damned good, but how hard it is to be objective about one's own work! Perhaps I was very wrong. There are always the doubts.

Bringing a new project in to a publisher is a jittery, suspenseful experience. This time was no exception. I waited until I knew that my editor, Liz Gordon, was out on her lunch hour. I crept into Harper and Row. I slipped the dummy onto her desk and hurried off. Carefully, I elected to do this on a Friday so that I could at least have a weekend of rest before waiting for the phone to ring—or not to ring—on Monday.

On the very next day, however, I was attending a small party given by the editor of another publishing house. To my horror, I saw Charlotte coming through the door. She had also been invited. Had she already seen the fables? Had she passed judgment on it? What if she hated it? I wanted to hide, but I knew that it would look silly if I jumped behind a sofa. Charlotte spotted me at once and moved quickly toward me across the room. She was smiling broadly. It was the same bright smile that I had seen in her office a year before. I think it was the nicest smile that I have ever seen. I knew right then that I was an official fabulist.

Mercifully, you will be relieved to hear, the later progress of *Fables* followed a smoother course. I thank Liz Gordon for helping me to tighten and polish my text, and I am grateful for her endless patience with all of my compulsive, last-minute word changes. I thank Kohar Alexanian, my designer, for somehow being able to read my mind's eye and to find the exact typeface that I could see in my head on the very first try. I thank her also for spending those endless hours and days at the printing plant with me while *Fables* was on the press.

I've been making books for children for a very long time. It has been twenty-one years since that rainy morning when I first came into Harper and Brothers to show my portfolio to Susan Hirschman. It was she who hung me up to dry and, to my astonishment, handed me my first manuscript to illustrate. So, in addition to again expressing my thanks to the committee, I wish to end with an appropriate literary quotation that I have found. By no coincidence at all, it has been taken from my own *Fables*. This evening I know that wishes on their way to coming true will not be rushed. Thank you all so much.

BIOGRAPHICAL NOTE

Van Williams

Arnold Lobel
by Elizabeth Gordon

Arnold Lobel is a genuinely modest man and a thoughtful, generous friend. He is also a consummate artist and illustrator, a writer of rich and resonant prose, and, consequently, the deserving winner of many awards and prizes including, of course, the 1981 Randolph Caldecott Medal for *Fables*.

One late afternoon on a cold January day near the end of my maternity leave the telephone rang. It was Joan Robins, Harper & Row's director of publicity, telling me that *Fables* had won the Caldecott Medal. The decision had been reached considerably earlier in the day, but no one had been able to find Arnold to tell him the glorious news. Among those of us in the children's book field, it is no secret on what day the Newbery and Caldecott Medals are announced, and many an artist and author have stayed by their phones just in case. How like Arnold to go about his normal, daily routine without thinking about the awards, without dwelling on official recognition.

I was lucky enough to be the first person to reach Arnold to tell him he had won, and his joy was spontaneous and infectious. He even bumped his head on a wayward cabinet door in his excitement, a bump that found its way into his Caldecott acceptance speech.

Arnold's modesty is deeply ingrained. It informs his work and the way he approaches people and new interests. When he has a new book to show me, he waits until I am out of the office (some ESP elf must work with him because he never slips up) and then leaves a large package in a plain brown wrapper on my desk. It is one of my favorite sights.

Inside the plain brown wrapper there is—always—one of the most complete, thoughtfully put together dummies I have ever seen. Arnold believes strongly that he should never show anything that he doesn't feel is finished and is his best work. He is amazed when I tell him how sloppy many dummies and sketches and manuscripts are, how *preliminary,* how incomplete. This is not to criticize other authors and illustrators—all of whom must work in the way that suits their creative energies best—but to point up how Arnold's modesty about his own work and achievements does not allow him to show other than his best, polished work.

His thoughtfulness is apparent, too, in that he thinks the whole procedure through, right to my desk. How might I feel sitting there, looking at his work? He leaves the package and goes home so I don't feel cramped and restricted by his presence. Of course, he wants me to call right away, and I do, but he has allowed me the freedom to sort through my own reactions without pressure. For us, this results in good editorial exchange—honest but not raw.

The first book of Arnold's that I worked on was *Mouse Soup,* published in 1977. Since then he has written and illustrated more than twenty books. The number alone is impressive, but more so is the variety of subject and style. After Arnold graduated from art school (Pratt Institute), he tried advertising but found he hated it, and then, like most beginning artists, he put together a portfolio and began knocking on doors. At Harper & Row, he was given a manuscript to illustrate, *Red Tag Comes Back,* and his first book—sixty-four pages of salmon swimming upstream— was born. Although to this day Arnold feels far less comfortable writing than illustrating, he did realize he could write stories, too, and in 1962 he wrote and illustrated *A Zoo for Mister Muster.* "The Prospect Park Zoo was just across the street from our apartment in Brooklyn," Arnold recalls, and the Lobels were frequent visitors. "The children were particularly fond of the vultures and the ice cream."

Frog and Toad came about in a similar way. One summer the Lobels took a house near a swamp in Vermont. Arnold spent a great deal of time watching frogs and toads—both outdoors and in the house. The difference in personality soon became apparent, and Arnold saw that these two amphibian characters could provide a perfect literary vehicle for his own feelings and "adult preoccupations."

All of Arnold's characters from Grasshopper and Owl (who Arnold describes as a psychotic) to the characters of *Fables* had their genesis in Arnold's own experiences.

Our whole office staff remembers the fun we had when Arnold first delivered *Fables*. We only had to look around us to find Ostrich, Camel, Rhinoceros, the poor old Dog—right in the office next door or at the drawing board down the hall. I always wondered who Arnold had in mind when he created those marvelous animal collections of human foibles and idiosyncrasies.

Arnold now lives by another park—Washington Square Park in Manhattan—in a handsome and comfortable apartment filled with books, records, and video tapes. The apartment is on the first floor, and by adjusting the shades on his windows, Arnold can become a very close observer of the rich and varied life that is always going on in and around the park. (Before the apartment was finished and the windows were still bare, Arnold was as much observed as observer, and one passerby even asked to come in and use the bathroom.) Selfishly, I hope Arnold leaves his shades open often, for I know many characters will find their way through those windows and onto the pages of a new book. Given Arnold's considerable artistic talents and his genuine warmth and interest in people, these characters are sure to touch adult and child readers alike and linger long in our memories.

The Caldecott Medal 1982

JUMANJI

written and illustrated by CHRIS VAN ALLSBURG

published by HOUGHTON MIFFLIN COMPANY 1981

BOOK NOTE

Judy and Peter discover in the park a box with a game in it: JUMANJI. Left alone at home for the afternoon, they take out the game board and find instructions, beginning, "Jumanji, a young people's jungle adventure especially designed for the bored and restless," and ending, "Once a game of Jumanji is started it will not be over until one player reaches the golden city." Peter's first move lands on a space marked "Lion attacks"—and suddenly, on top of the piano, there is a lion, which chases him around the house. Judy's move brings in a troop of monkeys who create havoc. Other moves bring a monsoon, a lost guide, a rhinoceros stampede, an eight-foot snake, and an erupting volcano to the living room, all of which frighten the children until Judy is able to roll the right dice and finish the game. Immediately everything returns to normal. Peter and Judy hastily drop the game in the park where they found it. Their parents return with friends, and the children work on a picture puzzle. One guest, Mrs. Budwing, remarks that her sons don't finish puzzles and never read instructions. Looking out the window, Judy and Peter can see the Budwing boys walking out of the park carrying the Jumanji game.

    The black-and-white illustrations are full page, and each is drawn from an unusual angle, which often foreshortens figures and objects and enlivens the composition. The full range of gray and black tones gives a strong three-dimensional effect. To create such a rich range the artist used Conté pencil with Conté dust.

Caldecott Medal Acceptance
by Chris Van Allsburg

I prepared for this speech by reading speeches of other Caldecott medalists. It seems there are certain traditions, such as describing where you were and what you were doing when the Caldecott Committee chairman called with the news. I was in my bed, and I was sleeping. Disbelief and sleepiness combined to inspire the following reaction to Gail Sage's phone call: "Uh ... gee." Throughout the conversation Gail must have wondered if she'd dialed the right number. How could someone who spoke only in monosyllables write a book? Afterward, as I lay in bed, a terrible thought came to me. What if the ALA had a secret clause, a clause that allowed the Caldecott Committee to reverse its decision if the recipient was found to be torpid, unresponsive, and dull-witted? If only I'd taped the conversation, I could prove to friends that I had been, for a little while, the Caldecott medalist. But no call followed telling me there had been a mistake. When I saw the announcement in the newspaper, I knew I was safe.

Other speech traditions are descriptions of one's childhood involvement with books and art. In my elementary school we had art twice a week. I loved those days. Children often use a slight fever as an excuse to stay home from school, drink ginger ale, and eat ice cream in bed. Once, in the second grade, I felt feverish at breakfast but concealed it from my mother because it was an art day. Midway through the morning art class, my teacher noticed that I looked a little green. Ordinarily it wouldn't be unusual, but paint wasn't being used that day. She took me out into the hall where we children left our coats and boots and asked if I felt O.K. I said I felt fine and then threw up into Billy Marcus's boots. I was profoundly embarrassed. The teacher was very comforting. She took me to the nurse's office, and my mother was summoned. I went home, drank ginger ale, and ate ice cream in bed.

There was another occasion when my physical health and my passion for art collided. When I was eight, my friend Russell and I became voracious stamp collectors. I loved those tiny little pictures. We wanted all our relatives to take a vacation in the

Ukraine and write us lots of letters. After three weeks of looking at nothing but stamps, I got a fever—the flu again. In my delirium, all I could see was a stamp picturing the Lewis and Clark expedition. I was there, too, with Lewis and Clark, standing in front of a timber fort with our Indian guides, but we never went anywhere. When I pulled out of the fever, I gave all my stamps to Russell. To this day I'm a terrible letter-writer, no doubt because of my lasting aversion to stamps.

There was a great deal of peer recognition to be gained in elementary school by being able to draw well. One girl could draw horses so well, she was looked upon as a kind of sorceress. (Everyone else's horses looked like water buffalo.) Being able to draw cartoon characters was a good trick, too. Pluto and Mickey always impressed friends. I specialized in Dagwood Bumstead, a little too sophisticated, perhaps, to be widely appreciated.

But the status gained by these skills wanes as one gets older. Certain peer pressures encourage little fingers to learn how to hold a football instead of a crayon. Rumors circulate around the schoolyard: Kids who draw or wear white socks and bring violins to school on Wednesdays might have cooties. I confess to having yielded to these pressures. Sixth grade was the last time I took art in public school. My interests went elsewhere.

Then, in college I enrolled in art classes as a lark. At that time I was quite naïve about the study of art. As a freshman I received a form that listed the courses I would have, their times and places, and the necessary materials. One course, described simply as "Fgdrw," met at eight o'clock in the morning. I did not know what Fgdrw meant, but the materials required were newsprint and charcoal. I went to the appointed room and was surprised to see an older woman wearing a terry-cloth robe and slippers. I thought, "What? Does she live here or something? Maybe we're here too early, and she hasn't had time to dress." Then she took off her bathrobe, and I deduced the meaning of Fgdrw.

During that year the art classes I took as a lark became more important and involving than any of my other classes. In fact, it took me five years to get my undergraduate degree because I never let liberal arts courses get in the way of making art. Going to classes like philosophy and French upset my rhythm, my pace. So I just skipped them, which upset my credit requirements (and my parents, too). It was clear I had a fever again. The fever to make art.

Actually, fever may be a misleading description of my own rather deliberate approach, but there is a constant urge to create. I am fascinated by the idea of making something real that at one point is only an idea. It is challenging and beguiling to sense something inside, put it on paper (or carve it in stone), and then step back and see how much has got lost in the process. The inevitability of losing some of the idea in trying to bring it to life is what keeps me working. I am always certain that next time, I'll lose less.

Ideas themselves have varied origins. In writing and illustrating *Jumanji,* the inspiration was my recollection of vague disappointment in playing board games as a child. Even when I owned Park Place with three hotels, I never felt truly rich, and not being able to interrogate Colonel Mustard personally was always a letdown. Another motivating element for *Jumanji* was a fascination I have with seeing things where they don't belong. The pictures in newspapers of cars that have run amok and crashed into people's living rooms always get my attention. There's the room, almost normal: sofa, TV, amused home-owner, end tables, and the front half of an Oldsmobile. It occurred to me that if an Oldsmobile in the living room looked that good, a herd of rhinoceros could have real possibilities.

I am surprised now that my fairly recent discovery of the illustrated book as a way of expressing ideas did not happen earlier. It is a unique medium that allows an artist-author to deal with the passage of time, the unfolding of events, in the same way film does. The opportunity to create a small world between two pieces of cardboard, where time exists yet stands still, where people talk and I tell them what to say, is exciting and rewarding.

It is also rewarding to receive mail from people who appreciate your work. The first letter I received as a result of having a book published came from a man in Cleveland. I don't remember his name, so I'll use a pseudonym. His letter was written with red Magic Marker on tissue paper. "Dear Mr. Van Allsburg," he wrote, "I love your work. Do you think life as we know it will exist in the year 2000? Yours truly, Frank Selmer." More recently, I received a letter from Alexandra Prinstein (her real name) from Delaware: "Dear Mr. Van Allsburg. I love the books you write. I am so glad your books are so weird because I am very weird. I think you are weird but great. I wish a volcano and flood would be in my room when I am bored. I am happy I am only five because I have lots more years to enjoy magical gardens and crazy games in books by you. Love Alexandra. P.S. I have a younger brother Peter too."

Other rewards of writing and illustrating are meeting and working with people like Walter Lorraine, my editor at Houghton Mifflin, and Anita Silvey, Houghton's publicity person. I would like to thank both of them for their support and guidance.

While I'm thanking people, I would also like to thank Jan Vermeer, for the way he used light; Edgar Degas, for the way he composed; Max Klinger, for the way he told a story; Federico Fellini, for making films that look the way they do; André Kertesz, for the photos he took; Winsor McKay, for little Nemo; H.C. Westermann, for the things he made; Gustav Stickley, for the way he built a chair; and Harold, for his purple crayon. I'm indebted to them all; I aspire to the excellence of their achievement.

And thank you to Alexandra and all the other children who have written to me, and to the children who come up to me at book signings to tell me how much they like *Abugazi* and *Pajami*. Some people may contend that there is no image more charming than a child holding a puppy or kitten. But for me that's a distant second. When I see a child clutching a book, especially my book, to his or her tiny bosom, I'm moved. Children can possess a book in a way they can never possess a video game, a TV show, or a Darth Vader doll. A book comes alive when they read it. They give it life themselves by understanding it.

Finally, I would like to thank the ALA and the Caldecott Committee for bestowing this great honor on me. Some artists claim praise is irrelevant in measuring the success of art, but I think it's quite relevant. Besides, it makes me feel great.

BIOGRAPHICAL NOTE

Chris Van Allsburg
by David Macaulay

When Chris won the Caldecott Medal, I heard about it first from his wife Lisa. That wasn't surprising. As long as we've been friends, Chris has never actually announced any of his triumphs. The information either seeps out inadvertently during a conversation, or it comes directly, with great pride and enthusiasm, from Lisa. Chris's modesty is genuine, and it should not be confused with a lack of confidence. He knows he's good; we've all told him he's good; and more important, he knows *why* he's good. But there is an inevitable distrust of praise, especially when it comes so quickly.

There are certain mundane requirements of every biographical sketch, including age, place of birth, siblings, and amusing quirks. I will dispose of these as quickly as possible. They are: between thirty and thirty-three, Michigan, one (female)—and a reluctance to fly. The last is bad news for Houghton Mifflin's promotional programs but good news for me because most people will never meet Chris and therefore will have little choice but to believe what I tell them.

Looking back over *The Garden of Abdul Gasazi, Jumanji,* and *Ben's Dream* (all Houghton), I think it is clear that houses big and small have been the main sets around and inside of which Chris's dramas unfold. Just as these houses are essential to his tales, so the Van Allsburg house is essential to mine. 114 is not an imposing edifice. At first glance it might even appear normal. Architecturally, it is just another American interpretation of a slightly Scandinavian-possibly-Bavarian woodman's cottage built just before 1920 by a neo-Victorian. In short, it is Carl Larsson's house bronzed.

Only gradually does one become aware of the house's true character and, more important, of the true characters of its inhabitants. There is a well-maintained 4-H sign by the front door. As far as I know, it is the only 4-H sign displayed so prominently on a house in Providence. This isn't surprising, considering the size of the city's farming population. At the other side of the front door is a bell which has been out of order for so long that even the most recent hand-written "knock" sign has abandoned the aging Scotch Tape for better things. This is an uncharacteristic detail, given Chris's concern for order, but it does display a sort of reassuring fallibility.

Inside the house a large stuffed raven and a smaller stuffed crow perch atop the glass-doored bookcase which houses the seldom warm television. The glassy-eyed *corvus corax* often sports a miniature Red Sox batting helmet indicative of Chris's interest in athletics and concern for the welfare of animals. On the mantel are two carved giraffes, a lithograph of a lion, and a bust of Dante. These are indicative of Chris's love of classical literature and admiration for exotic wild animals. Cecil, a Siamese cat of almost human persuasion, is the only living exotic animal residing at 114. Other shelves proudly display the growing collection of cast-metal Statues of Liberty and bulldogs indicative of Chris's patriotism and curious interest in pugnacious domestic animals.

Also on display are four pieces of Chris's sculpture. The first is a coffee cup falling off a cylindrical cabinet, as if nudged by some unseen elbow. The contents of the cup pour permanently over the rim because the cup, the coffee, and the cabinet are all made meticulously out of wood. In the dining room are three bronze cones. Each is caught at a particular moment of impact with an invisible missile, and each rests on a turned oak base inset with a marble top. The description of the impact is so convincing, you can almost hear it, not to mention feel the rush of wind.

The largest room in the house is the recently completed absolutely-from-scratch-no-old-materials-used-authentic-late-1930s kitchen—complete with red-and-white checkered tile band above the counter and a raised four-seater booth. Second only to his fear of flying is Chris's fear that the first thing any new owner of the house would do is modernize the kitchen.

The second largest room in the house is upstairs, and it is the studio. It is the modest sky-lit space roughly seven by thirty feet in which Alan P. Mitz, Abdul G., Judy, Peter, and Ben, and—over Cecil's objections—Fritz first appeared on paper. The calm of the studio is gently reinforced either by the mellow sounds of 103 or the more classical sound of 89.5 on Chris's FM dial.

It is here on most days that Chris and Cecil can be found—Chris hunched over the drawing board, Cecil hanging by his front paws from a door frame. Occasionally, Cecil joins Chris at the drawing board. Although he rarely gives his impressions of a drawing, he has been known to leave his impressions on a drawing. In those instances the serenity of studio life is shattered. Cecil, having been temporarily and unexpectedly airborne, continues to watch from a distance, as his master and trainer attempts to remove, or at least blend, a combination of paw print and claw mark into the fragile surface of the drawing.

In no time all is forgotten and forgiven. Once again, particles of graphite or pastel dust ride the currents dancing in the beams of light which find their way past the shades on the skylights. After a particularly demanding or gratifying stretch of drawing, the sounds of the radio are often replaced by the sounds of live music. Chris is a self-taught musician of little promise who owns, among other instruments, a tenor and an alto recorder. In order to play both the lead line and the accompanying harmony he has learned to play the instruments simultaneously with his nose. It is an unusual and slightly unsettling sight.

When he's not in his studio, Chris is probably at school or asleep. Professor Van Allsburg teaches a number of classes in the illustration department at the Rhode Island School of Design. In addition to his rigorous drawing courses with their emphasis on careful observation and technical proficiency, he also offers a class called "Design Your Own Country." Students are required to produce a number of visual documents, including posters and postage stamps, which illustrate and in effect prove the existence of their own imagined countries. What the sneaky devil has done in the guise of play is introduce students to the two main elements of illustration—elements so clearly visible in his own work. The first is the use of imagination—these countries must not only be created but also understood in some depth by their creators. The second is the development of technical skills without which the students would not be able to communicate and support their inventions.

Chris is a demanding teacher and is respected for it. The standards he sets for his students are high—but not as high as those he sets for himself. If Chris has a competitive streak, it is evident only in his determination to make each of his drawings better than the one that preceded it. It is perhaps his abhorrence of mediocrity that stands out above all his other virtues and quirks. His refusal to accept anything of inferior quality or of tainted integrity is as evident in his work as it is in all other aspects of his life, even including how much cheese one should expect when one orders a double cheeseburger. For Chris no detail is insignificant, no technical problem insurmountable, no challenge to the imagination too great. And no biographical sketch is entirely accurate.

The Caldecott Medal 1983

SHADOW

translated and illustrated by MARCIA BROWN

from the French of BLAISE CENDRARS

published by CHARLES SCRIBNER'S SONS 1982

BOOK NOTE

A poet, Blaise Cendrars, and an artist, Marcia Brown, each tell us what Shadow is—one with words inspired by African shamans and storytellers, the other with images inspired by African experience and the poet's words. Shadow is mute; it is blind; it does not sleep; it has no hunger. It is frightening; it is a trickster; yet it is full of life; it goes everywhere; it is magic; it is a game, a dance.

The words and visual images of each double-page spread are totally interdependent and together create a strong mood. The art is collage prepared with cut and pasted forms, some cut from black paper, some carved on wood blocks and printed in white on tissue. The backgrounds are washes and blottings of paint.

Caldecott Medal Acceptance
by Marcia Brown

Of course, this is a very happy occasion for me, and I am grateful to all of you here and not here who have made it possible. I suspect it took a certain courage for those on the Caldecott selection committee to choose *Shadow* for a third medal. I am grateful for their courage.

My publisher, Charles Scribner, Jr., has trusted me through work on quite a few books by now, and especially on this one. Monica Brown Lamontagne, production manager at Scribner's, by her integrity and her acute eye on proofs and press, assured the look I had hoped for. Dai Nippon of Japan printed it beautifully. Olga Richmond, the designer, and David Toberisky gave it their meticulous care. Lee Deadrick, then my editor, from the beginning of my interest in Blaise Cendrars's prose poem, believed in the book and had the grace and kindness to put no impossible pressure on me while I allowed it to grow. And I am more grateful than I can ever express to close friends—they know who they are—who stood by me during a painful hiatus in my work on *Shadow* and by their faith in me and the book enabled me to finish it in strength.

I am especially happy that my being here coincides with your reestablishing this ceremony as a banquet; so once again we break bread together. I have attended several of these occasions—some up here, some down there. Wherever one is, one cannot help but feel on this night a sense of celebration and pride that we are all somehow one in work very much worth doing, despite occasional "weary dismals" during the year.

A long time ago I found, in Italy, a little book of proverbs collected from various peoples of Black Africa. Their pithy pertinence can leaven my words.

. . .

Proverb: "It's true that I killed an elephant; however, it's not true that I carried him home on my shoulders."

Have you looked down from a high hill or tower on traffic patterns around a well-engineered intersection? Drivers trust each other; they trust their own ability to drive and react quickly. They trust the reactions of their own machines. There are remarkably few accidents, considering the number of vehicles on the roads. They all seem held, as it were, in orbit by invisible threads of trust.

Proverb: "The tongue is a lion; if you let it run free, it will eat you up."

Illustrators often find themselves in an ironical position. Much of what they say about their work has to be after the fact because they think in images, not in words. Yet if they can't talk, heaven help them!

Proverb: "When you hear a good talker, don't agree with him all at once. What is hiding in the corner has not come out yet."

Many years ago, when I was a storyteller in The New York Public Library, I was fascinated by a little book in the French collection of the Central Children's Room: *Petits Contes Nègres pour les Enfants des Blancs,* published in France in 1929, with semi-abstract and somewhat sophisticated illustrations. Margery Bianco translated that book and published, in 1933, *Little Black Stories for Little White Children* (Payson & Clarke), with handsome woodcut illustrations that suggested African wood carvings. The one piece in the French of Blaise Cendrars that Mrs. Bianco did not translate was "La Féticheuse" or "The Sorceress."

I have been haunted for years by the mysterious atmosphere created by Blaise Cendrars as he evoked Shadow, a spirit coming to life in firelight, wandering in and out of memory, taking part in rituals that gave meaning to life, at times a mirror image of life.

Although the poem had been told more often to adults than to children (hauntingly, by Maria Cimino of The New York Public Library's Central Children's Room), I felt that in the 1980s the prose poem might have meaning for American children. Levels of awareness might be probed that might not have been reached so easily in 1933. We have grown, and we have also suffered a great deal, since 1933. Perhaps we have learned something about ourselves.

A trip to East Africa in 1975 showed me a land of dazzling light that carved bold shapes relentlessly against mysterious shadow, colorful rocks still displaying the scars of the geological upheavals that had formed them, savannahs of golden grasses, and brilliant sunsets before the sudden fall of night. Proud peoples seemed caught between past and present. Magnificent animals were both hunters and prey. The shadow of scavengers hung greedy over the burning land.

One of my strongest impressions was of timelessness, a kind of innocence in which man lived with nature in a way barely imagined by Western man.

My challenge, if I were to make a book of "Shadow," as I had come to call the poem to myself, would be to incorporate the images that had formed in my head from reading the poem with impressions gained from travel in Africa, with records of anthropologists who had very recently tried to record ways of life that are constantly changing and absorbing influences from other societies and, in some cases, are disappearing altogether.

I recognized another challenge: to suggest the element of play with an idea that is implied in the text. I do not think that Cendrars ever imagined himself to be recording a piece of ethnic literature—even though *Shadow* is told in a form suggestive of some kinds of storytelling prevalent in Africa—any more than Picasso's "Les Demoiselles d'Avignon," incorporating impressions of African masks, professed to be a record of those masks. It was a new creation. *Shadow* was in no way to be a documentary performance. Poets, children, and artists often delight in mixing the real and the unreal, intuitively aware that each feeds an understanding of the other. I trusted children to understand many more emotional levels of shadow than the obvious.

Cendrars, and that was not his real name, was in Africa over fifty years ago. He wrote of people living in pastoral and agricultural societies where Nature was beneficent but had to be appeased by ritual for the loss of vital forces taken from the earth. The explosive energy of dance, of song, of storytelling, of all the components of ritualistic ceremonies in which the whole community shared, restored these vital forces, and equilibrium was maintained.

. . .

Proverb: "No matter how calm the lake, in it there may be crocodiles."

. . .

I was quite aware of the possible nonacceptance of the book on an African subject because I am white. Also, the book, as I had conceived it, would be very expensive to print and produce properly. I gave my publisher every chance to be released from our agreement. Scribner's decided to trust me and gave me possibly the best printing of all my books, one that united tonalities that had been executed over many months, with a long interruption in between.

. . .

Proverb: "If you have tried in vain to fish with the sea low, try to fish at high tide."

. . .

I wanted to make the book as vivid as I could, to speak to any child, regardless of color. We all share fear, discovery, loss, and a sense of play.

At one time, I toyed with the idea of photography as a medium for *Shadow*. I would work with images created by a trained dancer. The book would have been very different. I decided to work out my own images. At one time, I had hoped to cut wood blocks for the pictures. Arthritic pain in my hands forbade that. I think of African wood-carvers as sculptors the peers of any in the world, regardless of the original purpose of their carvings—not as works of art in the sense that we enjoy them in museums but as tools of ritual with enormous spiritual and evocative power.

The text was a poem. Black, stark cut-paper figures for people and animals could unify its many episodes and avoid the individualization of character that would limit imagination. I used the deep violet-blue shadows I had seen at dusk in Africa to suggest actual shadows. I cut wood blocks and printed them in white on translucent paper to suggest memories, spirit-images, and ghosts. The round-headed Fang masks suggest that one newborn may be closest to his ancestors. A community consists of the ancestors, the living, and those yet unborn.

When I had completed half the illustrations, I was forced to stop work for a year because of illness. I later worked out the method of blotting to suggest a land scarred by the history locked in its rocks. Fragments of blotted paper were pasted together to build up the landscapes I remembered.

I conceived the book as a kind of day that starts with sunset, moving into night. Probably because of the huge clouds of dust kicked up by running animals, sunsets in Africa can be awesomely brilliant before a brief dusk. The book moves through another day and ends again with the fire that brings Shadow to life.

Since the book was not to be a literal record, I did not wish to limit it to any one group. Clothing in temperatures that can easily hover near 125 degrees Fahrenheit is apt to be minimal, but I also wished to show gesture as probably the most vivid mode of communication among the various members of the human family. Bodily positions were suggested by my own numerous photographs taken in Africa, by recent photographs taken by Leni Riefenstahl of the Kau and Nuba peoples, and those of Michel Huet, who spent years recording dance rituals of many ethnic groups in Africa before they would pass from memory.

. . .

Proverb: "A beautiful neck has no need of a pearl necklace."

. . .

Translation is not retelling. I decry and fear the growing tendency to think that a translator has the right to change thought, intent, or style. I made my own translation, telling it over and over to myself, keeping in mind the shifting image of a wonderful dancer-storyteller, images darting from her pointed fingers.

When I read *Shadow* to Lee Deadrick, she immediately thought it could speak to children. We were a bit optimistic in thinking that French editors would be more careful of old records than we sometimes are. It took Lee and her staff almost a year of writing back and forth to France before we were able to ascertain ownership of rights and go ahead.

. . .

Proverb: "Children sing the song which they hear from their mother and father."

. . .

We know, from the child deep within ourselves, that children rarely speak of all they feel. We often violate their privacy and urge them to expose inner feelings that are withered in our scrutiny. I have often trusted children to accept poetic truth when their elders were worried and confused by terminology unfamiliar to them or were too literal of mind. There are levels of response in children we often make no attempt to reach, so anxious are we to cram their small skins full of practical skills ans information. We push them out of a time of precious reverie and inner growth at the price of stunted and shallow adult inner life. Worse, we are sometimes guilty of passing on to them fears, hates, all the baggage of our own pain, when there is often no need. One generation of twenty years can change mental climate a good deal.

. . .

Proverb: "Today and tomorrow are not the same thing."

. . .

The book was to be published as a children's book. Even though I never thought it for very young children, I felt that children would expect to find children in the illustrations. Along with dance, storytelling was often part of a ritual ceremony taking place in an open space in the village, attended by the inhabitants, old and young. I showed an audience of children for the storyteller, who tells his animal tales and passes along to his listeners the lore and wisdom of their society.

Shadow is often paradoxical. Playing with his idea, Cendrars moves back and forth between the shadow seen and known to the child as playmate, an accompaniment to all that lives in light, and shadow unseen, the ancestral past, the spirit that lives after life, after light, after fires are quenched. In no way did I wish to make a literal picture of African life, and indeed what picture book could undertake to show honestly the incredible diversity of a huge continent? Customs of pastoral peoples are not those of the forest, still less those of the cities that have grown so remarkably in the last half century. I would like to range as freely as the poet.

On the title page, a child steps out of her shadow, giving a backward look to the powerful ancestral images of the past. Some of the strongest possible means for instilling awe and reverence for ancestral spirits are the ritual dance masks. They absorb and control an energy released by the death of living creatures and make that energy available as a good, rather than as a surrender to chaos. When making the Bwa mask from Upper Volta, I worked until that mysterious transferal of spirit could take place, the leap from the spirit of the artist into the thing created. The evocation of spirit existing in the husk of an artist's creation is unmistakable when it occurs, the result of concentration and utter submergence of mind into material.

A child awakens in the night, perhaps for the first time startled at the thought, "What if I am not?" and feels the hole of nothingness, the negative of all positive.

In Africa, as Joseph Campbell has written, "Ash is the key to the sacred." Ash, what is left after fire, after growth, after purification, becomes the eyes of Shadow.

A child lifts a stone and uncovers shadow people squirming in the shock of light. A boy child, who had danced so gaily at noon, is lost. Shadow sits heavy on the heart in the evening, as a child seeks to comfort the grandfather who has lost his hunter son, his warrior son. And the poet sings with his lute to their joy, sings to their grief.

.   .   .

Proverb: "If a village burns, all see the smoke; but if the heart is in flames, no one notices."

.   .   .

Years ago, I told some of Cendrars's stories to children. I knew their power. My first chance to use my book *Shadow* with children came last year before it was published. I showed slides of my pictures and read the poem aloud to a second-grade class in a public school in a nearby town. The children were of many nationalities, many colors—half of them boat people from Laos, Cambodia, and Vietnam. Many had recently lost family members. Some were gifted in art, such as Phovanh Mekmorakoth from Laos, whose picture of a blackbird among little yellow-green orchids hangs on my studio wall; Eddie Pacific, who wrote, "Were we excellent when we read our stories?"; Ruth Ashby, who wrote, "You told us we were casting a shadow on you. You will remember us, won't you?"; and Paul Arbitelle, who wrote, "I'd like to be an artist because it's peace." As I read, shadows flickered over their faces.

. . .

Proverb: "Fruits do not shake off by themselves; someone is under the tree."

. . .

Vituperations tell a great deal more about those who utter them than about the work attacked. Self-appointed experts are often people who are distinguished—for their ignorance as well as for their arrogance. Their eagerness to take up cudgels for causes they appear barely to understand often seems to be purely careerist in intent. They need not concern us here, and their words had best be forgotten. My concern is for the people who do have an emotional stake in conflicts that confront us, who have suffered real pain and understandably do not wish the children they teach to suffer the same pain. They feel a passionate responsibility to protect children from stigma that is unjust. I would hope that they might also interpret their responsibility as one of leading children away from facile, indignant labels of stereotype into a feeling of pride in a distant background of which we are just beginning to perceive the worth.

Works of art from this background have proudly taken their place all over the world. Were they fashioned by so-called primitive people, these exquisite and powerful objects, with such subtlety and finesse of surface, with the inner power only true works of art possess? I think not. Regardless of whatever fad in art is having its heyday, art history has sifted out those works endowed with spirit, not photographic finish nor the product of antlike copying of nature.

Western man, in his arrogance, has left a wake of bruised peoples around the world. The seeking of power demands a putting down to build oneself up.

We are learning that what might have appeared, long ago, to be a meager spiritual and physical diet was far more sound than the endlessly diluted, manipulated fare we sometimes put up with because we think we have no control over it. In the paradox that psychology has taught us to recognize, Western man has envied the wealth of those he chose to label primitive, feared them because their lives were different, and eventually hated them because he had mistreated them.

. . .

Proverb: "What the arm cannot do, wisdom can."

. . .

We are now in a position of learning wisdom from people we had been taught to think of as primitive. Could children nearer in heritage to those roots be taught pride in them? Many of the rest of us bear in our heritage the shame of what might merit the words *bestial,* even *satanic*—certainly *inhuman.*

. . .

Proverb: "A drop of water can be the beginning of a deluge."

. . .

Why must we cling to the mental fix that an idea presented to a child be law forever after? Why is one example immediately frozen into an archetype? Or a stereotype? Do we really understand just what that word means? Where do our clichés come from, if not from fact?

. . .

Proverb: "A lie can produce flowers, but not fruit."

. . .

How are we to enable children to explore different modes of thinking and feeling if we exclude what we, in our literalness, cannot accept? There are those with wounds still open, from hurts some of us can hardly imagine, who are hypersensitive to any wind that seems harsh to barely healing flesh. Their expressions of dismay are honest. I ask them for their trust.

. . .

Proverb: "He who keeps asking and asking will not get lost."

. . .

Last year Julie MacRae published for Franklin Watts a beautiful and unaffectedly wise book by a great artist, the singer Janet Baker. It is a journal of her last year of singing in opera. Translate for yourselves her references to listening into those of looking:

The power of art is a person-to-person communication. It is meant for one ear, one heart at a time; one's own. What is received is unique, and cannot be got vicariously from listening to the remarks or the opinions of others. One must drink at the life-giving fountain for oneself. What is tasted there depends upon the individual.

For us, the performers, another sort of life-and-death struggle is going on. Our concern is how well we have prepared ourselves to do the job, mentally, physically, spiritually. Only we can know this, and even them, partially; all we can do is try our best at a particular moment, but it must be the best, nothing less.

Proverb: "Tasting the fruit, think with gratitude of who planted the tree."

. . .

Politicians and their ambitions notwithstanding, the more we learn of the mythologies of the world, the more we learn of the one creature, man. The great themes of his fears, his imaginings, his worship are legion and universal. As Joseph Campbell says in the prologue to his first volume in *The Masks of God* series, *Primitive Mythology* (Viking):

"and though many who bow with closed eyes in the sanctuaries of their own tradition rationally scrutinize and disqualify the sacraments of others, an honest comparison immediately reveals that all have been built from one fund of mythological motifs—variously selected, organized, interpreted, and ritualized, according to local need, but revered by every people on earth."

Come down from the height and watch the cars—cougars, sky hawks, thunderbirds, cobras, and rabbits. We still keep our totemic distinctions. We are still tribal in our allegiances, in our exclusions from our own state of blessedness, and in our mistrust of those we exclude.

We are entering a period forecast hundreds of years ago, one that will probably be cerebral, calculated, terribly competitive for material gain or material survival, depending upon who and where you are. A great deal that is very precious to us may mean next to nothing to this coming generation and those following. But our joy must be in going forward, trusting each other and the children we serve, sharing the common purpose of recognizing the spark of life that can ignite and nourish spirit. Isn't that why we are here? Africa is slowly stepping out of its shadows. Isn't it time that we stepped out of our shadows?

BIOGRAPHICAL NOTE

Marcia Brown
by Janet A. Loranger

Thirty-seven years ago, Marcia Brown published her first picture book for children: *The Little Carousel*. On June 28, 1983, she received her third Caldecott Medal for *Shadow*. Those years from 1946 to 1983 have encompassed one of the most distinguished careers in American children's books. That her latest book has received such a signal honor and that she is the first illustrator to be awarded the medal three times are evidences of the undiminished vitality and richness of her contribution to the field. It is an uncommon achievement.

The nourishment of such a gift and such an achievement comes from many sources. Marcia grew up in several small towns in upstate New York, one of three daughters in a minister's family. Everyone in the household loved music and reading, and her father also passed along to her, especially, his joy in using his hands. From childhood Marcia was allowed to use his tools and learned to respect and care for them. And from her own workbench and tools, in later years, have come the wood blocks and linoleum cuts that illustrate such handsome books as *Once a Mouse* ...(1961), *How, Hippo!* (1969), *All Butterflies* (1974), and *Backbone of the King* (1966). Marcia feels that the most important legacy her parents gave her was a deep pleasure in using her eyes—for *seeing,* rather than merely for looking. Her keen delight in the details of nature and her acute observation of them are evident in all her books—most dramatically, perhaps, in the beautiful photographic nature books *Walk with Your Eyes, Listen to a Shape,* and *Touch Will Tell* (all Watts, 1979).

As a college student, Marcia was interested in botany, biology, art, and literature. During summer vacations she worked in Woodstock, New York, at a resort hotel and studied painting with Judson Smith, whose criticism and inspiration have remained an important influence in her life and art. After graduation she taught high school English, directed dramatic productions for a few years, and worked in summer stock. Some years later, she became a puppeteer in New York City and also taught puppetry for the extra-mural department of the University of the West Indies.

When Marcia moved to New York City, her interest in children's book illustration drew her to work in the Central Children's Room of The New York Public Library, where she gained invaluable experience in storytelling and an exposure to the library's large international and historical collections. Here, too, she received encouragement from such outstanding children's librarians as Anne Carroll Moore, Helen A. Masten, and Maria Cimino.

Marcia's particular interest in folklore and fairy tales is apparent to anyone familiar with her books. Marcia believes strongly that the classic tales give children images and insights that will stay with them all their lives. To each of these stories she has brought her own special vision, her integrity, and a vitality that speaks powerfully and directly to children.

A very important influence in her life and in her books has been the stimulus of travel—that mind- and eye-stretching jolt out of the usual. Marcia has traveled widely in Europe, Great Britain, Russia, East Africa, the Middle East, and the Far East, including China. If she has a "home away from home," it is Italy, the country with which she has felt most profoundly in tune. She lived in Italy, off and on, for four years, spending much of her time painting. *Felice* (1958) and *Tamarindo!* (1960) are books that grew out of her love for that country and her friendships with Italians. Marcia still writes to friends there, in Italian, and is able to converse with them in the language when she calls them on special occasions. France, too, has a special place in her life, and she spent over a year there; while living in Paris, she studied the flute with a member of the Paris Conservatory Orchestra. On a speaking trip to Hawaii she was so overwhelmed by the incredible beauty of the islands that she returned to spend many months and to do the research that was the basis for one of her most powerful books, *Backbone of the King,* a retelling of a great Hawaiian hero legend.

In the late 1960s Marcia gave up her long-time residence in New York City and moved to a small town in southeastern Connecticut. For the first time she was able to design and build a studio to fit her needs. It is a large room with a balcony at one end, a high ceiling with two skylights, and areas for doing painting, woodcuts, drawing, photography, sewing, and flute playing. The house is surrounded by hemlocks, and the woods nearby are filled with possums, raccoons, deer, squirrels, and birds. Not far from her property is the small river that provided the inspiration and the evocative winter photographs for her only filmstrip, *The Crystal Cavern,* published by Lyceum Productions in 1974. The plants, trees, wildflowers, and animals—and the changing seasons—are a constant source of stimulus and delight. Her greatest problem is finding time for all the interests she wants to pursue at home and also for going to New York to attend operas, ballets, concerts, and museums—and for traveling.

Most days, Marcia gets up early and spends some time reading while she has her breakfast. Just now, she is interested in the recently published book about a journey through the byways of America, *Blue Highways,* by William Least Heat Moon (Atlantic-Little). She finds many of the conversations the author had with residents of small, out-of-the-way villages the stuff of living folklore. Later, she might go to her studio and practice Chinese brush painting, a technique which first interested her in 1977 and which she began to study seriously, with a teacher, two years ago. Her paintings of lotuses, bamboo, plum blossoms, birds, and dramatic landscapes fill the walls of her living room and studio. She has begun to exhibit, along with other artists practicing the technique, and has sold several paintings.

If she has a sewing project, as she often does, Marcia will spend time on the studio balcony, where she has set up a sewing area. And each day, she faithfully practices her flute. She feels very fortunate to be studying with John Solum, a much-esteemed concert flutist, who lives in a nearby town. When she sews or paints, or works on illustrations, there is always music—as necessary to her as food. Her love of music and the dance and her deep understanding of them perhaps account, in part, for the grace, rhythm, and strength of her writing and illustration. Most certainly they are profound influences. Because her work requires solitude and long stretches of concentration, she often does not see as much of her friends as she would like to, but she accepts this fact as a price that must be paid.

Marcia Brown's books have unquestionably stood the test of time. Nearly all of them are still in print—a certain proof of their enduring hold on generations of children. Never has Marcia been interested in passing fashions in children's book illustration. She has worked in many media but not for the sake of variety; rather, she has always let the story and her feeling for it determine the medium and the style. Her particular vision and her uncompromising integrity have been rewarded in the past: two Caldecott Medals (for *Cinderella* in 1955 and for *Once a Mouse...* in 1962), six Caldecott Honor Books, two nominations for the Hans Christian Andersen Award, the University of Southern Mississippi Medallion for Distinguished Service to Children's Literature, and the Regina Medal. Now, after so many years of creating memorable children's books, Marcia stands in a unique position—one abundantly deserved. It is gratifying that the children's librarians of America, the dedicated people who bring children and books together, have honored her in so special a way.

The Caldecott Medal 1984

THE GLORIOUS FLIGHT: ACROSS THE CHANNEL WITH LOUIS BLÉRIOT JULY 25, 1909

written and illustrated by ALICE AND MARTIN PROVENSEN

published by THE VIKING PRESS 1983

BOOK NOTE

Louis Blériot, father of a large and charming family, is so inspired by the sound and sight of an airship flying over his city of Cambrai in France that, first, he drives his car into a cart full of pumpkins and cabbages and, second, he decides to build his own flying machine. His Blériots I, II, III, and IV do not rise off the ground, but V hops up; VI sails across a field, and Blériot VII actually takes to the air. An Englishman offers a great prize to the first man to fly across the English Channel, and as Blériot now has spent six years working up to his eleventh model, he is ready to accept the challenge in his Blériot XI. On July 25, 1909, he takes off alone in his airplane, and thirty-seven minutes later he lands in England—a glorious flight.

Full-color double-page spreads give adequate space to both men and machines. While the machines are technically correct in appearance, they are painted as charming objects in a style that blends with the interesting groupings of people against the French backgrounds. The Provensens have been interested in the history of flight for some time, and Martin Provensen is a pilot. The art was prepared in acrylic paints and pen and ink.

Caldecott Medal Acceptance
by Alice and Martin Provensen

While we were growing up during the years of the Great Depression, our families moved from town to town all over America. We would stay a year or two or three and then move on. The one constant which we both discovered by some rare good fortune was the library. That there were libraries with things about them that did not change, no matter where they were—Chicago, New York, Minneapolis, Boston, Washington, wherever—was a great comfort.

The clear light, the big tables, the books with their smell of paper and glue, the secret stacks like an Aladdin's cave full of gold, and the quiet, gentle librarians made the library a reassuring and inviting place.

Separately, we learned to find our way about the shelves and to discover the treasures there—P. G. Wodehouse (all forty volumes), Gene Stratton Porter and the magic of the Limberlost, the travel books—Richard Halliburton, Carl Akeley, Osa and Martin Johnson. We discovered the adventure stories of Rafael Sabatini and Talbot Mundy and Percival Christopher Wren. And we discovered the books in the art section. In those days art books had few color plates, but how hungrily we stared at those there were!

No matter where we moved or how often, the libraries were safe havens for us. We must have spent hundreds of hours during our childhood within their walls. In the course of growing up, our paths must have crossed many times—in Chicago, in Los Angeles, in school, in Museums—but we did not meet until we were both working in the same animation studio during the Second World War. Now we often wonder if we couldn't have been sitting across from one another at one of those library tables so long ago.

Since books and libraries are very much a part of both of our lives, it is not perhaps so surprising that the similar experiences we had in our youth led us to find a common profession. The question we are most often asked is, "How do you work together?" Everyone asks this of us because the stereotyped image of an artist is that of a lonely, starving figure working in a garret.

People have forgotten that the first book illustrators, the illuminators of the Middle Ages, worked in concert—one to paint the flowers, another to paint the figures, still another to do the background and the text. All through the Renaissance, artists' studios were little factories. The masters and their apprentices turned out marriage chests or murals, altar pieces or portraits, supplying the demand.

In any kind of work there is a great sense of support in having someone beside you whose skill and judgment you trust. It is true of bookmaking. There are so many decisions to be made—the page size, the choice of type, the paper, and the fitting of the pictures to the text. *We* start with the words. The story sets the style. No matter how fine the illustrations, unless they enhance the text, they fail. And we have had our failures. They are painful but valuable. Nothing teaches one so well as a mistake.

Little by little we learned something of the art of bookmaking—how to design not just a page but a whole book so it moves, so it is a unity. Our work in the animation studios taught us the concept of flow, linking one picture to another.

During our years at Golden Press, Pierre Martinot and Martin Connell and Frank Metz taught us the mechanics of signatures, binding, typography, and color separation. Later there were the designers, Grace Clark and Barbara Hennessy, who with enormous patience were able to translate our first roughs into feasible, affordable formats—teaching us the art of the possible.

There was and is so much to learn. The balance of light and dark in relation to type, all the complications and delights of color, the agony of the first printed proofs. It has taken us years of practicing the art even to begin to understand its complexity.

Making books for children is one of the very few areas left where old ways of working still apply. You have time to plan, to discard, to choose between alternatives, to explore possible solutions. Time, for artists of our temperament, is a necessity.

Although we admire the incredibly accomplished technique that is used in some book illustration, we do not try for too much polish, too facile a style. We like pictures that are a little clumsy, a little rough and lacking in finish. Children's drawings seem to us to be marvelous. If only we could draw like that!

We draw and paint to express our joy and excitement in life

and to communicate our feelings to children in the most direct and effective way. This is the essential problem for us—to find the right, the inevitable, pictures and words that say what we want to say. But illustrating a book involves two things that do not always go together. To keep the flatness of the page and the abstract design (without which the book falls apart) and at the same time to illustrate the story line are the primary considerations. It is exciting to try to find a new solution for each new book.

The mechanics of bookmaking can be taught and learned, but we believe that children's book writers and illustrators are born, not made. First, there must be a great drive, a need to draw and write for children—for the child in oneself. This is not the part of bookmaking one can learn; it is something one must have.

Too, there is something odd about spending your whole life in front of a piece of paper. Perhaps it is because of this oddness that most artists have an impulse toward working in secret, almost as if there were something subversive in the act of drawing and painting an image. The painter Degas said he painted a picture "in the same spirit as a criminal committing a crime." Given then these difficulties and strangenesses, it is easy to wonder at the ability of artists, especially husbands and wives, to work together.

The early artisans and architects, illuminators and scribes are, by and large, anonymous. It was the work that counted, not the personality of its maker. It is still the work that counts, and some artists have always found a way to join their individual styles and skills. Georges Braque, writing of the first days of cubism, said that he and Picasso "were roped together like mountain climbers to try and scale the peaks before us." To make a children's book may be a smaller mountain, but for us each new book is a new challenge. The form, the style, the spirit of one particular unique book must have something that touches our inner selves—that in some small way speaks for us both. Otherwise, no matter how fine the artwork, no matter how clever the writing, it is just another book.

For us *The Glorious Flight* is not just another book.

Our fascination with airplanes and the magic of flight began with the flying circuses performed above dusty fields on the outskirts of the midwestern cities where we lived. Martin learned to fly, not too many years ago, at an airfield famous for its fleet of

World War I aircraft, an experience which served to intensify our interest in early planes.

In telling the story of Louis Blériot and the first flight across the English Channel in a powered aircraft, we wanted to capture for children some of the incredible daring of the first days of flying when men in fragile boxes made of sticks and wire and linen lurched off cow pastures all over the world. They did not last long, those good old days. Men learned very fast. By 1914 quite efficient airplanes were gearing up for the war to be fought in the air. But there were a brief few years from about 1900 to 1910 when the amateur aviators and aircraft designers reigned supreme. The Wright brothers, Wilbur and Orville, were in the vanguard. At Kitty Hawk in 1903 they successfully flew the first powered airplane for a flight of eight hundred fifty-two feet in fifty-nine seconds. We know their glory.

The man who flew the English Channel in 1909, Louis Blériot, is not well known to Americans. He was a lovable, wonderful man as well as one of the great pioneers of aviation. Unskilled as a pilot, untutored as a designer (there were no teachers), he had to learn in the air. He was incredibly brave and enormously ingenious. His contraptions flapped, skipped, and sailed ponderously into that new element—the sky. If we caught just a flash of that great moment in our book about Papa Blériot, we consider ourselves lucky.

It has been suggested by some reviewers that *The Glorious Flight* has a message—"If at first you don't succeed, try, try again." This moral may be inherent in our story, but it was not a conscious intention. Rather, we wanted to write the story of a man with a passionate obsession to create something new, the successes and failures in his work toward that goal, and the moment of triumph that rewarded him.

For us, making new children's books is equally obsessive, and being here tonight is certainly one of those satisfying moments. We thank our publisher, Viking-Penguin, and our editors, Linda Zuckerman and Regina Hayes, for their encouragement and unfailing support.

And to the American Library Association for the great honor they have done us by awarding the Caldecott Medal to *The Glorious Flight,* thank you.

BIOGRAPHICAL NOTE

Alice and Martin Provensen
by Nancy Willard

Of all my visits to the Provensens' farm, there is one I shall never forget. My husband, my son, and I, along with Barbara Lucas, the editor of *A Visit to William Blake's Inn* (Harcourt), spent a delightful afternoon with Alice and Martin, who deserve a gold medal for their hospitality. It was high summer; goldenrod and Queen Anne's lace nodded on both sides of the road leading to the house. The pond gleamed like a bright carpet spread in the meadow where a horse browsed and several geese stood about, waiting to be admired.

We admired them. We gathered for lunch in the kitchen decorated with prints and engravings from old chapbooks which reminded me of my favorite pages in the Provensens' *Mother Goose Book* (Random). On a chair slept the cat who that very morning had presented Alice with a dead mouse. If I ever arrive at the Valley of Love and Delight praised in that lovely Shaker hymn "The Gift To Be Simple," I am sure it will be very much like an afternoon spent with Alice and Martin; it will be blessed with the humor and the harmony of these two artists, who this year have celebrated their fortieth wedding anniversary and the Caldecott Medal for the fifty-fourth book they have made together.

After lunch we followed Alice into the library, and she shared with us some of the rare books she had bound on her press: a three-volume edition of Leonardo da Vinci's notebooks and a book on falconry whose marvelous beasts move from page to page on a single line, much like the pages of *A Peaceable Kingdom: The Shaker Abecedarius* (Viking). The press, she explained, was in the studio. At the mention of the studio, we all looked eager, and Martin smiled: Would we like to visit the studio?

The barn holds the studio, the guest room, and the henhouse (entered by a ramp on which Martin has nailed rungs for the convenience of small tenants). Light from the skylight fell on the worktable and on a model Piper Cub in one corner. The walls were covered with an extraordinary number of sketches. Suddenly, Martin exclaimed, "Don't look! They're from a new book we're making!" I think none of us looked. He did divulge one secret, however. The new book had something to do with flying. Such was our introduction to *The Glorious Flight: Across the Channel with Louis Blériot* (Viking), which was awarded the 1984 Caldecott Medal.

Recently, I asked some students to tell me their favorite Provensen books. The class came up with nearly a dozen titles, including the first book, *Fireside Book of Folk Songs* (Simon) published in 1947 and still in print. They have illustrated art books, cookbooks, alphabet books, and the classics—for example, *The Illiad and The Odyssey* (Simon), *The Golden Treasury of Myths and Legends* (Golden Press), *Shakespeare: Ten Great Plays* (Golden Press), *Aesop's Fables* (Golden Press), *The Provensen Book of Fairy Tales* (Random). They have also brought thousands of children to the farm through the books inspired by it: *Our Animal Friends at Maple Hill Farm; The Book of Seasons* (both Random); *The Year at Maple Hill Farm; A Horse and a Hound, A Goat and a Gander; An Owl and Three Pussycats* (all Atheneum). Eight of their books have been included in *The New York Times* list "Best Illustrated Children's Books of the Year." For *Myths and Legends,* they received the Gold Medal of the Society of Illustrators. For *A Visit to William Blake's Inn,* a Caldecott Honor Book, they won the 1982 Boston Globe–Horn Book Award for illustration. I'm sure that when *The Glorious Flight: Across the Channel with Louis Blériot* was announced as the winner of the Caldecott, a great many people heaved a sigh of relief and said, "It's about time."

Quite as wonderful as their work is the way they work together—the remarkable rapport, the seamless blending of two imaginations. They make it sound easy.

We have been working together for so long that it has ceased to be a question of who does what. In any given finished illustration one of us may have done the first sketch, the other may have painted what we hoped was to have been a finished picture. It almost always has to be done over several times; we pass it back and forth between us until we are both satisfied. It is a happy collaboration. If one sometimes reaches a degree of frustration, there is a certain joy in giving up and saying, "Here, you do this one."

I remember with amusement a different kind of collaboration: the time a horse came down with a foot disease and Alice read Martin a whole book about life in China while he applied compresses every four hours to the horse's leg. "The animals we have drawn and written about, with one exception, we have now or have had over thirty years," Martin told me. "We've never had a cow; we brought in cows from the neighbors. That's poetic license. Most children adore animals, and some adults never outgrow this passion. I think we fit into that category, as you can see by the way we live." The way they live. One day a friend came to visit, and when he arrived, he found Martin bathing a sick rooster's foot. "The rooster was standing very quietly with one leg in the pail of solution. And our friend was astonished. Was this some religious rite—or what?"

Who can forget the names of those animals? Evil Murdoch, Potato Who Disappeared, Eggnog, Willow. The namer of beasts is Karen, the Provensens' daughter, now twenty-five and working as a music therapist in a California high school. She is her parents' strictest and most compassionate critic. "She made us aware of children's relationships to books, not as toys, not as teachers, but as something more special—as friends to hold, to cherish, to escape to, and to enjoy."

Henry James might have been describing the Provensens when he remarked, "Write from experience and experience only. Try to be one of the people on whom nothing is lost." Their experience includes past and present, near and far. They travel a great deal, and their sketchbooks travel with them. It is from these voluminous records that they draw material for books requiring settings that are foreign or historical or fanciful. They have traveled a long way since their first jobs at Walt Disney's studio, Alice working as an animator and Martin in the story department. "It was ideal training for book illustration," Martin has observed. "You'd be given a sequence, the barest outline, just a thread of narrative, and then it was up to you to invent. That was delightful. You could take it and play with it."

Their playfulness and inventiveness would have delighted the subject of their next book, Leonardo da Vinci, with whom they share a passion for matters of flight. *The Glorious Flight* was inspired partly by the Rhinebeck Aerodrome with its weekend demonstrations of early airplanes. Martin himself learned to fly; his instructor has a Blériot XI, the type of plane that flew the channel in 1909.

Flight and fables, music and myths, colors and cookbooks, seasons and animals; reading the Provensens, I come away richer and wiser.

"Animals are for me—and I think for Alice, too—wonderful guides to the unknown. And such wonderful guides they are! Wasn't it Einstein who said that the mysterious is the most wonderful thing a human being can know?"

Alice and Martin Provensen are guides to both the known and the unknown. And wonderful guides they are.

The Caldecott Medal 1985

SAINT GEORGE AND THE DRAGON

illustrated by TRINA SCHART HYMAN

retold by MARGARET HODGES

published by LITTLE, BROWN AND COMPANY 1984

BOOK NOTE

The princess Una has found a champion, the Red Cross Knight, who will fight the terrible dragon that has beset her father's kingdom. There are perils on the journey, and the knight, glimpsing the glorious High City from afar, wishes to go there. But he owes six years of service to the Fairy Queen, and he must first do brave deeds, such as killing dragons, for her. He meets the ferocious dragon and attacks again and again until the dragon throws him to the ground in flames. He falls into a spring of cool water and in the morning rises to challenge the dragon once more; he wounds the dragon, but again the monster casts him down in scorching flames. The Red Cross Knight falls under an apple tree which releases a healing dew, and in the morning he is able to rise again. This time he slays the dragon. The king opens the gates of the castle, and the king, the queen, men, women, and children come to celebrate and to praise Una and the Red Cross Knight. The gifts of riches the dragon slayer receives, he gives to the poor, but he marries Una, and even though he knows he will inherit the kingdom, he does not forget his promise to serve the Fairy Queen with good deeds. Thus he becomes known as Saint George. The author has adpated her retelling of the legend of Saint George and the dragon from Edmund Spenser's *Faerie Queene*.

    The full-color illustrations are set into frames that are repeated as borders for the pages of text. These borders are filled with decorative detail, such as flowers native to England, and with vignettes of action in the text, interwoven with unicorns, fairies,

Caldecott Medal Acceptance
by Trina Schart Hyman

I have waited a long time for this moment—ten years, to be exact. And now, I am so happy to be able to take this wonderful opportunity to tell all of you how deeply sorry I am and how much I regret the carving on the witches' table and the inscription on the tombstone. Not because I didn't mean every line of them—but simply because I'm sick to death of being asked to explain and apologize. Gotcha!

It has occurred to me, in a few weak moments since January fourth, that one of the reasons *Saint George and the Dragon* may have been selected for the Caldecott Medal is that it's the cleanest, most innocent, least likely-to-offend book I've ever illustrated. And if that's so—well, it wasn't my fault! I just draw what the story tells me to draw; this one happened to be pure in heart; that's all. Although once you've established a reputation, it seems to follow you around. Shortly after *Saint George* was published my friend Cyndy Szekeres called me up and said, "Oh, Trina, you devil dog, you! How sneaky and clever you were to make that apple tree a sexy naked woman reaching out for George!"

"What are you talking about, Cyndy? *What* naked woman?!"

"Come *on,* Trina! The *apple* tree!—you know—the one George is sleeping under! It's a nude woman, upside down! Terrific!"

Well, that apple tree on page twenty-two happens to live in my back yard, and if there's a naked lady in it, *I* never knew she was there. But when I hung up the phone, I realized that I was already mentally composing a letter of explanation and apology to answer the flood of outraged letters from parents and teachers and the Dallas Public Library. Happily, Cyndy is the only one who has ever seen the naked lady. And don't ask me to point it out to you, because I still can't see it!

I know what she means, though. One of the nicest things about being an artist is the ability to see things a little differently, a little more carefully, perhaps a little more imaginatively, than most other people do. To be able to see the possibilities in things; to see the magic in them, to see what it is that makes that thing inherently itself. And then, sometimes, to go beyond the surface of the thing and see what it is that the thing wishes to become: the cities that live in clouds, the landscapes that become sleeping bodies, the human face that becomes an animal, the tree that becomes a woman.

When I was a child, it was easy for me to see these transformations—the hidden souls of everyday things. At any moment the sky could produce a long-lost fairy-tale city; a chair would leer at me with the face of a demon; a leaf turned into an insect and hopped away; my sister turned to look at me with the face of a cat; or an apple tree changed, with the light, into a beautiful woman. It never occurred to me to disbelieve anything that I read in Grimms' fairy tales or in the Greek and Norse myths that I loved so much. It was quite clear to me that everything in the world was under a spell of enchantment, and that the most ordinary objects had secret lives of their own. Everything—the wind, the trees, coffee cups, toothbrushes—had a soul, a spirit. It therefore seemed the most natural and believable thing in the world that stones and birds should speak or that a frog should turn into a prince. My mother and father never discouraged this point of view—as a matter of fact I think they were rather tickled by what they called my "vivid imagination," and they had the good sense to take my fantasies in stride. If I mentioned that there was an angel on the roof, my father would agree that there probably had been. The year I became Little Red Riding Hood, my mother sewed me a very beautiful little red cape with a hood and usually remembered to call me Little Red Riding Hood rather than Trina. When I had to get a vaccination at the doctor's and was about to throw a fit at the sight of the needle, my mother told me not to worry—it was just like Sleeping Beauty being pricked by the spindle. And so I calmly took the shot in the arm and then proceeded to fall into a deep sleep that lasted for a hundred years.

We believed in fairies in my family. We believed in the power and magic and mystery that exists in nature, anyway. After all, if angels are living in the heavens, why shouldn't fairies be hidden in the forest or trolls in the earth? It is easy to see these things once you know they are there. And for me it has always been easier to draw a picture of what I've seen rather than to try to explain it with words. I drew a lot—I think I was born drawing. I drew because I needed to as well as for the sheer joy of it. And because I loved to draw—because I was an artist—I learned to look very carefully at things. I learned to watch closely and to remember what I had seen. I learned to look for those things that were hiding or waiting to emerge as well as at the outward appearances of things.

Of course, when you go to school, they do their best to knock it all out of you. Most of the grown-up world, it seems, is in a conspiracy to teach us to disbelieve in the magic we see so easily as a child—to deny the existence of those powerful images we see with our hearts rather than with our minds. So school was an unhappy and difficult time for me. A socially backward kid whose only attributes are a "vivid imagination" and a need to draw pictures all day long was not exactly appreciated in the public school system of Cheltenham Township, Pennsylvania. I was a further pain in the neck because in first grade I preferred reading Edith Hamilton's *Mythology* to following the fascinating saga of Dick and Jane and Spot, line by bumbling line. No one had ever told my parents that it wasn't cool to teach your kid to read books at a decidedly preschool age, and I was made to suffer in subtle ways for their innocent mistake. However, I was stubborn, and I was tough with the peculiar kind of toughness that timid children learn to develop. And the Brothers Grimm were strong—stronger than Dick and Jane, and stronger than my grade-school teachers.

Eventually, I learned to shut up about the angels and to do my real drawings at home, where they wouldn't be subjected to embarrassing questions. I learned to survive, and the fairies and angels survived with me. I have to look a little harder for them now, but I know they are still there because they have always been there. And one very good thing came out of those school years when I was a stranger in a strange land. It was always very clear to me—and to everyone else, too—exactly what I would do when I grew up. I would be an artist, and I would be the sort of artist who made pictures that told stories. It wasn't until the seventh grade that I learned about the word *illustrator,* but when I heard it, I knew that that was me.

I can't say that I've never wavered from that chosen course. I've always secretly wanted to be a ballet dancer, and once I wanted to be an organist. More realistically, I've always longed to be the sort of artist who simply paints pictures—big, mysterious, grown-up paintings on canvas—with oil paint. But I can't. I can't because there are too many stories in the world, too many books waiting to be illustrated, and not enough time to illustrate them all or to learn how to do it well enough. Besides, I have this consuming, fatal passion for books—the books themselves, the way they look and smell, the feel of them, and of course the stories that they have to tell. When I'm upset or depressed or unhappy, I go to a bookstore for comfort, the way other people go to a church or to a therapist. Books and illustrations are a part of me: They're not just what I do; they're what I *am*.

Twenty-five years ago, when I was just starting out as a children's book illustrator, I used to trot across the Boston Common at least once a month with my portfolio to show my latest efforts to Helen Jones, the children's book editor at Little, Brown and Company. Helen Jones was a tough, clear-eyed, no-nonsense Yankee lady. She was a feminist before we had even started using the word. She was smart, opinionated, had a wicked sense of humor, and did not suffer fools gladly. She cared deeply about children's books and knew everything there was to know about publishing them. I was terrified of her, and I fell in love with her at first sight. I badgered her with my portfolio until she finally gave me a book to do—a collection of Christmas stories and poems by Ruth Sawyer called *Joy to the World*. It was the start of a long—and for me tremendously enriching—and happy association. It was Helen who gave me my first book of fairy tales to illustrate and who was brave enough to publish a story I'd written called *How Six Found Christmas*. She gave me the chance to try my hand at illustrating every sort of children's book—picture books, young adult novels, mystery stories, folk tales. She also initiated me into the terrors of speaking before large groups of people. At Helen's insistence the first time I agreed to speak—and draw—was to a group of over one thousand grade-school children in John Hancock Hall in Boston. I guess she figured if I could survive that, I could speak anywhere! She took me to my first ALA convention and my first Newbery-Caldecott Awards dinner in 1964. She taught me almost everything I know about how children's books are made—how they are produced, marketed, and sold.

When Helen Jones died in 1973, I had one page left to do on a book I had begun at her suggestion. That book was *King Stork* by Howard Pyle. I finished the job, and then I fell apart. I honestly did not know how I was going to continue my work without her guidance and support. But I did, of course—I did because I had to and because she would have been furious with me if I hadn't. The subsequent books that I did for Little, Brown under Emilie McLeod and John Keller were *Snow White* and *Sleeping Beauty*—the kind of lavish picture-book fairy tales that Helen might have trusted me with by then if she had been alive. After that, my association with Little, Brown became sporadic. Things there had changed, as they were changing everywhere. I began working with various other publishers; I was involved with *Cricket* magazine and going through several interesting life crises, both personal and professional. During one of the most severe and frightening of these professional life crises, it was Kate and John Briggs and Holiday House who picked me up, dusted me off, and set me back on my feet again. It was they who helped me renew my faith in myself as an illustrator. It was they who suggested that I take the plunge and do that autobiographical picture book—*Little Red Riding Hood.* At that point I was even beginning to notice the fairies again.

Then, one day in the spring of 1983 I got a call from an assistant editor at Little, Brown and Company named Karen Klockner. They had a manuscript by Margaret Hodges—a retelling of "Saint George and the Dragon." Would I be interested in illustrating it? Well, sure—I would take a look at it. And from that first look I was hooked. Wow! It was good. It was better than good; it was extraordinary. "Okay, Helen," I muttered. "I'll do it." Later on that summer, I got another phone call—this time from Margaret Hodges. She and her husband were just off to England for a month—would it be possible for them to come to Lyme on their way back to meet me and talk about the book?

Now, there is an old, unwritten, but very sensible rule in children's book publishing that says you must never let the author and illustrator meet, at least not until after the book is on its way to the printer. It's a good rule because authors and illustrators almost never agree on how a book should be illustrated and, besides, they usually hate each other on first sight anyway. But I wanted to meet Margaret Hodges. I wanted to meet the woman who had crafted this extraordinaty bit of prose, and I knew that I also needed her help. I had lots of questions about *Saint George and the Dragon*—the most important one being, what period of history should I set this story in? As usual, with any book that has even the vaguest historical reference, there are piles of reference work to do because you've got to be careful about particulars. And in this instance we had Edmund Spenser, who was an Elizabethan, to deal with as well as George himself, whom nobody can seem to pin down to a particular period, never mind agree that he existed at all. So I told Margaret Hodges that I would be delighted to meet her and her husband and to please look for any kind of visual reference material on George that I could use for the book.

A month later, when I saw Margaret and Fletcher Hodges walking up my driveway, something magical happened to the landscape. I swear that the light changed. The trees became enchanted princesses; the clouds became castles; and the fairies came out of the flowers. It was a case of love at first sight, again. You can see this scene for yourselves on the back of the jacket for *Saint George*.

We decided during lunch to put our George in his own, vague, pre-Arthurian time, and not in Mr. Spenser's Elizabethan period. We decided that perhaps I could use Spenser's bits about the little sailors and their voyage to bring in something Elizabethan. Or that maybe I should make a parallel to the main story in the borders of the pages, using Elizabethan children doing a George and the Dragon Mummers' play. I had already decided to make this book my own version of an illuminated manuscript, with decorative, lavishly illustrated page borders. Amazingly, it turned out that we agreed completely on how this book should look. In other words Margaret said, "You do exactly what you think is best, Trina, and I'll like it!" Wonder of wonders! We spent the rest of the afternoon talking about fairies—Margaret believes in them, too. Fletcher and my friend Barbara talked about books. New friends, new beginnings, and an exciting new book to work on! Life can be kind.

Later on that summer there was a conference with Karen Klockner and Bob Lowe. Bob has been the art director for children's books at Little, Brown for as long as I have been doing books for them. We are the only two left who remember how it was in the old days with Helen Jones. While Helen was teaching me how to be an illustrator, Bob was teaching me how to talk to printers. It was good to be working with him again.

It was also good to work with Karen, who looks like a fairy-tale princess and who instantly displayed the qualities I admire most in an editor—the sensitivity and intelligence to leave me alone with the job and the confidence to say, "Call me if you need me."

To be left alone with the job is very important to me. I came into this world alone, and I'll go out of it alone, and each book I do is the same kind of birth and maybe the same kind of death, on a smaller scale. I don't do sketches, or preliminaries. I think about it, instead. I think about the story and about what it means and about how it can be brought to life in pictures. I think about the characters and what makes them tick and where they're coming from and where they might be going to. Who *are* these people? What do they like to eat for breakfast? How do they react in a situation that's *outside* this story? What are they *really* thinking while this story is happening to them? I think about the landscape. Where is this taking place? What time of year is it? What was the weather like? Was the sky in the fourth century the same as the sky we see now? Obviously, it wasn't. What was it like, then? Were the stars brighter, the light more pure, the colors clearer? What was this dragon like? *Were* there dragons? Of course there were. They still exist somewhere, I bet. So, what did he look like? What did *he* eat for breakfast?

I think about all this a lot. I think about it so much that eventually I start to dream about it. And when my dreams start to become the dreams of the characters in the book, when their reality becomes a part of my subconscious, when I can live in their landscape, when I put on the little red cape with a hood and tie the red ribbons under my chin, then I know what to do with my pictures.

When I'm halfway into a book, the people who know and love me best always say things like, "You haven't been *listening* to me.

I told you last week that the oil burner sounded weird!" Or, "What do you mean, you're not coming to my fiftieth birthday party! I told you about it months ago!" Or, "Hey, Trina, the bugs are only four months late. I'm going to shoot myself tomorrow, in case you're interested!" Or, "*Trina!* I *told* you about this person! He's very important to me! Where have you *been*?" Well, I've been in the book. That's where I live now, and it's hard for me to come out of it. I know that there's another world out there, going on about its business, but *my* world is right here with George and his valiant old horse and Una and the dwarf and the lamb and the donkey. And, wow! The dragon is right there, waiting for them! Hey, I know you can't hear it or see it or smell it or feel it the way I can, but wait for it! Wait a few days and I'll show you. I'll help you to see it the way it really happened!

Look. There are the fairies: They're listening, waiting. Fairies always know how the story will turn out. They stole George when he was a tiny baby. His mom left him in a field, just the way some moms today leave their babies in the car when they're shopping in the supermarket. So the fairies took him, and the fairy queen brought him up to be a warrior—strong and clean-limbed and pure-hearted and totally committed. And then she turned him free and said, "Go for it."

At just about the same time, here comes Una, looking for a hero to kill the dragon that's been destroying her father's kingdom. She's a very strong, self-confident, independent young woman. My research into fourth-century England told me that women were brought up that way. They hadn't invented the word *feminist* then, but they didn't have to. Women were expected to be self-sufficient and strong. Who else was going to run the kingdom when Daddy and Big Brother and the rest of the men-folk were off fighting wars? We haven't come such a long way, baby.

Una travels with the dwarf. I figured he was probably the household astrologer: a servant and at the same time a wise and learned man. Maybe he is a Jew or an Armenian or an Arab. Someone who was a cripple—an outsider: an observer, a visionary who was left behind by the Romans because he was too embarrassing or too clever to be taken back to Rome as a slave. I think that Una's mother, the queen, asked him to go along on this journey—to look after Una and, more important, to bring back a true report of what happened. She knows that Una is a dedicated and save-the-world idealist; but she also knows about sixteen-year-old girls. Una takes her pet lamb along, too—obviously for symbolic reasons. I guessed that she started out on her journey as soon as the roads were passable—maybe sometime in March. It took her about three months to reach the west coast of England to meet George just as he is riding out into the world for the first time. He is wearing a suit of chain mail that the fairies fashioned for him and a breastplate of cast-off Roman armor. He is bearing the sword that men will call Excalibur in some future time. His shield comes from the grave of an ancient hero and bears the symbol that the flag of England is based upon—the red cross.

The fairies are watching them. They know the beginning and the end of this story, but they're curious anyhow, which is one of the best things about fairies. They also know that they are at this time engaged in their own great and perhaps final battle with the angels of the new religion. The angels of Christianity are taking over in the battle for people's hearts and minds. So the fairies have sent their own changeling, their sweetest, most powerful hero, to do the dragon job—who will succeed in his quest and be called forever a saint on the Christian calendar.

It is one of the fairies' last, greatest jokes on the world. But Una and George know nothing about this and neither does the dragon. What is the dragon thinking through all this?

The dragon isn't evil or wicked. He isn't anything but an animal. What he's thinking about most is food and maybe a little stalking and hunting, and then he just wants to be left alone. Maybe he's irritable because he hasn't found a female dragon to mate with in the past hundred years or so. Who knows? The dragon is a nuisance, and he's terrifying, like most of the primal forces in nature, and so he has to die.

Every morning, unless the temperature is lower than ten degrees below zero, I take the same two-mile walk with the dogs. We go down to the river and then past Bernard Tullar's farm and back up the hill to our own road and then home. The landscape of our upper Connecticut River Valley is very like the west country of England and Wales—all sharp little grassy hills and wooded valleys and rocky fields. One misty morning in March, when I was taking this walk and thinking about what the dragon was thinking, I heard him coming towards me, across Bernard's cow pasture. I heard him first, like the sound of distant thunder, and then I saw him—I saw the huge shape of the dragon appear on the crest of the hill. And before I even had the chance to be frightened, he was gone.

A few days later, I got to the page where George kills the dragon. As I usually do, I read the text on that page over again for the thirty-seventh time, and then I read it five more times, just to make sure I'd got it right. And then I realized I couldn't do it. I often say "I can't do it" when all I really mean is that this is going to be very difficult. But this was different. How on earth was I going to show George—somehow having got between the dragon's huge jaws, stabbing his sword up through the roof of the monster's mouth and piercing his brain? Do you know what this would *look* like, *really*? Can you imagine the blood, the ghastliness, the *violence* of that scene. You think the carving on the witches' table was bad? I was horrified at the thought of what I had to do, and worse than that, I was stymied. I paced the floor for an hour, and then I made a desperate, unprecedented decision. I called Margaret Hodges. This was the only time in my entire professional career when I knew I was truly beaten—I had to call the author to ask what I should do. "Margaret, I wonder if you can help me. I'm just about to start on the spread where George kills the dragon, and I can't do it. I mean, I can't draw it. The whole thing is physically impossible, and, besides that, it's disgusting and gross."

"Oh, dear," said Margaret, "I do see what you mean! Well, Trina, why don't you just forget about all that and draw the scene *after* George has killed the dragon. That will be just as dramatic, and maybe it is the best solution."

I love you, Margaret Hodges. You're not just a vivid imagination—you're clever as well! It took me nine months to complete the illustrations for *Saint George and the Dragon*. I learned a lot during those months. I learned about herb-lore and ancient roses and wild flowers, when I decided to decorate my borders with whatever grew in the fields and hedgerows of fourth-century England. I learned that the Romans named England "Alba," for the many wild white roses that grew there. I learned that the ancient Celts and Britons were terrific weavers and dyers and metal-smiths. I learned that the richest and most valued color in those days was red—so I gave my angels red wings. I learned a lot about lizards and dinosaurs and other strange and wonderful reptiles. I learned about pre-Norman conquest sailing craft and pre-Arthurian armor and weapons. I learned that Winston Churchill wrote the best stuff about prehistoric England and that Arthur Rackham drew the best dragons in the world.

I learned that I could give everything I have—all of whatever talent and skill and craft and thought and love and guts and vision I possess to yet another picture book. And that when it was all finished and done with, it still wasn't good enough. I wish I could have done it better. I wish I could have made you *see* the dragon the way I saw him that morning on the hillside. I can see the fairies, but I still haven't learned how to draw them the way they really are. Not yet. Maybe next time. But now it's time to stop and time to say thank you.

Thank you, Mimi, for giving me my first fairy tales and for allowing me to believe in them.

Thank you, Helen Jones. I wish you were here.

Thank you, dear Barbara, for putting up with me through *Saint George,* and all the other books, too. And for taking all those beautiful slides of my pictures.

Thank you, Patricia McMahon, for keeping the dragons at bay.

Thank you, Karen Klockner, for being wise and understanding and sensible and courageous.

Thank you, Bob Lowe, for being there when I needed you, during the work on this book and the seventeen others that came before it. It's been a long time, and it seems that we're both good survivors.

Thank you, Margaret Hodges, for giving me a story so good that even after I'd read the same paragraph four hundred times in a row, the words shone just as pure and clean as if they'd been written with air and fire and stone.

And thank you, librarians and members of the American Library Association for awarding the Caldecott Medal to *Saint George and the Dragon.* You couldn't have given me a nicer surprise.

BIOGRAPHICAL NOTE

Trina Shart Hyman
by Katrin Hyman

When I was six years old, I wanted my mother to be like Laurie Bacon's mother. Laurie Bacon was my best friend, and her mother wore pretty dresses, baked cookies, belonged to the PTA, went to church, and volunteered her time to the first-grade class. My mother wore blue jeans and spent twelve hours a day, seven days a week, behind the drawing board. Trina is a person who works. She doesn't belong to the PTA or the League of Women Voters. She doesn't go to church. She doesn't play tennis; she isn't a serious gardener; she can't fix a car or knit a sweater. She hardly ever goes to the movies.

When I went to the first grade in 1969, I was the only kid in the entire school who was being raised by a single, working mother. And my mother really worked. When she sent me off to school in the morning, she was working; when I came home, she was working; and long after I went to bed at night, she was still at her drawing board. So when I think of Trina, I picture her hunched over her drawing board, a cigarette in one hand and a brush in the other. This image remains an important point of stability for me. It is the foundation on which I was able to grow to adulthood and on which I now build a life of my own.

My mother raised me with the idea that it's not very important what religion people follow or how much money they make or what country they come from. She taught me to value human beings for their humanness, their ability to feel strongly, to work hard, and to care for each other. Her illustrations celebrate these essential qualities that bind us together as a species.

I like Trina's work, in the same way that a lot of people like their mother's cooking. It's so familiar. How could I not like it? It seems to me that Trina's pictures accurately reflect the way she sees the world and the way she has encouraged me to see it. Her drawings show a sense of humor and an attention to detail that is characteristic of the attitude we try to maintain in our household. More important, she likes to draw real people, people who laugh and cry easily, people who have bad habits and good smiles.

Ever since Trina won the Caldecott, people have been calling up to congratulate her, and they always ask me, "Aren't you proud of your mother?" Well, yes. I am proud of her, but certainly not because she won an award. I'm happy for her, and I think it's nice that she's finally receiving this recognition. But I'm proud of Trina for surviving. I'm proud of her for managing to get through the hungry years without compromising herself or her artistic vision. I'm proud of her for having the courage to depict the world the way it really is, for drawing Black people who look like Black people—not like white people with Black skins—princesses who are really sexy, witches who are truly evil.

I'm now able to appreciate the fact that it's just not possible to work twelve hours a day and be the kind of mother who bakes cookies and goes to PTA meetings at the same time. Trina's not a "superwoman." She's an ordinary person who wanted to raise her family and own her home. She did it by taking any job she could get: textbooks, Little Golden Books, dozens of unmemorable children's stories. She nearly went blind from doing color separations. I think she nearly went crazy from a lack of free time, fresh air, and sunshine and from the constant pressure to keep her bills paid and her family intact.

The important thing is that she didn't get sick or become blind or go crazy. Instead, she worked hard and kept on growing as a person and as an artist. I remember my third-grade math textbook, which was illustrated by my mother. There are five cats that have to be matched up with the five balls of yarn. Each of the cats is different—they all have their own, distinct personalities. One of the cats is even winking, as if to say, "I know this is a stupid exercise, but you might as well go ahead and do it." Trina has a lot of conviction. She does the best job she can, whether she is illustrating a math textbook or a Grimm tale, making a bed or helping a friend.

She still works hard, but her twelve-hour days have become eight-hour days unless she is really behind on a deadline. She no longer does color separations, and she can choose her own projects rather than indiscriminately accept any work that comes her way. These days she spends a disproportionate amount of time on the phone talking to editors who call her up just to chat and traveling around the country to give lectures or participate in seminars about children's literature and book illustration. She is a little more fashion-conscious, although she still wears jeans ninety per cent of the time. But the structure of her life remains essentially unchanged.

Trina still lives in the large, falling-apart New Hampshire farmhouse she bought fifteen years ago. She shares the house with me and her best friend, Barbara Rogasky, who is an editor, photographer, and sometime-collaborator with Trina. There are also two dogs and four cats, and we have a herd of sheep we share with our neighbors across the road.

Barbara is the first person to wake up in the morning, usually by about five A.M. Trina and I have the unfortunate habit of waking up at about the same time, at eight o'clock, give or take half an hour. There is often a little struggle about who is going to get the first shower. I usually win.

After she has her shower, Trina puts on her eye make-up (she feels naked without it), gets dressed, and takes the dogs for a two-mile walk. Then she makes herself breakfast, which is invariably a soft-boiled egg, a piece of toast, and seventeen vitamin pills. After she has eaten and done the dishes, she makes a cup of instant coffee and brings it to her drawing board. If the day is a good one, she will have started work by ten o'clock—about the time the phone starts ringing.

Throughout the day there is a constant flow of phone calls, visitors, and minor crises. The sheep get out of their field, start walking down the road, and have to be chased home again. A lady who owns a bookstore in Rhode Island stops by to show Trina a sister-in-law's artwork. The UPS man comes. I call from town because my car has broken down again and I need a ride home. My grandmother calls with the daily weather forecast. The dog gets into a fight with a porcupine and has to have the quills picked out of his nose. Tom, the boy from across the road, comes over to sell us eggs and stays to watch Trina draw. I come downstairs to say "Hi" to Tom and sit for a while, watching Trina draw and describing in minute detail the movie I saw the night before last. Barbara comes downstairs to eat an orange, watch Trina work, and read the newspaper.

Sometimes we talk to each other over dinner, but more often we read. Every evening Trina reads the *Valley News* from front to back. When she is done, she goes back to work. Barbara and I disappear upstairs to read or work or watch television. The dogs and cats fall asleep in a circle around Trina's drawing board. Trina continues to work until, as she puts it, "I can't see any more." She puts down her brush, puts out the dogs, turns off the lights, and goes upstairs to bed with a book.

This day is typical in the life of Trina Schart Hyman. It's a little shorter than it used to be, but her routine hasn't changed very much from when I was growing up. Trina is still chained to her drawing board, though by now the chains are forged as much by habit as by necessity. But "Trina at her drawing board" is hardly an isolated, sterile world. It's the axis about which the life of this entire household revolves. It's a world filled with interesting people, interesting ideas, and perpetual activity.

Somehow, in the midst of all the furor, a number of widely read, well-loved books have been created and sent out into the world. Yet it still surprises me when people say things like, "Your mother is amazing—how does she do it?" I don't know how she does it. As far as I can see she just sits down every day and draws. Of course I know there's more to it, but her technique as an illustrator isn't very important to me. Neither is the final product. What I care about is that she's still there, where I know I can find her, still sitting and drawing. If Trina weren't at her drawing board, where would I bring my bruises to be kissed and made better? Who else wants me to describe the movie I saw the night before last?

The Caldecott Spectrum
by Barbara Bader

In its fifth decade the Caldecott Medal appears as entrenched as ever—a guarantee of optimum sales and eternal shelf-life, a certificate of achievement in the world outside children's books. And perhaps more than ever, it raises questions: Does the term "distinguished" inherently skew the award, toward ostensible importance and outward appearance? In honoring the artist's work alone, is too little notice taken of the book as a whole? From any point of view, there is much to be said for the attempt to give greater visibility to the runners-up, or Honor Books—if only they were fewer in number and the array looked less like proportional representation.

What the winners have in common is obvious enough: With a single exception, the ten under consideration are based on pre-existing, traditional-type material and thus stand forth as bearers of culture—the heritage of the ages or the contributions of folk societies. Four reflect the enthusiasm that sprang up in the Sixties for non-Western, tribal cultures: *Why Mosquitoes Buzz in People's Ears, Ashanti to Zulu, The Girl Who Loved Wild Horses,* and *Shadow.* Two others, *Noah's Ark* and *Saint George and the Dragon,* are straight picturizations of epic tales. *Fables* is in the Aesop-and-after tradition: probably the most conventional work to come from an original, idiosyncratic talent. *Ox-Cart Man* is Americana—and, as rendered, picturesque Americana. *The Glorious Flight* commemorates the early, insouciant days of aviation. That leaves *Jumanji*—not on a lonely peak, exactly, but as the one-in-ten without associations to propel or support it, without an external, validating function.

Much of the artwork is no more original, in its way, than the contents. In this era of wholesale revivalism and decorative plun-

Illustration by LEO AND DIANE DILLON

dering, this is perhaps not to be wondered at. The danger for illustration is the substitution of a manner for a thought-and-felt response, and the production of work that calls attention to itself at the expense of the subject-matter. Derivative or not, a great deal of artwork is in evidence here, inch for inch—buckets of color, masses of shading, heaps of pattern and ornament.

Some of the Honor Books of the period are significantly and hearteningly different. Fresh, authentic, immediate, and imbued

King Lion called the python, who came slithering, wasawusu, wasawusu, past the other animals. "But, King," he cried, "it was the iguana's fault! He wouldn't speak to me. And I thought he was plotting some mischief against me. When I crawled into the rabbit's hole, I was only trying to hide."

The king said to the council:
"So, it was the iguana
who frightened the python,
who scared the rabbit,
who startled the crow,
who alarmed the monkey,
who killed the owlet—
and now Mother Owl won't wake the sun
so that the day can come."

for *Why Mosquitoes Buzz in People's Ears,* retold by Verna Aardema, Dial, 1975, 9⅞ x 9⅞.

with feeling, they repay consideration not as alternatives to particular winners but as alternate ways of creating picture books.

For a look at the attributes that have been reaping top honors, no books are better to begin with than the two by Leo and Diane Dillon that captured the Caldecott in 1976 and 1977, *Why Mosquitoes Buzz in People's Ears* and *Ashanti to Zulu: African Traditions.*

Why Mosquitoes Buzz in People's Ears has a crisp, flavorful text

282 / *Barbara Bader*

by seasoned storyteller Verna Aardema based on a lighthearted cumulative African tale. As executed, the book is a showcase of graphic design and technical finesse. The color is luscious; the filmy air-brushed surfaces are seductive; the composition, in the abstract, is striking. But the pictures are complex, monumental, immobile: a pile-up of motifs, all clamoring for attention.

Without the text, the pictures are indecipherable; even with the text, they have to be puzzled out. When King Lion is reproaching the python for scaring the rabbit (see pp. 280-1), the iguana isn't actually at hand. The python speaks of him, complaining of his silence, his suspicious refusal to speak. If any single motif first catches the eye, it's the iguana, jaws agape—presumably "plotting some mischief," as the python recalls fearing. One can allow that the Dillons wanted to be imaginative, and not illustrate the scene literally; that would also explain why the python, allegedly crying out in self-defense, is pictured mum and glum. But this is literalism, too, of a more rudimentary sort: showing the off-stage reference as if the audience were unable to imagine it without visual aid.

On the next page it's the iguana's turn to appear in person and speak in his own defense. But the fun of his doleful re-entry has been dulled, as much of the nonsense is sapped throughout, by overloading the simple plot-scheme and obscuring the repetitive go-round. Think of successful visualizations of other cumulative tales—Robert McCloskey's *Journey Cake, Ho!* or William Holdsworth's *Little Red Hen,* or such modern classics as *The Five Chinese Brothers* and *Ask Mr. Bear.* In each, the tale is told in terms of the handful of characters, and its spirit is kept intact.

The Dillons' *Ashanti to Zulu,* in turn, derives directly from a species of cultural anthropology: Margaret Musgrove's assemblage of so-called African traditions—actually customs and practices—tribe by tribe. The multiplicity of African tribes, with names that span the alphabet (unto Quimbande, Xhosa, and Zulu), allowed for an ABC of tribes that also has the lineaments of a directory. As an introduction to African people and ways of life, however, the book is little more than a collection of curios, and in some respects misleading. Many of the customs and practices identified with a particular tribe are widespread (as a prefatory note acknowledges). Tribes are not generally identified with the customs and practices characteristic of their ways of life:

M/ Masai (mah·sigh´) men groom their long thick hair with red clay and cow grease. Dozens of tiny neat braids flow over their strong lean shoulders. Pulled and looped into fancy styles, the braids flop heavily when they run or jump. It is Masai custom for the women to shave their heads and wear pounds and pounds of jewelry made of beaded iron and copper wire. They soothe the skin under the heavy wires with special leaves and grease.

Illustration by LEO AND DIANE DILLON
for *Ashanti to Zulu: African Traditions,* written by Margaret Musgrove, Dial, 1976, 10 x 12½.

Illustration by PETER SPIER

Nothing is said, for instance, of the pastoral, nomadic, or warrior traditions of the Masai. (Their renowned stature and bearing, not irrelevant to their dress and body-adornment, also go unnoted.) Neither are the customs and practices, however significant or unusual, explained: "A wealthy Quimbande man," we're simply told, "can have many wives." Polygamy and peer-grouping, Ga stew and Masai hair-styling, are presented on an equal, unstructured basis. If the subject were European peoples, or for that matter Native American tribes, would we ascribe value to such a superficial aggregation of facts?

The illustrations are said by the Dillons to typify the life and milieu of each tribe, and to be accurate in detail "though in some cases [the] different elements would not ordinarily be seen together." To whatever extent this may be true, it is vitiated by the similar appearance of the illustrations overall (see page 283). A

for *Noah's Ark,* Doubleday, 1977, 10⅜ x 8.

golden bronze haze suffuses the paintings, literally and figuratively robbing them of "local color." Lean, statuesque figures, impassive or occasionally grinning, are arranged in symbolic groupings; there is no descriptive or narrative reality. The stylistic effect—along with certain incidental motifs (the ambiguous lion in the Masai example, the unknown birds in the Ndaka picture)—predominates over the specific content.

In its oversize, hard-cover form, the book is certainly imposing. The stately borders, conspicuous framing, and surface-"finish" call to mind the gift books, with tipped-in plates, of early four-color process reproduction. It may be felt that gilt-edged packaging confers dignity, even majesty, on the African peoples represented; but a hard look at African art, now on display in museums from Brooklyn to Seattle, will reveal a strength and majesty that come from within the art itself.

Illustration by DAVID MACAULAY

Peter Spier's sketchy lines, gentle washes, and disheveled air contrast pleasingly with the Dillons' polished artifice. Unfortunately, the easy manner appropriate for *A Fox Went Out on a Chilly Night* is not up to the challenge of Noah's Ark, subject of his 1978 Caldecott winner.

The Biblical tale of Noah and family setting afloat with a

The drawbridge connected the castle to the end of a twenty-five-foot-high stone ramp. Anyone wishing to enter the castle would have to climb the ramp and then be exposed to attack by the soldiers along the walls.

The postern gatehouse was also finished at this time and it too had a drawbridge.

for *Castle,* written by David Macaulay, Houghton, 1977, 9 x 12.

paired-up menagerie lends itself naturally to humorous embellishment and provides episodes of high drama. E. Boyd Smith did it to an anecdotal turn, missing no detail of animal or human behavior. In the outstanding latter-day version, *A for the Ark,* Roger Duvoisin achieved a picture-book triumph—putting the animals into the Ark in alphabetical order, letting the text carry the scrip-

Next morning she was wakened by a loud neighing. A beautiful spotted stallion was prancing to and fro in front of her, stamping his hooves and shaking his mane. He was strong and proud and more handsome than any horse she had ever dreamed of. He told her that he was the leader of all the wild horses who roamed the hills. He welcomed her to live with them. She was glad, and all her horses lifted their heads and neighed joyfully, happy to be free with the wild horses.

Illustration by Paul Goble

tural weight of the Flood, then reversing the alphabet for the animals' safe departure. A more recent, straight embodiment by Warwick Hutton eschews incident and, in its generalized pallor, foregoes emotional or dramatic force.

Spier's *Noah's Ark* is at once elaborate and feeble. On the front endpapers, a contrast is drawn between war-and-desolation and Noah peaceably tending his crops; overleaf, on the half-title page, the Ark is a-building; the title-page spread shows the assembling

for *The Girl Who Loved Wild Horses,* written by Paul Goble, Bradbury, 1978, 8 x 10.

of provisions; then comes an old Dutch moralizing rhyme ("They were killed/For the guilt/Which brought all/To the Fall"), neither particularly suited to children nor eloquent in itself. The rest is wordless picturization, in a combination of large scenes and small comic-strip-like vignettes. (See pp. 284–5.)

As description, the jacket copy is unintentionally apt: "A host of animals, in all shapes and sizes, parade across the colorful pages." (Well, not all that colorful; mainly a range of paintbox

Crossing trestles.

Illustration by DONALD CREWS

pastel tones.) The animals, that is, are a throng: little characterized and seldom individuated. Most of the anecdotal detail is as trite as Mrs. Noah's horrified reaction to the mice. For want of significant and distinguishable detail, the scenes tend to blur, on land and aboard ship alike.

Weaker still are the Flood scenes, where a featureless, monotonous sky meets a listless sea. The Ark itself is a mere tub, without firm structural contours, stoutness, or heft: a surprising lapse in a mariner and ship-model-builder like Spier. In one clever bit, however, he uses four successive panels to show the water rising and raising the Ark little by little above the flooded Earth. Along the byways of folk history, which afford greater scope for such light touches, his work has looked much better.

A 1978 runner-up, coincidentally, was David Macaulay's magisterial *Castle:* an Ark of a sort, too, as he conceived and depicted

for *Freight Train,* written by Donald Crews, Greenwillow, 1978, 9⅝ x 8.

it. Macaulay—need it be said?—combines a rare historical imagination, a keen eye, a gift for topographical and structural delineation, and a deep sense of the human condition. Watching his Welsh castle take shape, element by element, one enters into the lives of workers, farmers, townsfolk. The cutaway view is as characteristic of Macaulay, in one or another form, as the aerial panorama, in a variety of perspectives (see pp. 286–7). Yet mechanical drawing is no more to be found than a careless line. Timbered roof, thatched roof, and shingled roof each has its character, as each human figure, however minute, has a characterizing gesture, a characteristic stance. From raw beginnings to spectral end, virtuosity, sensitivity, and vision coalesce.

Though some of the varied winners do demonstrate technical competence and others have an ingratiating personality, little can be said for the 1979 selection, Paul Goble's pseudo-Plains-Indian

The Girl Who Loved Wild Horses. The story is a thin, maudlin conceit, shallowly rooted in Indian folklore (the Animal Husband motif) but more in keeping with a romantic, Western theme, the prepubescent girl's infatuation with horses. Goble's illustrational style, modeled after the flat planes and silhouetted forms of Plains-Indian skin painting (see pp. 288–9), produces some bold design effects in scenes of running horses, the sort of scenes for which the originals are famous. But once the horse leaves the herd, and the setting and tenor of the story change, the illustrations become stilted, arbitrarily stylized, art-moderne absurdities. Native American art gains nothing by such misconceived and vacuous emulation, well-intended as it may be.

Among the 1979 Honor Books was Donald Crews's *Freight Train:* a stellar example of the simple, assured work for younger children—conceptually interesting and visually exciting—that

Illustration by BARBARA COONEY

hasn't been taking top prize. Crews, who bowed with *We Read: A to Z*, is a designer who is also an interpreter and a dramatist. His books have an internal, expressive dynamic. In this instance, his subject is the passage of a freight train, and that alone: not where it's coming from or going to, or what it's carrying—but rather, the experience of a watching child, extended and expanded. Because the quintessential designer book, by Paul Rand and others, has tended to be sterile, it's worthwhile to compare Crews's train crossing a trestle with the well-known image in *Sparkle and Spin*. Where Rand's train is a toylike abstraction of flat forms, Crews employs four modes of illustration for his four visual configurations (see pp. 290–1). The supporting banks are solid color, naturalistically outlined; the trestle is a linear grid, in two shades of brown, that is at once a built structure and an illusionistic, op-art-like tease; the train, rushing onward, has turned into a

for *Ox-Cart Man,* written by Donald Hall, Viking, 1979, 10¼ x 8⅛.

until he came to Portsmouth
and Portsmouth Market.

streaming, streamlined blur; the smoke forms a shaded, slower-moving cloud canopy. The one constant, fittingly, is the checkered band of the tracks. The few words, in turn, are unobtrusively integrated with the pictures. Different in color from opening to opening, they become part of the total composition—never more so than on the last page, where the once-again-empty track is accompanied by the single word *gone*. Unity and compression ramify.

A certain irony inheres in the award of the 1980 Caldecott Medal to Barbara Cooney for the illustrations to *Ox-Cart Man*—for, had Donald Hall's laconic, unsentimental text been entrusted to a similarly inclined illustrator, it would have been a different book entirely. Here as in her other Early American evocations, Cooney's primitivist paintings are cheery and utterly likable. Her

Illustration by RACHEL ISADORA

Every day on the way home from school, Ben stops by the Zig Zag Jazz Club.

perky countryfolk sparkle. Her sacrificial ox is a charmer. Her scenes are knowingly composed to show and tell. She's also a thorough-going illustrator. When we hear that the Ox-Cart Man packed "a bag of wool," "a shawl his wife wove," and "five pairs of mittens his daughter knit," we see him carrying the bag, his wife holding the shawl, his daughter displaying the five pairs of mittens (each helpfully and prettily—if not-so-realistically?—a different color).

We might even wonder, faced with those staring figures, if she's joking—gently twitting the conventions of American primitive art, perhaps the taciturn ways of old-time Yankees, too. But the immaculate landscapes and tidy Portsmouth scenes speak another language, winsome and quaint (see pp. 292–3). Look at the cunning curved paving, the demure undulations of the bare trees.

for *Ben's Trumpet,* written by Rachel Isadora, Greenwillow, 1979, 9⅝ x 7⅞.

He watches the musicians practice.

Illustration by ARNOLD LOBEL
for *Fables,* written by Arnold Lobel, Harper, 1980, 8 x 11½.

Look only at the silhouetted hat brims—deft typecasting by headgear, yet anything but innocent limning.

The family in chiaroscuro by the fireside (shades of Georges de la Tour), the fiery March sky setting off the sugar maples, serve as reminders that light effects have long been a Cooney forte. (Remember especially *The Owl and the Pussycat*.) Yet a reader has only to turn away from the pictures, and concentrate on the concrete images and solid rhythms of the text, to be aware that Cooney has given it a light and springy cast—softening and broadening to the verge of stereotype what William Kurelik or Mary Azarian would have made vigorously real.

Still, no aesthetic law dictates absolute simplicity or homespun earthiness either. *Ben's Trumpet*, a 1980 runner-up, is a showy book, and alongside Rachel Isadora's recent portrayals of infancy, artificial. Anyone who recalls the Topolski drawings for Arna Bontemps's *Lonesome Boy*—also about a black boy's yearning for a trumpet in Jazz Age days—may find Isadora's projection all surface by comparison. Yet *Ben's Trumpet* has a natural, brilliant theatricality, such as one finds on the musical stage, putting Art Deco design and decor to appropriate and intense purpose. Call it sincere artifice.

It's also a workout for the eye (see pp. 294–5). Ben slouches against the door of the Zig Zag Club, surrounded by emblems of sophisticated night life and, in the border, spotlighted silhouettes of the after-dark revels. Opposite, the rehearsing musicians and their instruments are one, and instantly recognizable if as yet immaterial. Absorption and longing, shoddiness and glamour, are in the first picture; pure music-making is in the second. Easy as the pictures are to read, they don't pall. Isadora's patterns and devices have a life of their own, beyond decoration or evocation. Later, when Ben sees "the trumpeter from the Zig Zag Club!", the facing page explodes in fragments of prefigured pattern. Isadora also knows when to hold back, to let figure drawing alone convey emotion. Designing grandly, she tries not to overdo.

No admirer of unassuming proficiency, unforced merriment, and plain good-fellowship can regret the award of a Caldecott Medal, in 1981, to Arnold Lobel. And the worst one can say of *Fables* is that it's the closest he has come to being boring.

As fables the twenty little stories of Lobel's invention are a so-

so lot, more often lame than pithy—lacking the tightness and directness, the combination of inevitability and unexpectedness, of the classic examples. One problem, perhaps, is that many of the animal characters aren't in character; they just stand in, looking foolish, for one or another human foible. "The Crocodile in the Bathroom," "The Baboon's Umbrella," "The Ostrich in Love," "Madame Rhino and Her Dress," belong to this number—each looking extra-foolish out of incongruity. This is the role that animals commonly play in picture-book tales with a moral, where the humor is heightened and the lesson is eased by the silliness.

The book-design, with its sedate framing and respectful white space, puts the pictures on formal exhibit—as in a gallery; and Lobel has indeed approximated full-scale, four-square paintings. But it is no accident that Aesopian fables, centered on a single point of conflict and inherently graphic, have attracted illustrators through the ages, while painters have sought out the more ample and complex situations of classical myth. In the illustration for "King Lion and the Beetle" the two figures do epitomize the mighty and the humble, so there is some excuse for the cumbersome collar and heavily modeled drapery, and the confontation between them dominates the scene (see page 296). But in Lobel's natural hand, in spontaneous, cartoony sketches or comic stylizations, the work would have had more sparkle and less ponderousness.

Chris Van Allsburg—whose first work, *The Garden of Abdul Gasazi*, was a 1980 Honor Book; who then won the 1982 Caldecott for *Jumanji;* and whose honors grow—is probably best regarded as a popular phenomenon. A master of theatrical effects and suave magic-realism, he delivers visual shocks and thrills and a single Romantic message—about how kids are wiser, in their credulity, than grownups: the old poet's notion of the loss of imagination with the loss of innocence, moved up to the age of the knowing child and the obtuse parent.

Jumanji has a superlative jacket—as a poster and a trailer—enhanced by omitting Van Allsburg's name (deemed unnecessary: distracting and self-evident?). A comparison with *Fables,* similar in format, points up the excellence of the interior design, too: type of a darkness and weight and character to set off the infinitely modulated grays, the molded forms and precisionist textures of

Illustration by CHRIS VAN ALLSBURG
for *Jumanji*, written by Chris Van Allsburg, Houghton, 1981, 10⅝ x 9¾.

the Conté pencil drawings.

Through use of perspective, scale, and lighting, the drawings make the banal look eerie, as when the bespectacled boy and pigtailed girl—with (anachronistic) toys abandoned at their feet—sit down to play the game. They telegraph the children's reactions to the ensuing disorder in dumb show—the boy's stupefaction ("He couldn't believe his eyes") at the sight of the lion on the piano, the girl's gasp on seeing the monkeys in the kitchen. They pitch the onlooker into the picture space, and the pictured forms at the on-

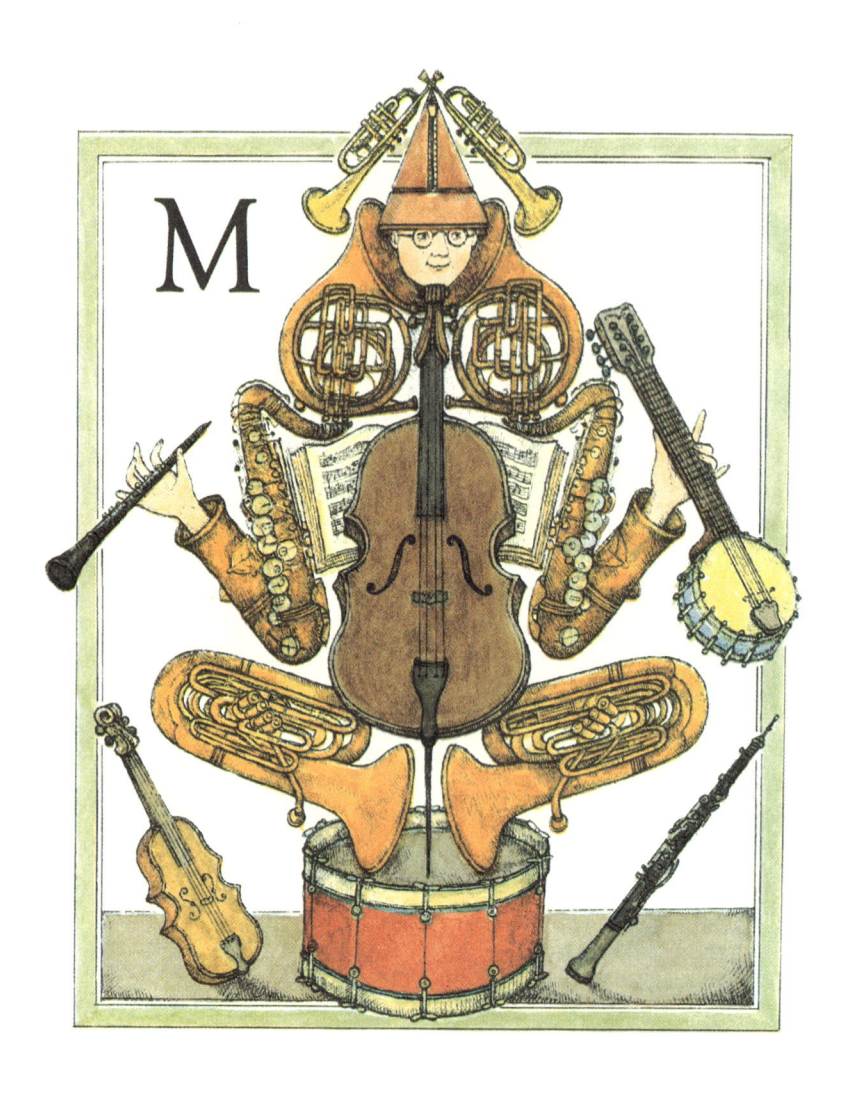

Illustration by Anita Lobel

looker, in a razzle-dazzle of 3-D cinematics and baroque *trompe l'oeil* (see page 299).

The terror, though, is of a neutral, painless sort—unthreatening alongside, say, Hansel and Gretel. There's no real mystification, by comparison with the likes of Arthur Yorinks's *It Happened in Pinsk*. As an imaginary construct, the whole thing is formulaic: The children have only to say the magic word *JUMANJI* to dis-for *On Market Street,* written by Arnold Lobel, Greenwillow, 1981, 7¾ x 9⅞.

pel the danger, sending the diamond-spotted snake back into the flower-spotted upholstery. And, in the dénouement, an unthinking adult remark lets us know that the hazardous game will go on—whereupon we see two new children bearing it away. The illustration, manipulative and matter-of-fact, leaves nothing to the imagination either. What can be said for it, as can also be said of certain high-impact poster imagery, is that it stays in the mind.

Illustration by MARCIA BROWN

If *Ben's Trumpet* is one exception to the aridity of historic reconstructions, *On Market Street,* a 1982 runner-up, is another: a witty adaptation by Anita Lobel of an old illustrational mode, the composite figures of eighteenth-century trade engravings, done in the original rococo style.

From the first, in the trim peasant decor of *Sven's Bridge,* the delicate splendors of *The Seamstress of Salzburg,* the captivating

for *Shadow,* translated by Marcia Brown, Scribner, 1982, 8½ x 11.

exotica of *Peter Penny's Dance,* Lobel has shown herself to be an innate antiquarian. She feels herself into period modes and manners the way a performer does—an actress or a dancer—and then creates something of her own, at once credible and amusing.

On Market Street, keyed to words by Arnold Lobel, puts her decorative invention beguilingly on exhibit. "M/Musical Instrument" and "N/Noodles," for example, form a complementary pair (see pp. 300–1): the first playing on the resemblance of French horn, saxophone, and so on to parts of the human anatomy; the second fashioning a vision of female frippery out of today's gourmet array of noodles—noodles in bunches and noodles in rows, noodle ribbons and ruffles and bows. No academic archaism here. No mere imitation or stylization either.

With Marcia Brown's *Shadow,* the 1983 Caldecott winner, we are back in Africa—the phantasmic Africa that Western pulse-beats once quickened to. It was Brown who, in *Once a Mouse,* produced the first Third World blockbuster picture book (for which she also won her second Caldecott); and *Shadow,* adapted from the French original of Blaise Cendrars's 1929 *Little Black Stories for Little White Children,* could stand as her claim to continued pre-eminence.

It's not a comfortable book, either for youngsters or for the ordinary onlooker. A succession of high-keyed images are strung on a metaphorical, discontinuous, often cryptic and paradoxical text;

Illustration by VERA B. WILLIAMS

there is no letup in the clash of light and dark, the clamor of earth and sky, near and far, interpenetrating shapes and indeterminate space. With every opening a bleed—no white space, no framing, no visual connections or transitions—the overall design lacks stability and coherence.

But oh the vitality! Even the procession threading its way across the distant desert, an image familiar from a hundred movies, is unhackneyed—a file of individually articulated beings, of differing ages and conditions. Closer up, isolated in thought as "night falls," each form has an independent existence; (see pp. 302–3) they're inward silhouettes, aware and unaware of the delicate, wraithlike phantoms stirring in the dusky glow. Whatever is wrong with the book, it doesn't lack art-interest—see the use made of different media, the compositional subtleties, the contrast of exactitude and ambiguity—nor is it without dramatic effect.

The Honor Books that year included Vera Williams's all-round

for *A Chair for My Mother,* written by Vera B. Williams, Greenwillow, 1982, 10½ x 8.

I tried out our chair in the back of the truck. Mama wouldn't let me sit there while we drove. But they let me sit in it while they carried it up to the door.

This is more like it. Here is «BLÉRIOT II,» a glider. Big enough to hold a man. Papa has not yet learned to pilot, so Gabriel Voisin, his good friend, will fly.

Illustration by ALICE AND MARTIN PROVENSEN

triumph, *A Chair for My Mother*. Probably not since Ezra Jack Keats's first Peter books has there been a work so genuinely childlike in its outlook, so finely knit, so down-to-earth and sumptuous.

Changing times have had their effect, symbolized by the shift from *Peter's Chair* to *A Chair for My Mother*. The fatherless household, the working mother, are outward differences; the family is an emotional and material unit, not child-centered, and part-and-parcel of what it would be fair to call a working-class culture. Important events occur, time elapses. A fire necessitates a move to a new bare apartment; neighbors and relatives contribute spare goods; Mama still has only a "hard kitchen chair" to rest in after work. Hence the jar slowly filling with coins.

A motorboat will tow it into the air as the glider has no motor. All is in readiness. Gabriel gives the signal.

---

for *The Glorious Flight,* written by Alice and Martin Provensen, Viking, 1983, 10 x 8¼.

The water-color pictures, the picture-and-text pages, are correspondingly rich and ripe: a matter of vibrant color in league with forceful, varied design. A paragraph could be written about the freehand borders: the dead blooms after the fire, the bank-note scallops when the coins are changed for ten-dollar bills, the store pennants celebrating the purchase of the chair. The armchair itself is not only a comfortable resting place and an object of beauty but, implicitly, a protection and a throne (see pp. 304–5). There is feeling—tenderness, humor, concern—in the quietest look. There is a world of comment in the sweeping view of the bank floor. A transparent wash brings the text pages alive.

Of the winners, the most fully realized is a curiosity: Alice and Martin Provensen's *The Glorious Flight*—which not only harks

Illustration by TRINA SCHART HYMAN
for *Saint George and the Dragon,* retold by Margaret Hodges, Little, 1984, 10 x 9.

back to their *Charge of the Light Brigade* but is totally at odds with their more characteristic, archly primitivist work, in *A Visit to William Blake's Inn, The Peaceable Kingdom,* and numberless others. (See pp. 306–7.)

The Provensens are professionals, resourceful and technically accomplished. But folkish material seems to induce in them a simplistic response, a resort to fanciful elaborations of architectural ornament, to costumed figurines and cunning ornamental animals. *The Glorious Flight* is an honest spoof, sophisticated and sly, that carries no such excess baggage. The humor is inherent in the situation: Papa Blériot's sudden obsession with flying machines, the repeated smash-ups and instant recoveries ("It sails across a whole field before it hits a rock. No so bad!"), the consummate poise. In the Provensens' rendering, Gallic lightness and playfulness, and pictorial echoes of the period (the camera poses, the sepia tones), combine with airy, limpid sea and water effects for a buoyant ensemble: adult but not out of reach.

Trina Schart Hyman's *Saint George and the Dragon*, the 1985 winner, uses an ancient English legend and illustrious art-models to slight effect, interpretively or aesthetically. The book is executed in a commonplace illustrational style descended from the English graphic artists of the 1860s, with decorative embellishments in the later, Howard Pyle manner. Strong outlines provide a linear substructure and, though the framing obtrudes, a distinct compositional thrust (see page 308). In one particular composition, George eyeing the fallen dragon, the juxtaposition of the dragon's winding coils and the upright figure of the knight packs a dramatic punch: a powerful foe has been vanquished. But the dragon is a monster in this rendering, not the embodiment of evil.

Everything is clear; everything is included as stated. But if there are no obscurities, omissions, or deviations, neither are there any subtleties or nuances, emotional overtones or undertones. Nothing is added to the text but conventionalized forms in conventional poses (like the two hearty, strapping peasants in the lower right-hand corner, a compositional device and good-earth motif dear to certain travel poster landscapes). The picture-page framing permits of an occasional pictorial aside, or flourish, meaningless in itself (the child's face at lower left); otherwise the framing is extraneous, except insofar as it suggests a medieval picture window, incongruously, and unites the two facing pages in a design scheme that is probably the book's most prominent feature. The border decorations on the text pages, which might be the one good justification for the scheme, are banal as motifs and vapid as pictured forms (where in Pyle's work, and the illuminated manuscript originals, they are suggestive, animated, enticing). The whole, indeed, is a pretentious invocation of past illustrational glories, which it cheapens rather than enhances: the definition of *kitsch*.

Illustration by Paul O. Zelinsky
for *Hansel and Gretel,* retold by Rika Lesser, Dodd, 1984, 11¼ x 8.

For contrast, there is Paul Zelinsky's runner-up, *Hansel and Gretel.*

Finished, old-masterly paintings are perilous in picture books. The incidents they illustrate seldom sustain the requisite breadth and depth of treatment. They substitute plastic (that is, modeled, molded) for graphic values, and lie uneasily on the book page—like reproductions. Enclosed, self-contained, complete, they allow of no pictorial flow; coming one after the other, they permit little of the variation in mood and tempo natural to narrative.

Zelinsky's *Hansel and Gretel* does not so much surmount these problems as render them, in large measure, immaterial. Partly, the reason is the story. Among the familiar nursery tales, Hansel and Gretel has special weight as an account of child victims; of children cruelly treated by a vicious mother and a weak father, and threatened anew by a false grandmotherly benefactor lurking behind a sugary facade.

Zelinsky's handling is direct and reserved—without pathos or melodramatics. In two grave pictures—the father's near-empty-handed return, the mother's malevolent urgings—we have the children's plight. A full moon then casts a luminous glow over a pastoral scene of deceptive yet heartening tranquility as Hansel gathers up the pebbles that will, he hopes, save them. What evil can prevail against this image of purity and gentleness, transcribed in the flat planes of cottage roof and wall, the balanced masses of light and dark, the delicately modeled figures of the waiting Gretel and the squatting Hansel?

Agitation, even torment, is the message of the children's second departure—seen in the elongated, distorted figures; the skewed perspective; the whiplash of the road (see page 310). In a change from the first departure, the father's mute, stooped misery has become an agony that is almost an outcry. The house in the woods, with its gimcrack confections (the peppermint-stick loops edging the path, the whipped-cream chimney pots), is then disturbingly unreal—and properly so.

The word *distinguished,* with its connotations of merit, importance, and cultural esteem, might well apply to Zelinsky's *Hansel and Gretel.* It might apply, surely, to Macaulay's *Castle.* But for the best interests of picture books as a whole, it is perhaps too lofty a term. Under its shadow, technique and facility may be too easily confused with art, and aspiration too easily equated with accomplishment. Creativity, expressiveness, integrity of ends and means, resonance or sheer delight: In children's picture books, as in any art form, these deserve to come first.

The Newbery and Caldecott Medal Honor Books 1976–1985

The Newbery Medal Honor Books

1976 THE HUNDRED PENNY BOX
Written by *Sharon Bell Mathis*
Illustrated by *Leo and Diane Dillon*
Published by Viking 1975

DRAGONWINGS
Written by *Laurence Yep*
Published by Harper 1975

1977 A STRING IN THE HARP
Written by *Nancy Bond*
Published by Atheneum 1976
A Margaret K. McElderry Book

ABEL'S ISLAND
Written and illustrated by *William Steig*
Published by Farrar 1976

1978 RAMONA AND HER FATHER
Written by *Beverly Cleary*
Published by Morrow 1977

ANPAO: AN AMERICAN INDIAN ODYSSEY
Written by *Jamake Highwater*
Published by Lippincott 1977

1979 THE GREAT GILLY HOPKINS
Written by *Katherine Paterson*
Published by Crowell 1978

1980 THE ROAD FROM HOME: THE STORY OF AN ARMENIAN GIRL
Written by *David Kherdian*
Published by Greenwillow 1979

1981 THE FLEDGLING
Written by *Jane Langton*
Published by Harper 1980

A RING OF ENDLESS LIGHT
Written by *Madeleine L'Engle*
Published by Farrar 1980

1982 RAMONA QUIMBY, AGE 8
Written by *Beverly Cleary*
Published by Morrow 1981

UPON THE HEAD OF THE GOAT: A CHILDHOOD IN HUNGARY, 1939-1944
Written by *Aranka Siegal*
Published by Farrar 1981

1983 GRAVEN IMAGES
Written by *Paul Fleischman*
Illustrated by *Andrew Glass*
Published by Harper 1982

HOMESICK: MY OWN STORY
Written by *Jean Fritz*
Illustrated by *Margot Tomes*
Published by Putnam 1982

SWEET WHISPERS, BROTHER RUSH
Written by *Virginia Hamilton*
Published by Philomel 1982

THE BLUE SWORD
Written by *Robin McKinley*
Published by Greenwillow 1982

DOCTOR DE SOTO
Written and illustrated by *William Steig*
Published by Farrar 1982

1984   THE WISH GIVER
   Written by *Bill Brittain*
   Illustrated by *Andrew Glass*
   Published by Harper 1983

   SUGARING TIME
   Written by *Kathryn Lasky*
   Illustrated with photographs by *Christopher G. Knight*
   Published by Macmillan 1983

   THE SIGN OF THE BEAVER
   Written by *Elizabeth George Speare*
   Published by Houghton 1983

   A SOLITARY BLUE
   Written by *Cynthia Voigt*
   Published by Atheneum 1983

1985   THE MOVES MAKE THE MAN
   Written by *Bruce Brooks*
   Published by Harper 1984

   ONE-EYED CAT
   Written by *Paula Fox*
   Published by Bradbury 1984

   LIKE JAKE AND ME
   Written by *Mavis Jukes*
   Illustrated by *Lloyd Bloom*
   Published by Knopf 1984

The Caldecott Medal Honor Books

1976 STREGA NONA
   Retold and illustrated by *Tomie de Paola*
   Published by Prentice-Hall 1975

   THE DESERT IS THEIRS
   Illustrated by *Peter Parnall*
   Written by *Byrd Baylor*
   Published by Scribner 1975

1977 THE AMAZING BONE
   Written and illustrated by *William Steig*
   Published by Farrar 1976

   THE CONTEST
   Adapted and illustrated by *Nonny Hogrogian*
   Published by Greenwillow 1976

   FISH FOR SUPPER
   Written and illustrated by *M. B. Goffstein*
   Published by Dial 1976

   THE GOLEM: A JEWISH LEGEND
   Written and illustrated by *Beverly Brodsky McDermott*
   Published by Lippincott 1976

   HAWK, I'M YOUR BROTHER
   Illustrated by *Peter Parnall*
   Written by *Byrd Baylor*
   Published by Scribner 1976

1978 CASTLE
   Written and illustrated by *David Macaulay*
   Published by Houghton 1977

   IT COULD ALWAYS BE WORSE
   Retold and illustrated by *Margot Zemach*
   Published by Farrar 1977

1979 FREIGHT TRAIN
Written and illustrated by *Donald Crews*
Published by Greenwillow 1978

THE WAY TO START A DAY
Illustrated by *Peter Parnall*
Written by *Byrd Baylor*
Published by Scribner 1978

1980 BEN'S TRUMPET
Written and illustrated by *Rachel Isadora*
Published by Greenwillow 1979

THE GARDEN OF ABDUL GASAZI
Written and illustrated by *Chris Van Allsburg*
Published by Houghton 1979

THE TREASURE
Retold and illustrated by *Uri Shulevitz*
Published by Farrar 1979

1981 THE BREMEN-TOWN MUSICIANS
Retold and illustrated by *Ilse Plume*
Published by Doubleday 1980

THE GREY LADY AND THE STRAWBERRY SNATCHER
Illustrated by *Molly Bang*
Published by Four Winds 1980

MICE TWICE
Written and illustrated by *Joseph Low*
Published by Atheneum 1980
A Margaret K. McElderry Book

TRUCK
Illustrated by *Donald Crews*
Published by Greenwillow 1980

1982   ON MARKET STREET
        Illustrated by *Anita Lobel*
        Written by *Arnold Lobel*
        Published by Greenwillow 1981

       OUTSIDE OVER THERE
        Written and illustrated by *Maurice Sendak*
        Published by Harper 1981

       A VISIT TO WILLIAM BLAKE'S INN: POEMS FOR INNOCENT AND EXPERIENCED TRAVELERS
        Illustrated by *Alice and Martin Provensen*
        Written by *Nancy Willard*
        Published by Harcourt 1981

       WHERE THE BUFFALOES BEGIN
        Illustrated by *Stephen Gammell*
        Written by *Olaf Baker*
        Published by Warne 1981

1983   A CHAIR FOR MY MOTHER
        Written and illustrated by *Vera B. Williams*
        Published by Greenwillow 1982

       WHEN I WAS YOUNG IN THE MOUNTAINS
        Illustrated by *Diane Goode*
        Written by *Cynthia Rylant*
        Published by Dutton 1982

1984   LITTLE RED RIDING HOOD
        Retold and illustrated by *Trina Schart Hyman*
        Published by Holiday 1983

       TEN, NINE, EIGHT
        Written and illustrated by *Molly Bang*
        Published by Greenwillow 1983

1985 HANSEL AND GRETEL
Illustrated by *Paul O. Zelinsky*
Retold by *Rika Lesser*
Published by Dodd 1984

HAVE YOU SEEN MY DUCKLING?
Written and illustrated by *Nancy Tafuri*
Published by Greenwillow 1984

THE STORY OF JUMPING MOUSE
Retold and illustrated by *John Steptoe*
Published by Lothrop 1984

A Decade of Children's Books: A Critic's Response
by Ethel L. Heins

In the writings of Michelangelo one often finds the idea that a statue, rather than being a human concept shaped into solid reality in stone, is actually something the sculptor discovers and then releases, with each blow of his chisel, from inside the marble. An optimist might have supposed that the creation of this essay would come about in much the same way; after all, among the mere twenty-nine thousand children's books published in the ten years 1975-1984 (the Newbery and Caldecott Medals were awarded 1976-1985) the comparatively few worth discussing, pro or con, would take shape and prod the memory of a fairly experienced reviewer. A realist, however, knew that the total output of the decade would have to be initially considered; how then to tackle the massive job? It was also obvious that a thorough scrutiny of the books would be voluminous in scope, and the findings, at best, statistical and encyclopedic. What is more important is to consider the tendencies of the era—the economic and social situations—and to mention significant books. Perhaps these examples, rather than defining the characteristics of the period, will reveal the interplay of forces that create a dynamic pattern.

One of the striking aspects of the books published for children and young adults during the past ten years is that so many of the observable trends were logical and emphatic continuations of what had begun in the mid-1960s. Before that cataclysmic time, especially just before and after midcentury, both Paul Hazard and Walter de la Mare were the patron saints of children's literature, and their spirits hovered over much of the writing about the subject. Not only had they given children's books a status, but they had glorified them and set the standards for their creation. In the 1950s sex and violence in explicit terms were still unthinkable, and although the dark side of life was not ignored, didacticism was abhorred, and the emphasis remained on traditional good taste and literary quality. Of course, children's writers were not normally concerned with clinical situations—the abused or retarded child or the deeply troubled child. Nor was the imbalance of society's views of certain ethnic and racial groups a major theme—as yet.

Then came the revolutionary sixties, and the adolescent—or teenager—arrived at new independence; younger brothers and sisters soon clamored for more freedom, resulting in the loss of innocence of American childhood so clearly perceived by psychologists. Old taboos dropped away like autumn leaves, and varieties of social didacticism began to alter the very countenance of children's literature. Moreover, gaining wide acceptance was another approach to children's books and reading, which seemed to cast away traditional standards, as determined adults were bent on using books to solve not only the personal problems of children but also the dilemmas of society. And social reformers, with nonliterary assaults on children's books, led the unwary to assume that the ancient tales of poets and storytellers as well as the whole body of creative writing for children were to blame for injustice and entrenched bigotry. For example, while proponents of the women's movement disdained conventional heroines and mined folklore for tales with strong female protagonists, Bruno Bettelheim's influential book, *The Uses of Enchantment: The Meaning and Importance of Fairy Tales,* paradoxically stressed the therapeutic and psychological value of classic stories. By the mideighties, however, there were perceivable signs that children's books would once again be viewed as literature rather than as instruments of propaganda and persuasion.

By now it is a familiar fact that both the economic distress and the political climate of the 1970s dealt swift and painful blows to school and public libraries, from which they have even now scarcely recovered. Federal funds previously available either vanished or were deflected away from books. For publishers, survival has often meant pragmatism rather than idealism. One response has been to do small print runs of items that sell quickly: reissued classics in flashy format; homogenized mediocrity in endless series of fact and fiction; sports, movie, or television tie-ins; and a torrent of trivia—toys, games, and puzzles, all published in the guise of books. And strong backlists of fiction, folklore, poetry, and nonfiction—formerly a publisher's financial backbone—became a luxury; with libraries and schools unable to afford the books nor publishers the warehouse costs, more and more excellent books of the recent past slipped into oblivion.

Ironically, while institutional markets were shrinking, book selling for children has been enjoying a renascence. Perhaps parents in this country began to heed insistent cries that students were demonstrating not only a steady erosion of reading skills but an appalling decline in general verbal proficiency. In addition, as a result of recent research into infant development, a new generation of parents has been trying to expose its children to books at an early age. Thus, books for babies have become supremely marketable—colorful board books, pop-ups, and other beguiling manipulative items of instant attraction to purchasers.

To add confusion to a rapidly changing industry, the picture of publishing itself has become kaleidoscopic; diversifying conglomerates acquire and later divest themselves of established publishing firms, while other publishers amalgamate in self-defense. Commercial pressures grow more intense, and the predictions of sales staff more influential. The literary book, the unusual book, the book without assured popularity are all considered risky ventures. In 1977 John Rowe Townsend, ruminating in a *Horn Book* article on the future of children's books, concluded that they are "something rather small, individual and intimate, trying to survive in an age when the trend is heavily toward the large-scale, the impersonal, the mass-produced."

Are children's books indeed surviving? Are there ominous signs of deterioration? Which of the time-honored elements and which of the discernible trends of the late sixties and early seventies have endured? And which books may possibly become the classics of the past decade?

Book illustrators have been liberated by the sheer wizardry of modern printing technology, and despite the constraints of economics they seem to be limited only by their own talent, imagination, and judgment. Yet many picture books of the past ten years were technically brilliant, but empty, vessels. Pictures have often lacked a sense of composition and of narrative direction as though the artist were using the book as a portfolio or an art gallery, creating a complex graphic orchestration that overwhelmed a simple text and obscured what should have been clear and comprehensible. The decade saw a return to inappropriate surrealism and a fad for fussy, pseudo-Oriental work that attempted to impose on children a purely adult nostalgia for decadent chinoiserie; one thinks of Leonard Lubin's unfortunate *The Perfect Peach* and of his *Aladdin and His Wonderful Lamp*. Evident, too, in many books was an over-dependence on decorative borders for a cozy ethnic effect—an obvious visual cliché.

Creators of picture books have also been liberated in another way by philosophical changes in acceptable subject matter—changes signaled partly by the publication in 1963 of *Where the Wild Things Are,* a book that has continued to open ways into previously uncharted territory for the young. Some picture-book makers attempted for a time to borrow Sendak's graphic hallmarks, and others tried to explore the young child's inner feelings with limp stories and pretentious pictures. Imitators corrupted Sendak's radical new concern for children's emotional lives and his conviction that their fears and anxieties could achieve catharsis through the metaphor of fantasy. At the same time his revolutionary ideas were being incorporated into *realistic* picture books that burdened children with thinly veiled information about the concerns of adults. Thus, earnestly intruding into picture books were handicapped friends or siblings, aging grandparents, death, single parents, and even—of all things—thumb-sucking. But when any theme is subjected to the imagination of a creator, the result can be a work of emotional depth; for example, Tomie de Paola's *Now One Foot, Now the Other,* a poignant, unsentimental story of a little boy and his ailing grandfather, or *My Friend Jacob* by Lucille Clifton and Thomas di Grazia, an uncommon story of two boys—a small, eager Black child and his large, retarded white friend.

The explosion of color in the psychedelic art of the sixties and a general infatuation with the visual continued through the next decade and into the eighties, with weak, shrinking texts and the insistent encroachment of the pictorial. The traditional standard of a delicate balance between art and text would appear to have become redundant; yet in the May-June 1985 *Horn Book* Ava

Weiss, one of the most respected art directors in publishing, stated a venerable point of view: "The perfect picture book is an art form in which two separate disciplines, literature and art, merge to create a new, integrated whole."

During the past decade established illustrators continued their productivity, several of them achieving the Caldecott Medal and other honors. And in the best work there was no lack of beauty, of innovation, of integrity. Edward Ardizzone, Edgar Parin d'Aulaire, Roger Duvoisin, Don Freeman, and Ezra Jack Keats—their most important work all completed by the mid-1970s—died before the middle of the eighties. Maurice Sendak finished his long-awaited, most ambitious and challenging book, *Outside Over There*, a severely disciplined work whose many-layered story is haunting and metaphoric, whose artwork is mature and masterly. Testimony to Sendak's view of the picture book as "a beautiful poetic form," *Outside Over There* marks the completion of his trilogy whose theme is "how children master various feelings . . . and manage to come to grips with the realities of their lives."

William Steig published several picture books during the decade, with some repetitiveness, as in *Caleb and Kate,* and some purely adult allusions, as in *Gorky Rises;* but he reached new heights of originality and childlike humor with *Doctor DeSoto*, which the Newbery Medal Committee had the percipience to declare an Honor Book for its verbal storytelling. Barbara Cooney, having won her second Caldecott Medal, ended the decade with a burst of new creativity, doing some of the finest work of her long, splendid career. *Miss Rumphius*, a miniature biography and a beautiful, out-of-the-ordinary picture book, was neglected by both the Caldecott Medal Committee and the Notable Children's Books Committee; nevertheless, it has been enthusiastically received by children. John Burningham's *Come Away from the Water, Shirley,* a brilliantly conceived and composed fantasy constructed on a double irony, explores and bridges the gap between the private imaginary world and the public demeanor of a wonderful poker-faced little girl. And in *The Snowman* Raymond Briggs made the most eloquent wordless picture book yet, a work of lyrical beauty and dramatic intensity.

Vigorous new talent made definitive statements during the ten years from 1975 to 1984 in the work of such diverse stylists as

Molly Bangs, Ann Jonas, Warwick Hutton, Diane Goode, Nancy Tafuri, and Vera Williams. Unquestionably, Chris Van Allsburg's work heralded a virtuosity as unique as his instantaneous success. His sculpturesque figures and architectural forms and his tonal range of grays in concert with black and white all add emotional force to his illustrations. And when he burst into full color with *The Wreck of the Zephyr,* one saw intensified the characteristics of his work—beauty of composition, confident drawings, a striking use of light and shadow, a sense of clarity and solidity, and the intriguing ambiguity of illusion and reality.

In total contrast, one notes the emergence in 1975 of James Stevenson, joining a prestigious list of authors-illustrators who, doing double duty as artists for *The New Yorker,* had years before started what proved to be a picture-book tradition. Earlier there were, among others, Syd Hoff, Robert Kraus, Mischa Richter, William Steig and, later in the decade, Frank Modell and Charles Martin—artists who approached childhood sympathetically, but obliquely and unsentimentally. His initial book, *"Could Be Worse,"* showed Stevenson to be a purveyor of genuine entertainment, drawing with the sureness and the deceptive breeziness of Quentin Blake and skilled in the fine art of glorifying nonsense.

The enormous expansion of books for the very young has inspired some hastily prepared, tawdry offerings, often with an emphasis on noisy graphics. But many picture books seem to speak clearly and directly to the little child and intuitively to reflect the interests, the curiosity, the small dilemmas, the thought patterns, and the behavioral responses of early childhood. For example, the work of Shirley Hughes, Rosemary Wells, John Burningham, Tana Hoban, Helen Oxenbury, Eric Carle, Janet and Allen Ahlberg, and Nancy Tafuri can surely help to establish between parent and child the habit of "verbal give-and-take" that Dorothy Butler recommends so indisputably in one of the period's most persuasive parents' aids—*Babies Need Books.*

It is paradoxical that while the decade witnessed a drastic falling-off in the publication of folk-tale collections, the folk story in picture-book form continued to proliferate. It can almost be said that in 1947 Marcia Brown, with her sturdy *Stone Soup,* unwittingly engendered a new trend, if not an industry. Retellers plundering the world's folklore have been busily adapting—and often truncating and bowdlerizing—favorite tales, even tackling the challenging subtlety and wisdom of Hans Christian Andersen, sending forth a stream of derivative, unintegrated picture books with elaborate, theatrical illustrations. And editors show no signs of relinquishing such a treasury of ready-made, royalty-free texts. Songs, poetry, and Biblical stories have been repeatedly pictured; and a much-loved short lyrical poem of Robert Frost was actually dismantled line by line to provide captions for largely irrelevant, though handsome, illustrations. Relying on traditional material, Paul Galdone has been repeating himself again and again, with none of the verve, humor, and freshness he demonstrated a generation ago; while Susan Jeffers and Mercer Mayer, in the same way, have denied their early promise and submerged their real talent.

Of course, some illustrators have distinctively captured the essence—the flavor—of folklore and poetry. Consider the great diversity of style and subject. Tomie de Paola's quintessential *Strega Nona* established him as a major figure, although he has been too prolific, and his style too reiterative. Charles Mikolaycak has done strong, beautiful work for another rendering of an old story—*Baboushka*—and for *Peter and the Wolf,* which is not a folk tale but has recently been treated as such in several inappropriately pictured editions. Other proud products of the decade are Uri Shulevitz's *The Treasure,* Nonny Hogrogian's *The Devil with the Three Golden Hairs,* and Margot Zemach's *It Could Always Be Worse,* a universal numskull story illustrated with deep-toned water colors of beauty, humor, and gusto. Ed Young's brilliant but restrained paintings for the Chinese Cinderella tale *Yeh-Shen* are among his most striking achievements; and Warwick Hutton's illustrations for *Beauty and the Beast,* for Susan Cooper's *The Silver Cow,* and for several Old Testament narratives are masterpieces of cool painterly elegance. And for its simplicity and honest beauty Erik Blegvad's pictorial accompaniment for *The Three Little Pigs* is a model of perfection. Two books from England are noteworthy: a daring, provocative *Hansel and Gretel* illustrated by an exciting innovator, Anthony Browne, and Alfred Noyes's romantic ballad, *The Highwayman,* made into a new visual adventure for older children by the outbursts of expressionism in the striking illustrations by Charles Keeping. Both books—in Aidan Chambers's words—"give us something truly modern, reflecting how we think now and what we think about; and they give us something old, brought to life with fresh, reinvigorated, and reinvigorating energy, so that tradition is kept alive and is woven into the pattern of today."

Some years ago, Barbara Cooney, with visual references authentic and beautiful, made three picture books of Greek myths; all are out of print. One must wonder why, with so little classical literature available for younger readers, Gerald McDermott chose to render the Roman myth of Ceres and Proserpina in an oversized, explosive picture book—in this case, employing a kind of violent expressionism fortunately rare in children's books.

Adults who have acted as a link between young children and books know that the favorites are still the ones in which firm verbal storytelling, with Aristotle's beginning, middle, and end, is counterbalanced by readable narrative artwork. For the small child's appetite for story is insatiable. But while artists have grown more and more dependent upon retold tales from myth, legend, and folklore, there has been a distinct tendency to depart from strong, original, imaginative, often humorous texts. Pretentious, eccentric fantasy has been abundant. For this reason Mary Rayner's *Mr. and Mrs. Pig's Evening Out* arrived as a rare gem, almost the equal in dramatic strength, suspense, and humor of the 1969 *Sylvester and the Magic Pebble;* it is ironic that both books brought down upon their creators a storm of misguided protest. And one must acknowledge with profound respect and appreciation the contribution of Arnold Lobel to the I-Can-Read series, especially his matchless diminutive stories about Frog and Toad. But how many picture books of 1975-1984 will rival the durability of *Horton Hatches the Egg, Blueberries for Sal, The Happy Lion,* or Tomi Ungerer's *The Three Robbers*? How many contemporary picture-book characters will assume the status of emblematic heroes—the kind of vital, individualistic personalities young readers found plentiful in the past—like Little Tim, Madeline, and Harold (of the purple crayon) or the anthropomorphic Ferdinand, Peter Rabbit, Babar, Lyle, Curious George, and Harry the dirty dog?

Picture books by Black artists and writers were, disappointingly, not as abundant as one might have expected. The greatly gifted Tom Feelings, neither prolific nor commercially inclined, produced *Something on My Mind,* an album of sensitive, forceful drawings of Black children which inspired the fragments of poetic prose by Nikki Grimes; and the even more beautiful and trenchant *Daydreamers* in which eloquent, soul-searching portraits of young people again evoked a verbal response—this time Eloise Greenfield's extended poem, which added spiritual illumination. The best work of Leo and Diane Dillon, of course, was awarded Caldecott Medals; and Lucille Clifton continued to contribute emotionally truthful, understated texts, especially for *My Friend Jacob*—mentioned above—and for *Amifika,* both illustrated by Thomas di Grazia, who died toward the end of the decade. Rosa Guy made a beautifully cadenced translation of a Senegalese folk tale for *Mother Crocodile*—"*Maman Caïman*," illustrated with luminous paintings by John Steptoe. But not until the end of the decade did Steptoe again provide both text and illustrations; retelling an extended North American Indian animal fable and forsaking his characteristic color and style, he made exciting use of black, white, and shades of gray in *The Story of Jumping Mouse.* Ashley Bryan, with his own rhythmic retelling of one of the Ananse tales from the Antilles, fashioned an enchanting little book, *The Dancing Granny.* And Donald Crews presents subject matter of universal interest to young children, consistently providing them with an abundance of information and delight—all expressed in bold, inviting graphics.

Perhaps symptomatic of the caution and conservatism evident among publishers is the fact that few picture books from Western Europe and Japan seemed to make their way across the oceans; on the other hand, the decade saw some imports that injected originality and vitality into the American scene. Foremost among the younger European illustrators is Lisbeth Zwerger, a gifted artist who has been working modestly and poetically with Grimm and Andersen stories as well as with some nineteenth-century literary fairy tales.

Not the first picture book to win the Mildred L. Batchelder Award for translation was Toshi Maruki's *Hiroshima No Pika,* a work whose subject and expression definitively marked it for an intermediate—or even older—audience. Telling and showing what happened on the morning of August 6, 1945, are a direct, plain-spoken text and naturalistic paintings whose shocking force for young people could be compared with the impact on adults of Picasso's *Guernica.* Yet also from Japan has come the rich flowering of the extraordinary work of Mitsumasa Anno. Published in 1975, *Anno's Alphabet: An Adventure in Imagination* is an uncanny exercise in visual delusion into which a searching look reveals the subtle deception that transforms the realistically painted letters into astonishing three-dimensional forms. And Anno's *Journey* books, with their silent traveler astride his horse pursuing his tranquil way across time, space, and double-page spreads, are minutely detailed, wordless picture books full of pictorial witticisms, anachronisms, and astonishing discoveries.

It is perhaps fitting to close a discussion of picture books with some thoughts on a trend particularly dismaying at a time when so many treasures of children's literature have been going out of print: the publication of modern classics in ornamental, expensive newly illustrated editions. Is this fashion another manifestation of the desperate struggle to capture an adult market beguiled by superficial glamor? Much of the new illustration is mannered, undisciplined work, heavy with color and extraneous detail, lacking pictorial or stylistic consistency, and carelessly eclectic or shamelessly imitative.

Everything about Allen Atkinson's new artwork for Beatrix Potter's timeless classics is outrageously wrong: the intitial conception, format, atmosphere, coloration, and graphic inaccuracies. One needs only to think of William Pène du Bois's quiet, lyrical drawings for Rumer Godden's *The Mousewife,* a miniature epic of heroism, captivity, and freedom, to realize how poorly the story is served by Heidi Holder's coy, sentimental illustrations. Why erase the enduring impression of Ernest Shepard's crisp, impeccably right drawings for *The Reluctant Dragon* with Michael Hague's muddy, crowded paintings? Was it necessary to have his sumptuous, ponderous new editions of *The Lion, the Witch and the Wardrobe, The Hobbit, Alice in Wonderland,* or *The Wind in the Willows*? And did the market need, when *The Velveteen Rabbit* passed into the public domain, seven or eight new editions of the oversweet story, all competing with one another?

Critical judgments are naturally subjective, and one runs the risk of being accused of purism. Literature should be viewed anew by each generation, and illustration can retain the ethos, the spirit, of a work even with new approaches. But in adding modern illustration to older books, one must avoid a deadening homogenization and maintain, as always, a spiritual relationship between text and pictures.

Among picture books, critics have long sought works of artistic quality and excellent texts. But what do these conceptual terms actually mean? Obviously, there are no absolutes, nor is there unanimity among critics, publishers, or even artists themselves. More inflexible is the fact that the picture book in all its abundance and diversity may well be the richest—and at present the most contestable—form of children's literature. But it is a literature blessed with brave new talent—artists who are creating their images to heighten the child's perception of the world and of life. And among established artists there are still adventurous innovators who freshen their work by refining their art, changing their directions and constantly renewing the sources of their inspiration.

The tenacious realism that continued to dominate children's fiction also seems to have shifted its center of gravity. During the decade 1975-1984 books at either end of the age span appeared to be proliferating by leaps and bounds—picture books and young adult novels. At the same time one notes a distant decline in the sort of domestic stories, fantasy, and adventure tales that for so long satisfied the preadolescent's voracious hunger for story. Moreover, even in books not specifically aimed at teenagers, the characters grew perceptively older; adolescence, or puberty, suddenly became more interesting than childhood.

Long before the recent decade came the demise of the old-fashioned family story that celebrated the home as a place of safety and stability, whatever the circumstances. Family love transcended all misfortune, and the mother had the role of nurturer and protector, courageous and reliable. Today this cozy security has vanished as children have been confronted with social and human problems instead of shielded from them. Within the domestic unit the psychological aspect of the child has assumed importance, and it is the child who must often take decisive action to make up for the insufficiency of the parent. Indeed, a commanding theme in contemporary children's novels is the lack of understanding, of communication, between child and adult. Probably for this reason some writers were comfortable with a bygone period; thus, the Great Depression became the setting for, among others, Crystal Thrasher, who conveys a sense of family and community in her stories of Indiana, and Robert Burch, who refreshingly invokes an earlier mood in *Ida Early Comes over the Mountain,* a story of a rustic Mary Poppins caring for four motherless children in rural Georgia.

That children should not be protected from the full range of human emotions was surely not a new idea, nor was realism an invention of the sixties; for artistic, intuitive writers have always tried to present to children—in their own terms—the tragedy and exaltation of life. But what with social upheaval and a preoccupation with popular psychology, the writers' eager acceptance of liberated subject matter and emancipated vocabulary generated an explosion of fiction dealing with alcoholism, child abuse, death, divorce, drugs, murder, psychotic parents, suicide, teenage pregnancy—with or without abortion—and various diseases from anorexia nervosa to cancer, until it appeared that adolescents were indeed suffering all "the heartaches and the thousand natural shocks that flesh is heir to." Moreover, with many of the so-called problem novels totally centered on the angst of the protagonist narrating the story, the result is often a linguistically impoverished, cliché-ridden confession—an acknowledged legacy of the earlier and far more literary *Catcher in the Rye.*

Ironically, perhaps in reaction, perhaps as a sign of the country's mood of nostalgic discontent, there appeared in the past decade the publishing phenomenon of paperback teenage romances. Back in the apathetic fifties a host of honest, capable authors were writing innocent but perceptive love stories for a generation as yet unsophisticated. But even with a return to a national climate of conservatism, it must be admitted that these neat, laundered novels are a hypocrisy—an aspect of adults' wistful yearning for a vanished orderly time. It has been argued, of course, that such stories—along with other series of simplistic formulaic fictions—can lure young readers into reading. But, contrived by slick writers, the books share no insights, no vision of the world and of life;

although they have the trappings of realism, they lack reality and are nothing but sugary deceptions.

During the late sixties and early seventies the thrust of the new realism not only gave impetus to Judy Blume and her numerous, though less notorious, imitators, but it also brought about significant works of imaginative and emotional intensity, such as Paul Zindel's *The Pigman,* Mollie Hunter's *A Sound of Chariots,* the Cleavers' *Where the Lilies Bloom,* and Felice Holman's *Slake's Limbo* as well as Isabelle Holland's *The Man Without a Face* and Robert Cormier's *The Chocolate War.* And in the recent decade the new candor also encouraged the publication of books like Jan Slepian's *The Alfred Summer,* Cynthia Voigt's *A Solitary Blue,* Marilyn Sachs's *A December Tale,* and Rosa Guy's *The Disappearance*—all of which struck a fine balance between subject matter and literary quality.

So the frank acceptance of change offered unusual freedom not only to mediocre writers of ephemeral problem novels but to writers of sensitivity and narrative skill. And children's literature has weathered the storm because such notable authors have been able to absorb contemporary permissiveness without injuring the integrity of their work. Thus, the decade witnessed two magnificent books dealing with death—*Tuck Everlasting* and *Bridge to Terabithia;* and both of them presented the solemn subject in terms of a human experience significant on a child's level. In the same way, some writers incorporated episodes frankly sexual in nature, not necessarily in explicit terms but alluded to as an integral part of a developing narrative. In fact, sexuality itself is one of the themes of Ursula LeGuin's *Very Far Away from Anywhere Else,* a subtle novel that faces the dichotomy between sex and love and that implicitly provides a rebuttal to much present-day teenage fiction.

In reconsidering the familiar, reliable authors who persevered during the past decade, one is impressed that in an age of overt contemporary realism, they were not constrained by genre, nor were they limited by time or place or personae; in certain instances they invented new locales or even used some of the devices of fantasy to extend their themes. The work of many English writers was visibly underscored by imaginative power.

Alan Garner's *Stone Book* quartert was shaped by the influence of place, history, and linguistics on character and plot. With their graceful writing and emotional realism, Nina Bawden's *The Peppermint Pig* and *The Robbers* and Jane Gardam's brilliant, witty *Bilgewater* explored character as did Philippa Pearce's *The Way to Sattin Shore,* in which a plot is gradually activated as mystery and suspense unfold. Joan Aiken continues to be in a class of her own, with her exuberant, energetic stories unabashedly crowded with characters, action, and detail. In *Tulku* the ever-versatile Peter Dickinson chose China and Tibet as the setting for the adventures of American, English, and Oriental personalities; and in *The Seventh Raven,* like Robert Cormier, he demonstrated that a modern universal issue—terrorism—could be made into literature. Jill Paton Walsh worked with a variety of settings and themes—from the dilemmas of life and character in *Unleaving,* through *A Chance Child,* which made both history and time-slip fantasy serve to depict the agonies of children during the Industrial Revolution, to the victorious conclusion of *Gaffer Samson's Luck.* Tempering his observational realism with inventiveness, John Rowe Townsend wrote such novels as *Dan Alone* and *Kate and the Revolution,* straightforward narratives, and *Noah's Castle* and *The Visitors,* which rely on a speculative future. And from Australia came Patricia Wrightson's astonishing blend of geriatrics and aboriginal spirit lore in a remarkable piece of storytelling, *A Little Fear.*

In this country, too, well-established writers, while refusing to be shackled by fashion, produced some notable, original, and thoroughly contemporary work. In his *Westmark* trilogy Lloyd Alexander created a new realm to present an adventurous drama of the conflict between politics and morality. Katherine Paterson's novels ranged from historical fiction, *The Master Puppeteer,* through her two Newbery Medal books to the wryly humorous realism of *The Great Gilly Hopkins*—a runaway favorite with children—and then back to the past with nineteenth-century China in *Rebels of the Heavenly Kingdom.* Eleanor Cameron developed a sense of synchronicity in *Beyond Silence* and also wrote three engaging books about the child Julia, inspired by material antedating the events of *A Room Made of Windows.* In a traditional, classic style Paula Fox developed *One-Eyed Cat,* a novel extraordinary for the clarity of its prose, its reticence, and its concrete sensual imagery. Outstanding among their other achievements are Betsy Byars's tragicomic, eloquent *The Pinballs;* M. E. Kerr's *Little Little* with its blending of satire, sardonic wit, and compassion; and the Cleavers' *Trial Valley,* the sequel to *Where the Lilies Bloom,* which is strong in story but lacking its predecessor's poetic beauty, as well as such other novels centering on the authors' independent, tough-minded, interesting female personalities as *The Kissimmee Kid* and *Hazel Rye.* And Robert Cormier continued to write with devastating immediacy, especially *I Am the Cheese,* a chilling technical triumph, and *After the First Death,* a prophetic look at international terrorism. Moreover, it must be affirmed that Cormier deals with tragedy rather than with hopelessness; perhaps his work may be epitomized by a statement of Archibald Cox, the Harvard law professor and special prosecutor in the Watergate case: "Contemporary literature and the arts tell of man the absurd, the pervert, and the dropout, but rarely of man the hero or even the tragic, for the tragic requires a degree of nobility, and it is the fashion to forget Prometheus's reach and see only the chains."

To characterize Virginia Hamilton as a Black writer engrossed in the Black experience is a lackluster description falling far short of her own marvelous leaps of imagination. In the midseventies she plunged into an enormously productive period, publishing eight novels in a decade, all echoing with "African dream, family truths, and even speculations on the future." *Arilla Sun Down* and *Sweet Whispers, Brother Rush* are daring, inventive, and challenging—even demanding—while *The Magical Adventures of Pretty Pearl* is a fantasy that interweaves Black folklore with her own family history.

The decade began auspiciously enough for Black literature but failed to reveal any impressive new talent. Having already written several forceful young adult novels, Sharon Bell Mathis published a single book and was not to be heard from again. *The Hundred Penny Box,* beautifully illustrated by the Dillons, is a quietly intense, timeless story about a little boy and his ancient great-grandaunt. Walter Dean Myers proved to be a competent and versatile storyteller; his best works feature vivid, humorous dialogue and are full of the joys and frustrations of young adolescents and a knowledge of the New York street scene. Rosa Guy's *The Disappearance* is a mature and fearless novel—an exposure, transcending race and environment, of fear, loneliness, desperation, and pride. Mildred Taylor progressed from a simple incident in *Song of the Trees* to a penetrating chronicle of a family surrounded by a hopelessly racist society in *Roll of Thunder, Hear My Cry* and *Let the Circle Be Unbroken.*

Although a degree of sardonic humor and satire has worked its way into children's books, the absence of good comic writing has, for some years, been noted with regret. Surely, to sensitize the young and to offset the dehumanizing effects of the mass media, books should have emotional depth—a wide range of human feeling, including that rare quality, humor. A world—or a literature—without mirth would be terrifying; and if life is irrational and ludicrous as well as perilous and cruel, comedy can reveal as much about our plight as tragedy. Daniel Pinkwater, who manages to address young people of all ages, should be mentioned for his singular, offbeat plots and characters. Beverly Cleary's wonderfully real, enduring Ramona remains the prototype with whom other such fictional children will inevitably be compared. On an older level Lois Lowry's *Anastasia* stories and Judy Blume's *Superfudge* are less timeless and represent the urban middle-class comedy of manners. Much the same can be said of Sheila Greenwald's books even though she can attain heights of genuine humor, as in *It All Began with Jane Eyre*. Ellen Conford has made a successful career of ferreting out the wry incongruity in plausible everyday situations—as has Constance Greene. Imported from England, Helen Cresswell's *Bagthorpe Saga,* especially its initial volume *Ordinary Jack,* struck Americans as a hilarious example of British lunacy but, unaccountably, failed to amuse her compatriots and left them disappointed with a gifted writer. Two other authors exploited entirely different facets of comedy. A rare literary descendent of Mark Twain, Sid Fleischman created in *Humbug Mountain* a fine extravaganza in which he added his own wit and expert storytelling to a rich vein of tall-tale frontier humor. And E. L. Konigsburg, without aiming over the heads of children, wrote *Journey to an 800 Number,* a highly ingenious satire on contemporary mores peopled with some of her most eccentric yet vulnerably human characters.

It would be fruitful to examine all of the reasons why the strong historical novel has ceased to be claimed by enthusiastic young readers. One of the obvious explanations is that in an age of stunning technology young people are much more intrigued by the present and the future than they are by the past. And ours is a country often accused of lacking a real sense of history. In any case, historical fiction, with a perceptible shift in emphasis, has continued to be published. One notes a more individualized kind of story, with more sensitivity to personal dilemma and triumph, suffering and survival, than was found in the older type of historical adventure. This tendency is apparent in Rosemary Sutcliff's two novels about Roman Britain—*Frontier Wolf* and *Song for a Dark Queen*—and in such other works as Louise Moeri's *Save Queen of Sheba*, Jill Paton Walsh's *A Parcel of Patterns,* Scott O'Dell's *Sarah Bishop,* Erik Christian Haugaard's *The Samurai's Tale,* Elizabeth Speare's *The Sign of the Beaver,* and Jean Fritz's *Homesick;* and also in the powerful fiction about the Second World War and the Holocaust, the two often acting together to dramatize elements of the Nazi era: Myron Levoy's *Alan and Naomi,* Haugaard's *Chase Me, Catch Nobody!,* Doris Orgel's *The Devil in Vienna,* and Uri Orlev's *The Island on Bird Street.*

Despite a flurry of activity in all branches of American historical work during the Bicentennial period, one observes in the past decade a decline in sustained biographical writing; instead, there was an abundance of brief, timely, illustrated books, often in series. Of course, there were substantial contributions from Jean Fritz, such as *Stonewall* and *The Double Life of Pocahontas,* along with Polly Schoyer Brooks's *Queen Eleanor: Independent Spirit of the Medieval World.* David Kherdian's *The Road from Home: The Story of an Armenian Girl* must be mentioned as well as some significant memoirs of the Holocaust experience—Aranka Siegel's *Upon the Head of the Goat* and Ilse Koehn's *Mischling, Second Degree.*

In considering fantasy, one now observes its overlapping with science fiction. Some time-slip stories interpolate the future into the present, rather than revisit the past from the present. Some invented lands and peoples are created to provide high adventure; some only for the purpose of magic. And dragons and trilogies are equally involved in the plotting of extended fantasy and of science fiction. Moreover, both genres are still preoccupied with the polarizing of good and evil, although in science fiction the concept is now overlaid with political or social morality, as in Jan Mark's *The Ennead,* in William Sleator's *Interstellar Pig,* and in some of Helen Hoover's novels, especially *The Delikon* and *The Shepherd Moon.* One motif—the earth after a nuclear attack— appears in Robert O'Brien's *Z for Zachariah* and in Monica Hughes's *Beyond the Dark River;* and Hughes went on to write her *Isis* trilogy based on the idea of a planet with an intergalactic radar system.

During recent years Susan Cooper concluded *The Dark Is Rising* sequence with *The Grey King* and *Silver on the Tree,* and Mary Norton brilliantly rounded out her famous saga with *The Borrowers Avenged.* Other authors produced striking single books based on folklore, as Mollie Hunter did in *A Stranger Came Ashore,* or on a philosophical concept, as Natalie Babbitt did in *Tuck Everlasting,* one of the great creations of the period, which implicitly deals with the subject of immortality. Some writers continued to straddle the realms of realism and fantasy. Patricia Wrightson, beginning with *The Ice Is Coming,* developed a trilogy rooted in Australian aboriginal folklore. And in New Zealand Margaret Mahy combined realism with an overlay of the supernatural—ghosts—in *The Haunting* and possession by an evil spirit in *The Changeover.* A traditional form of fantasy, the anthropomorphic animal tale, appeared in William Steig's deliciously tongue-in-cheek *Abel's Island* and in several of Dick King-Smith's broadly humorous stories—for example, *The Mouse Butcher* and *Babe: The Gallant Pig.* In *The Voyage of QV66* Penelope Lively wrote an entertaining animal story blending fable, science fiction, and good-humored satire.

The influence of Tolkien and of Ursula LeGuin's brilliant trilogy was still observable in the invented lands and the heroic protagonists—many of them women—in the trilogies of Patricia McKillip and also of Anne McCaffrey and Jane Yolen, whose stories witness the glorification of the dragon as a mythic figure. Robin McKinley's heroic fantasies, *The Blue Sword* and *The Hero and the Crown,* are overlaid with elements of legend; and moving much closer to folklore—indeed, bridging the gap—is her *Beauty,* an ingenious recasting of a fairy tale into a full-length novel. But the dominant new figure in fantasy has been Diana Wynne Jones whose narrative inventions, admittedly somewhat uneven, combine ingredients of folklore, science fiction, literary allusion, and humor to form an attractive body of work—found especially in *Dogsbody, The Magicians of Caprona, The Homeward Bounders* and *Fire and Hemlock.*

The roots of fantasy literature lie, of course, in the great bedrock of oral tradition. In the early twentieth century, concurrent with the lively new interest in storytelling, a rich heritage of folk tale, myth, legend, and saga made its way into books for young people; and after the Second World War publishers offered an abundance of folk tales gathered from all over the world. Yet we have suffered a great loss, for a treasury of collections has gone out of print while few new books have taken its place. Christie Harris and John Bierhorst have continued to gather American Indian material, and Ashley Bryan made two delightful books of African tales. Probably the major work of the decade was Jamake Highwater's *Anpao: An American Indian Odyssey,* a hero saga created from a diversity of inherited tales. Interestingly, the changes that attached themselves to fiction for children also affected the retellings of myths and legends. For older readers Norma Johnston wrote novelistic narratives based on Greek mythology, and Rosemary Sutcliff completed a trilogy on Arthurian material, about which—she said—she was more concerned with real people than with magic and marvels, thus bringing the work much closer to the modern novel.

One of the victims of the economics of publishing and of the lassitude of readers has been the translated book. In recent years, despite glowing reviews and the impetus of the Mildred L. Batchelder Award, the sales figures of novels from abroad have been dismal. Certainly underappreciated are Irina Korschunow's *A Night in Distant Motion* and *Who Killed Christopher?,* a modern story of adolescence. And of the decade's Batchelder winners—selected, unhappily, from a sparse field—there are nonetheless some first-rate, absorbing books: Cecil Bødker's *The Leopard,* Christine Nöstlinger's *Konrad,* Harry Kullman's *The Battle Horse,* Astrid Lindgren's *Ronia, the Robber's Daughter,* and Uri Orlev's *The Island on Bird Street.*

And what of the new authors? Many of them have already been

mentioned. But perhaps the most significant trend is the fact that gifted writers are turning their backs on trendiness. In England Robert Westall, after his astonishing accomplishment in *The Machine Gunners,* established himself with substantial work ranging in many directions, combining sharp observation of adolescents with plot elements of psychological terror or patterns of sheer fantasy. Jan Mark, in addition to her realistic contemporary stories, has explored the importance of the individual in such novels as *Divide and Rule* and *Aquarius,* in which she created new terrestrial realms. In America Nancy Bond in her first book mingled the here-and-now with ingredients of Welsh folklore and then continued her graceful probing of personalities—the ebb and flow of their often turbulent interactions—in such diverse novels as *Country of Broken Stone* and *A Place To Come Back To.* Laurence Yep introduced himself as an interpreter of the Chinese experience in California; and recognition has come to the unclassifiable Paul Fleischman and to Patricia MacLachlan, who displays craftsmanship, humor, and a total disregard for prepackaged problems.

To rephrase an earlier question: is children's literature surviving? More than surviving, it is flourishing—in diversity, imaginative thrust, and receptiveness to change. And as never before, the timeless human significance of story is now being stressed. Virginia Hamilton put it this way: "The challenge ... is to deal with the truth through youth literature with an evolvement of a fiction of compassion, hope, and humor." And Nina Bawden put precisely the same idea another way: "If a children's writer presents his characters honestly and is truthful about their thoughts and their feelings ... he can also show [his readers] a bit of the world, the beginning of the path they have to tread; but the most important things he has to offer is a little hope, and courage for the journey."

Index of Titles Mentioned

A & The, or William T. C. Baumgarten Comes to Town, 58
A for the Ark, 287
Abel's Island, 315, 340
Aesop's Fables, 260
After the First Death, 337
Aladdin and His Wonderful Lamp, 326
Alan and Naomi, 339
Alfred Summer, The, 335
Alice in Wonderland, 332
All Butterflies, 250
Amazing Bone, The, 319
Amifika, 331
And It Rained, 58
Angels and Other Strangers, 90
Anno's Alphabet, 332
Anpao: An American Indian Odyssey, 315, 341
Aquarius, 342
Arilla Sun Down, 337
Ashanti to Zulu: African Traditions, 180, 181-87, 191-92, 279, 281-85
Ask Mr. Bear, 282

Babe: The Gallant Pig, 340
Babies Need Books, 328
Baboushka, 329
Backbone of the King, 250, 252
Bagthorpe Saga, 338
Battle Horse, The, 341
Beauty, 139, 142, 147, 151, 340
Beauty and the Beast, 329
Behind the Back of the Mountain, 170, 180
Behind the Golden Curtain, 15
Ben's Dream, 234
Ben's Trumpet, 297, 302, 320
Beyond Silence, 336
Beyond the Dark River, 340
Big Tiger and Christian, 89
Bilgewater, 336
Blue Sword, The, 140, 147, 151, 161, 316, 340
Blueberries for Sal, 330
Book of Seasons, The, 260
Borrowers Avenged, 340
Box of Delights, 13
Bremen-Town Musicians, The, 320
Bridge to Terabithia, 35-38, 38-44, 46, 157, 335

Caleb and Kate, 327
Castle, 290, 319
Chair for My Mother, A, 306-7, 321

Chance Child, A, 336
Changeover, The, 340
Chanticleer and the Fox, 216
Charge of the Light Brigade, 308
Chase Me, Catch Nobody!, 339
Chocolate War, The, 335
Cinderella, 253
Come Away from the Water, Shirley, 327
Contest, The, 319
"Could Be Worse," 328
Country of Broken Stone, 342
Cow Who Fell in the Canal, The, 201

Dan Alone, 336
Dancing Granny, The, 331
Dark Is Rising, The, 3, 9, 10, 13, 15, 155, 340
Dawn of Fear, 15
Daydreamers, 331
Dear Mr. Henshaw, 120-31, 161
December Tale, A, 335
Delikon, The, 340
Desert Is Theirs, The, 319
Devil in Vienna, The, 339
Devil with the Three Golden Hairs, The, 329
Dicey's Song, 105-6, 107, 108, 115, 159, 160
Disappearance, The, 335, 338
Divide and Rule, 342
Doctor DeSoto, 316, 327
Dogsbody, 341
Door in the Hedge, The, 151
Double Life of Pocahontas, The, 339
Dragonwings, 315

Ellen Tebbits, 134
Ennead, The, 340

Fables, 220-25, 226, 228, 279, 297-98
Felice, 251
Figgs & Phantoms, 54, 58
Fire and Hemlock, 341
Fireside Book of Folk Songs, 260
Fish for Supper, 319
Five Chinese Brothers, The, 282
Fledgling, The, 316
Fox Went Out on a Chilly Night, The, 202, 286
Franklin Stein, 58
Freight Train, 292, 320
Friendly Wolf, The, 206
Frog and Toad, 221
Frontier Wolf, 339

343

344 / Index of Titles Mentioned

Gaffer Samson's Luck, 336
Garden of Abdul Gasazi, The, 234, 320
Gathering of Days, A: A New England Girl's Journal, 1830–32, 62–64, 65–69, 71, 73, 158–59
Ghost in a Four-Room Apartment, 58
Girl Who Loved Wild Horses, The, 204–9, 279, 291–92
Glorious Flight, The: Across the Channel with Louis Blériot July 25, 1909, 254–58, 260, 262, 279, 307–9
Golden Treasury of Myths and Legends, 260
Golem, The: A Jewish Legend, 319
Gorky Rises, 327
Graven Images, 316
Great Gilly Hopkins, The, 46, 79, 82, 87, 315, 336
Greenwitch, 16
Grey King, The, 3–6, 7, 10, 16, 155–56, 161, 340
Grey Lady and the Strawberry Snatcher, The, 320

Hansel and Gretel, 311, 322, 329
Happy Lion, The, 330
Haunting, The, 340
Have You Seen My Duckling?, 322
Hawk, I'm Your Brother, 319
Hazel Rye, 337
Henry Huggins, 125, 133–34
Hero and the Crown, The, 136–48, 151, 155, 161–62, 164, 340
High King, The, 155
Highest Hit, The, 99, 100
Highwayman, The, 329
Hiroshima No Pika, 331
Hobbit, The, 332
Homecoming, 108, 116, 117, 160
Homesick: My Own Story, 316
Homeward Bounders, The, 341
Horse and a Hound, A Goat and a Gander, A, 260
Horton Hatches the Egg, 330
Household Tales of Moon and Water, 101
How, Hippo!, 250
How Six Found Christmas, 267
Humbug Mountain, 338
Hundred Penny Box, The, 315, 337

I Am the Cheese, 337
Ice Is Coming, The, 340

Ida Early Comes Over the Mountain, 334
Illiad and The Odyssey, The, 260
Interstellar Pig, 340
Island of the Grass King: The Further Adventures of Anatole, 100
Island on Bird Street, The, 339, 341
It All Began with Jane Eyre, 338
It Could Always Be Worse, 319, 329
It Happened in Pinsk, 300

Jacob Have I Loved, 74–76, 76–85, 88–89, 159, 164
Jenny, 87
Journey Cake, Ho!, 282
Journey to an 800 Number, 338
Joy to the World, 267
Jumanji, 229–33, 234, 279, 298–301

Kate and the Revolution, 336
King Stork, 268
Kissimmee Kid, The, 337
Konrad, 341

Land of Dreams, The, 97
Leopard, The, 341
Let the Circle Be Unbroken, 338
Like Jake and Me, 317
Lion, the Witch and the Wardrobe, The, 332
Listen to a Shape, 251
Little Black Stories for Little White Children, 240
Little Carousel, The, 250
Little Fear, A, 336
Little Little, 337
Little Red Hen, 282
Little Red Riding Hood, 268, 321
Lonesome Boy, 297

Machine Gunners, The, 342
Magical Adventures of Pretty Pearl, The, 337
Magicians of Caprona, The, 341
Man Without a Face, The, 335
Mandrake, 15
Marzipan Moon, The, 103
Master Puppeteer, The, 45, 46, 79, 90, 336
Merry History of a Christmas Pie, The, 100
Mice Twice, 320
Midnight Folk, The, 13
Mischling, Second Degree, 339
Miss Rumphius, 327
Mr. and Mrs. Pig's Evening Out, 330

INDEX OF TITLES MENTIONED / 345

Moose, Goose & Little Nobody, 58
Mother Crocodile—"Maman Caiman," 331
Mother Goose Book, 259
Mouse Butcher, The, 340
Mouse Soup, 227
Mousewife, The, 332
Moves Make the Man, The, 317
My Friend Jacob, 326, 331
Mysterious Disappearance of Leon (I Mean Noel), The, 54, 58

Night in Distant Motion, A, 341
Noah's Ark, 43, 89, 193–200, 202–3, 279, 286–90
Noah's Castle, 336
Nothing Ever Happens on My Block, 53
Now One Foot, Now the Other, 326

Of Nightingales That Weep, 46
Oh, Were They Ever Happy, 197
On Market Street, 302–4, 321
Once a Mouse . . . , 250, 253, 304
One-Eyed Cat, 317, 336
Ordinary Jack, 338
Our Animal Friends at Maple Hill Farm, 260
Outside Over There, 321, 327
Over Sea, Under Stone, 8, 9, 15
Owl and the Pussycat, The, 297
Owl and Three Pussycats, An, 260
Ox-Cart Man, 210–15, 279, 294–97

Parcel of Patterns, A, 339
Peaceable Kingdom: A: The Shaker Abecedarius, 260, 308
Peppermint Pig, The, 336
Perfect Peach, The, 326
Peter and the Wolf, 329
Peter Penny's Dance, 303
Peter's Chair, 306
Pigman, The, 335
Pinballs, The, 337
Place To Come Back To, A, 342
Provensen Book of Fairy Tales, The, 260

Queen Eleanor: Independent Spirit of the Medieval World, 339

Ramona and Her Father, 134, 315
Ramona Forever, 135
Ramona Quimby, Age 8, 134, 315
Rebels of the Heavenly Kingdom, 336

Red Tag Comes Back, 227
Reluctant Dragon, The, 332
Ring in the Prairie, The: A Shawnee Legend, 180
Ring of Endless Light, A, 316
Road from Home, The: The Story of an Armenian Girl, 158, 315, 339
Robbers, The, 336
Roll of Thunder, Hear My Cry, 18–21, 21–30, 34, 156, 338
Ronia, The Robber's Daughter, 341
Room Made of Windows, A, 336
Runaway Ralph, 128

Sailing to Cythera: And Other Anatole Stories, 100
Saint George and the Dragon, 263–74, 279, 309
Samurai's Tale, The, 339
Sarah Bishop, 339
Save Queen of Sheba, 339
Seamstress of Salzburg, The, 302
Seventh Raven, The, 336
Shadow, 238–49, 250, 279, 304–5
Shakespeare: Ten Great Plays, 260
Shepherd Moon, The, 340
Sign of the Beaver, The, 317, 339
Sign of the Chrysanthemum, The, 46, 87
Silly Songs and Sad, 58
Silver Cow, The, 329
Silver on the Tree, 15, 16, 340
Slake's Limbo, 335
Slave Dancer, The, 155
Sleeping Beauty, The, 268
Smoky the Cowhorse, 131
Snow White, 268
Snowman, The, 327
Solitary Blue, A, 160, 317, 335
Something on My Mind, 331
Song for a Dark Queen, 339
Song of the Trees, 26, 34, 338
Sound of Chariots, A, 335
Sparkle and Spin, 293
Spectacles, 58
Stone Book, 336
Stone Soup, 328
Stonewall, 339
Story of Jumping Mouse, The, 322, 331
Stranger Came Ashore, A, 340
Strega Nona, 319, 329
String in the Harp, A, 315
Sugaring Time, 163, 317
Superfudge, 338
Sven's Bridge, 302

Sweet Whispers, Brother Rush, 316, 337
Sylvester and the Magic Pebble, 199, 330

Tamarindo!, 251
Tattooed Potato and Other Clues, The, 54
Ten, Nine, Eight, 321
Three Little Pigs, The, 329
Three Robbers, The, 330
Thunder Hill, 201
Thy Friend Obadiah, 199
Touch Will Tell, 251
Treasure, The, 320, 329
Trial Valley, 337
Truck, 320
Tuck Everlasting, 335, 340
Tulku, 336
Twenty-two, Twenty-three, 58

Uncle Terrible: More Adventures of Anatole, 99
Unleaving, 336
Upon the Head of the Goat: A Childhood in Hungary, 1939–1944, 316, 339
Uses of Enchantment, The, 324

Very Far Away from Anywhere Else, 335
Visit to William Blake's Inn, A: Poems for Innocent and Experienced Travelers, 93–98, 103–4, 159–60, 163, 259, 260, 308, 321
Visitors, The, 336
Voyage of QV66, The, 340

Walk with Your Eyes, 251
Way to Sattin Shore, The, 336
Way to Start a Day, The, 320
We Read: A to Z, 293
Westing Game, The, 50–57, 58, 157–58, 163
Westmark, 336
When I Was Young in the Mountains, 321
Where the Buffaloes Begin, 321
Where the Lilies Bloom, 335, 337
Where the Wild Things Are, 326
Who Killed Christopher?, 341
Who, Said Sue, Said Whoo?, 58
Why Mosquitoes Buzz in People's Ears, 169–74, 180, 183, 191, 192, 279, 281–82
Wind in the Willows, The, 332
Wish Giver, The, 317
World's Greatest Freak Show, The, 58
Wreck of the Zephyr, The, 328
Year at Maple Hill Farm, The, 260
Yeh-Shen, 329

Z for Zachariah, 340
Zoo for Mister Muster, A, 227

*Index by Author of Titles Mentioned**

Aardema, Verna, *Why Mosquitoes Buzz in People's Ears,* il. by Leo and Diane Dillon, 169–74, 180, 183, 191, 192, 279, 281–82
Aardema, Verna, edited by, *Behind the Back of the Mountain,* il. by Leo and Diane Dillon, 170, 180
Alexander, Lloyd, *The High King,* 155
   Westmark, 336
Anno, Mitsumasa, *Anno's Alphabet,* il. by the author, 332

Babbitt, Natalie, *Tuck Everlasting,* 335, 340
Baker, Olaf, *Where the Buffaloes Begin,* il. by Stephen Gammell, 321
Bang, Molly, *Ten, Nine, Eight,* il. by the author, 321
Bang, Molly, illustrated by, *The Grey Lady and the Strawberry Snatcher,* 320
Bawden, Nina, *The Peppermint Pig,* 336
   The Robbers, 336
Baylor, Byrd, *The Desert Is Theirs,* il. by Peter Parnall, 319
   Hawk, I'm Your Brother, il. by Peter Parnall, 319
   The Way to Start a Day, il. by Peter Parnall, 320
Bettelheim, Bruno, *The Uses of Enchantment,* 324
Bennett, Dorothy, edited by, *Golden Mother Goose Book,* il. by Alice and Martin Provensen, 259
Bianco, Pamela, selected by, *The Land of Dreams,* il. by the selector, 97
Bierhorst, John, edited by, *The Ring in the Prairie: A Shawnee Legend,* il. by Leo and Diane Dillon, 180
Bishop, Claire H., *The Five Chinese Brothers,* il. by Kurt Wiese, 282
Blegvad, Erik, illustrated by, *The Three Little Pigs,* 329
Blos, Joan W., *A Gathering of Days: A New England Girl's Journal, 1830–32,* 62–64, 65–69, 71, 73, 158–59
Blume, Judy, *Superfudge,* 338
Bødker, Cecil, *The Leopard,* trans. by Gunnar Poulsen, 341
Bond, Nancy, *Country of Broken Stone,* 342
   A Place To Come Back To, 342
   A String in the Harp, 315
Boni, Margaret Bradford, edited by, *Fireside Book of Folk Songs,* il. by Alice and Martin Provensen, 260
Bontemps, Arna, *Lonesome Boy,* il. by Feliks Topolski, 297
Briggs, Raymond, illustrated by, *The Snowman,* 327
Brittain, Bill, *The Wish Giver,* il. by Andrew Glass, 317
Brodsky, Beverly, *The Golem, A Jewish Legend,* il. by the author, 319
Brooks, Bruce, *The Moves Make the Man,* 317
Brooks, Polly Schoyer, *Queen Eleanor: Independent Spirit of the Medieval World,* 339
Brown, Marcia, *All Butterflies,* il. by the author, 250
   Backbone of the King, il. by the author, 250, 252
   Felice, il. by the author, 251
   How, Hippo!, il by the author, 250
   Listen to a Shape, il. by the author, 251
   Little Carousel, il. by the author, 250
   Once a Mouse . . . , il. by the author, 250, 253, 304
   Stone Soup, il. by the author, 328
   Tamarindo!, il. by the author, 251
   Touch Will Tell, il. by the author, 251
   Walk with Your Eyes, il. by the author, 251
Bryan, Ashley, retold by, *The Dancing Granny,* il. by the reteller, 331

---

* This list is confined to juvenile titles and books pertaining to children's literature.

Index By Author

Burch, Robert, *Ida Early Comes over the Mountain,* 334
Burningham, John, *Come Away from the Water, Shirley,* il. by the author, 327
Butler, Dorothy, *Babies Need Books,* 328
Byars, Betsy, *The Pinballs,* 337

Cameron, Eleanor, *Beyond Silence,* 336
   A Room Made of Windows, 336
Carroll, Lewis, *Alice in Wonderland,* il. by Michael Hague, 332
Cendrars, Blaise, *Little Black Stories for Little White Children,* trans. by Margery Bianco, 240
   Shadow, trans. and il. by Marcia Brown, 238–49, 250, 279, 304–5
Cleary, Beverly, *Dear Mr. Henshaw,* il. by Paul O. Zelinsky, 120–31, 161
   Ellen Tebbits, il. by Louis Darling, 134
   Henry Huggins, il. by Louis Darling, 125, 133–34
   Ramona and Her Father, il. by Alan Tiegreen, 134, 315
   Ramona Forever, il. by Alan Tiegreen, 135
   Ramona Quimby, Age, 8, il. by Alan Tiegreen, 134, 315
   Runaway Ralph, il. by Louis Darling, 128
Cleaver, Vera and Bill, *Hazel Rye,* 337
   The Kissimmee Kid, 337
   Trial Valley, 337
   Where the Lilies Bloom, il. by James Spanfeller, 335, 337
Clifton, Lucille, *Amifika,* il. by Thomas di Grazia, 331
   My Friend Jacob, il. by Thomas di Grazia, 331
Cooney, Barbara, *Miss Rumphius,* il. by the author, 327
Cooney, Barbara, adapted by, *Chanticleer and the Fox,* il. by the adapter, 216
Cooper, Susan, *Behind the Golden Curtain: A View of the U.S.A.,* 15
   The Dark Is Rising, il. by Alan E. Cober, 3, 9, 10, 13, 15, 155, 340
   Dawn of Fear, il. by Margery Gill, 15
   Greenwitch, 16
   The Grey King, 3–6, 7, 10, 16, 155–56, 161, 340
   Mandrake, 15
   Over Sea, Under Stone, il. by Margery Gill, 8, 9, 15
   The Silver Cow, il. by Warwick Hutton, 329
   Silver on the Tree, 15, 16, 340
Cormier, Robert, *After the First Death,* 337
   The Chocolate War, 335
   I Am the Cheese, 337
Cresswell, Helen, *Ordinary Jack,* 338
Crews, Donald, *Freight Train,* il. by the author, 292, 320
   Truck, il. by the author, 320
   We Read: A to Z, il. by the author, 293

de Paola, Tomie, *Now One Foot, Now the Other,* il. by the author, 326
   Strega Nona, retold and il. by Tomie de Paola, 319, 329
Dickinson, Peter, *Tulku,* 336;
   The Seventh Raven, 336
Duvoisin, Roger, *A for the Ark,* il. by the author, 287

Fatio, Louise, *The Happy Lion,* il. by Roger Duvoisin, 330
Flack, Marjorie, *Ask Mr. Bear,* il. by the author, 282
Fleischman, Paul, *Graven Images,* il. by Andrew Glass, 316
Fleischman, Sid, *Humbug Mountain,* il. by Eric von Schmidt, 338
Fox, Paula, *One-Eyed Cat,* 317, 336
   The Slave Dancer, il. by Eros Keith, 155

INDEX BY AUTHOR / 349

Fritz, Jean, *The Double Life of Pocahontas*, il. by Ed Young, 339
   Homesick: My Own Story, il. by Margot Tomes, 316, 339
   Stonewall, il. by Stephen Gammell, 339

Gardam, Jane, *Bilgewater*, 336
Garner, Alan, *The Stone Book*, 336
Goble, Paul, *The Girl Who Loved Wild Horses*, il. by the author, 204–209, 279, 291–292
Goble, Paul and Dorothy, *The Friendly Wolf*, il. by Paul Goble, 206
Godden, Rumer, *The Mousewife*, il. by William Pène du Bois, 332
Goffstein, M. B., *Fish for Supper*, il. by the author, 332
Grahame, Kenneth, *The Reluctant Dragon*, il. by Ernest Shepard, 332
   The Wind in the Willows, il. by Michael Hague, 332
Greenfield, Eloise, *Daydreamers*, il. by Tom Feelings, 331
Greenwald, Sheila, *It All Began with Jane Eyre*, 338
Grimes, Nikki, *Something on My Mind*, il. by Tom Feelings, 331
Grimm, Jakob and Wilhelm, *The Devil with the Three Golden Hairs*, ret. and il. by Nonny Hogrogian, 329
   Hansel and Gretel, adapt. from a translation by Eleanor Quarrie, il. by Anthony Browne, 329
   Sleeping Beauty, ret and il. by Trina Schart Hyman, 268
   Snow White, trans. by Paul Heins, il. by Trina Schart Hyman, 268
Guy, Rosa, *The Disappearance*, 335, 338
   Mother Crocodile—"Maman Caiman", il. by John Steptoe, 331

Hall, Donald, *Ox-Cart Man*, il. by Barbara Cooney, 210–15, 279, 294–97
Hamilton, Virginia, *Arilla Sun Down*, 337
   The Magical Adventures of Pretty Pearl, 337
   Sweet Whispers, Brother Rush, 316, 337
Haugaard, Erik Christian, *Chase Me, Catch Nobody!*, 339
   The Samurai's Tale, 339
Highwater, Jamake, *Anpao: An American Indian Odyssey*, il. by Fritz Scholder, 315, 341
Hodges, Margaret, adapted by, *Saint George and the Dragon*, il. by Trina Schart Hyman, 263–74, 279, 309
Hogrogian, Nonny, adapted by, *The Contest*, il. by the adapter, 319
Holdsworth, William, retold by, *Little Red Hen*, il. by the reteller, 282
Holland, Isabelle, *The Man Without a Face*, 335
Holman, Felice, *Slake's Limbo*, 335
Hoover, Helen, *The Delikon*, 340
   The Shepherd Moon, 340
Hughes, Monica, *Beyond the Dark River*, 340
Hunter, Mollie, *A Sound of Chariots*, 335
   A Stranger Came Ashore, 340
Hutton, Warwick, retold by, *Beauty and the Beast*, il. by the reteller, 329
Hyman, Trina Schart, *How Six Found Christmas*, il. by the author, 267
Hyman, Trina Schart, retold by, *Little Red Riding Hood*, il. by the reteller, 268, 321

Isadora, Rachel, *Ben's Trumpet*, il. by the author, 297, 302, 320

James, Will, *Smoky, the Cowhorse*, il. by the author, 131
Jones, Diana Wynne, *Dogsbody*, 341
   Fire and Hemlock, 341
   The Homeward Bounders, 341
   The Magicians of Caprona, 341
Jukes, Mavis, *Like Jake and Me*, il. by Lloyd Bloom, 317

Keats, Ezra Jack, *Peter's Chair,* il. by the author, 306
Kerr, M. E., *Little Little,* 337
Kherdian, David, *The Road from Home: The Story of an Armenian Girl,* 158, 315, 339
King-Smith, Dick, *Babe: The Gallant Pig,* il. by Mary Rayner, 340
   The Mouse Butcher, il. by Margot Apple, 340
Koehn, Ilse, *Mischling, Second Degree,* 339
Konigsburg, E. L., *Journey to an 800 Number,* 338
Korschunow, Irina, *A Night in Distant Motion,* trans. by Leigh Hafrey, 341
   Who Killed Christopher?, trans. by Eva L. Mayer, 341
Krasilovsky, Phyllis, *The Cow Who Fell in the Canal,* il. by Peter Spier, 201
Kullman, Harry, *The Battle Horse,* trans. by George Blecher and Lone Thygesen-Blecher, 341

Langton, Jane, *The Fledgling,* 316
Lasky, Kathryn, *Sugaring Time,* phot. by Christopher G. Knight, 163, 317
Lear, Edward, *The Owl and the Pussycat,* il. by Barbara Cooney, 297
LeGuin, Ursula, *Very Far Away from Anywhere Else,* 335
L'Engle, Madeleine, *A Ring of Endless Light,* 316
Lesser, Rika, retold by, *Hansel and Gretel,* il. by Paul O. Zelinsky, 311, 322
Levoy, Myron, *Alan and Naomi,* 339
Lewis, C. S., *The Lion, the Witch and the Wardrobe,* il. by Michael Hague, 332
Lindgren, Astrid, *Ronia, The Robber's Daughter,* trans. by Patricia Crompton, 341
Lively, Penelope, *The Voyage of QV66,* 340
Lobel, Anita, *The Seamstress of Salzburg,* il. by the author, 302
   Sven's Bridges, il. by the author, 302
Lobel, Arnold, *Fables,* il. by the author, 220-25, 226, 228, 279, 297-98
   Frog and Toad, il. by the author, 221
   Mouse Soup, il. by the author, 227
   On Market Street, il. by Anita Lobel, 302-4, 321
   A Zoo for Mister Muster, il. by the author, 227
Louie, Ai-Ling, retold by, *Yeh-Shen: A Cinderella Story from China,* il. by Ed Young, 329
Low, Joseph, *Mice Twice,* il. by the author, 320
Lubin, Leonard, adapted by, *Aladdin and His Wonderful Lamp,* il. by the adapter, 326

Macaulay, David, *Castle,* il. by the author, 290, 319
McCloskey, Robert, *Blueberries for Sal,* il. by the author, 330
McKinley, Robin, *Beauty,* 139, 142, 147, 151, 340
   The Blue Sword, 140, 147, 151, 161, 316, 340
   The Door in the Hedge, 151
   The Hero and the Crown, 136-48, 151, 155, 161-62, 164, 340
Mahy, Margaret, *The Changeover,* 340
   The Haunting, 340
Mark, Jan, *Aquarius,* 342
   Divide and Rule, 342
   The Ennead, 340
Maruki, Toshi, *Hiroshima No Pika,* il. by the author, 331
Masefield, John, *Box of Delights,* il. by Faith Jaques, 13
   The Midnight Folk, 13
Mathis, Sharon Bell, *The Hundred Penny Box,* il. by Leo and Diane Dillon, 315, 337
Mikolaycak, Charles, retold by, *Baboushka,* il. by the reteller, 329
Moeri, Louise, *Save Queen of Sheba,* 339

Mühlenweg, Fritz, *Big Tiger and Christian*, il. by Rafaello Busoni, 89
Musgrove, Margaret, *Ashanti to Zulu: African Traditions*, il. by Leo and Diane Dillon, 180, 181–187, 191–92, 279, 281–85

Namovicz, Gene Inyart, *Jenny*, 87
Nicholds, Elizabeth, *Thunder Hill*, il. by Peter Spier, 201
Norton, Mary, *Borrowers Avenged*, il. by Beth and Joe Krush, 340
Nöstlinger, Christine, *Konrad*, trans. by Anthea Bell, il. by Carol Nicklaus, 341
Noyes, Alfred, *The Highwayman*, il. by Charles Mikolaycak, 329

O'Brien, Robert, *Z for Zachariah*, 340
O'Dell, Scott, *Sarah Bishop*, 339
Orgel, Doris, *The Devil in Vienna*, 339
Orlev, Uri, *The Island on Bird Street*, trans. by Hillel Halkin, 339, 341

Paterson, Katherine, *Angels and Other Strangers*, 90
  Bridge to Terabithia, il. by Donna Diamond, 35–38, 38–44, 157, 335
  The Great Gilly Hopkins, 46, 79, 82, 87, 315, 336
  Jacob Have I Loved, 74–76, 76–85, 88–89, 159, 164
  The Master Puppeteer, il. by Haru Wells, 45, 46, 79, 90, 336
  Of Nightingales That Weep, il. by Haru Wells, 46
  Rebels of the Heavenly Kingdom, 336
  The Sign of the Chrysanthemum, il. by Peter Landa, 46, 87
Paton Walsh, Jill, *A Chance Child*, 336
  Gaffer Samson's Luck, 336
  A Parcel of Patterns, 339
  Unleaving, 336
Pearce, Philippa, *The Way to Sattin Shore*, il. by Charlotte Voake, 336
Perrault, Charles, *Cinderella*, trans. and il. by Marcia Brown, 253
Phleger, Fred, *Red Tag Comes Back*, il. by Arnold Lobel, 227
Plume, Ilse, retold by, *The Bremen-Town Musicians*, il. by the reteller, 320
Prokofiev, Sergey, *Peter and the Wolf*, trans. by Maria Carlson, il. by Charles Mikolaycak, 329
Provensen, Alice and Martin, *A Book of Seasons*, il. by the authors, 260
  The Glorious Flight: Across the Channel with Louis Blériot July 25, 1909, il. by the authors, 254–58, 260, 262, 279, 307–9
  A Horse and a Hound, A Goat and a Gander, il. by the authors, 260
  Our Animal Friends at Maple Hill Farm, il. by the authors, 260
  An Owl and Three Pussycats, il. by the authors, 260
  A Peaceable Kingdom: The Shaker Abecedarius, il. by the authors, 260, 308
  The Year at Maple Hill Farm, il. by the authors, 260
Provensen, Alice and Martin, edited by, *Provensen Book of Fairy Tales*, il. by the editors, 260
Pyle, Howard, *King Stork*, il. by Trina Schart Hyman, 268

Quin-Harkin, Janet, *Peter Penny's Dance*, il. by Anita Lobel, 303

Rand, Ann and Paul, *Sparkle and Spin*, il. by Paul Rand, 293
Raskin, Ellen, *A & The, or William T. C. Baumgarten Comes to Town*, il. by the author, 58
  And It Rained, il. by the author, 58
  Figgs & Phantoms, il. by the author, 54, 58
  Franklin Stein, il. by the author, 58
  Ghost in a Four-Room Apartment, il. by the author, 58
  Moose, Goose & Little Nobody, il. by the author, 58
  The Mysterious Disappearance of Leon (I Mean Noel), il. by the author, 54, 58

Nothing Ever Happens on My Block, il. by the author, 53
Silly Songs and Sad, il. by the author, 58
Spectacles, il. by the author, 58
The Tattooed Potato and Other Clues, il. by the author, 54
Twenty-two, Twenty-three, il. by the author, 58
The Westing Game, 50–57, 58, 157–58, 163
Who, Said Sue, Said Whoo?, il. by the author, 58
The World's Greatest Freak Show, il. by the author, 58
Rayner, Mary, *Mr. and Mrs. Pig's Evening Out,* il. by the author, 330
    Rylant, Cynthia, *When I Was Young in the Mountains,* il. by Diane Goode, 321

Sachs, Marilyn, *A December Tale,* 335
Sawyer, Ruth, *Journey Cake, Ho!,* il. by Robert McCloskey, 282
    Joy to the World, il. by Trina Schart Hyman, 267
Schwartz, Stephen, *The Perfect Peach,* il. by Leonard Lubin, 326
Sendak, Maurice, *Outside Over There,* il. by the author, 321, 327
    Where the Wild Things Are, il. by the author, 326
Seuss, Dr., *Horton Hatches the Egg,* il. by the author, 330
Shulevitz, Uri, retold by, *The Treasure,* il. by the reteller, 320, 329
Siegel, Aranka, *Upon the Head of the Goat: A Childhood in Hungary, 1939–1944,* 316, 339
Sleator, William, *Interstellar Pig,* 340
Slepian, Jan, *The Alfred Summer,* 335
Speare, Elizabeth, *The Sign of the Beaver,* 317, 339
Spier, Peter, illustrated by, *The Fox Went Out on a Chilly Night,* 202, 286
    Noah's Ark, 43, 89, 193–200, 202–3, 279, 286–90
    Oh, Were They Ever Happy, 197
Steig, William, *Abel's Island,* il. by the author, 315, 340
    The Amazing Bone, il. by the author, 319
    Caleb and Kate, il. by the author, 327
    Doctor DeSoto, il. by the author, 316, 327
    Gorky Rises, il. by the author, 327
    Sylvester and the Magic Pebble, il. by the author, 199, 330
Steptoe, John, retold by, *The Story of Jumping Mouse,* il. by the reteller, 322, 331
Stevenson, James, *"Could Be Worse,"* il. by the author, 328
Sutcliff, Rosemary, *Frontier Wolf,* 339
    Song for a Dark Queen, 339

Tafuri, Nancy, *Have You Seen My Duckling?,* il. by the author, 322
Taylor, Mildred, *Let the Circle Be Unbroken,* 338
    Roll of Thunder, Hear My Cry, 18–21, 21–30, 34, 156, 338
    Song of the Trees, 26, 34, 338
Tennyson, Alfred Lord, *Charge of the Light Brigade,* il. by Alice and Martin Provensen, 308
Tolkien, J. R. R., *The Hobbit,* il. by Michael Hague, 332
Townsend, John Rowe, *Dan Alone,* 336
    Kate and the Revolution, 336
    Noah's Castle, 336
    The Visitors, 336
Turkle, Brinton, *Thy Friend Obadiah,* il. by the author, 199

Ungerer, Tomi, *The Three Robbers,* il. by the author, 330
Untermeyer, Louis, adapted by, *Aesop's Fables,* il. by Alice and Martin Provensen, 260

INDEX BY AUTHOR / 353

Van Allsburg, Chris, *Ben's Dream*, il. by the author, 234
   The Garden of Abdul Gasazi, il. by the author, 234, 320
   Jumanji, il. by the author, 229-33, 234, 279, 298-301
   The Wreck of the Zephyr, il. by the author, 328
Voigt, Cynthia, *Dicey's Song*, 105-6, 107, 108, 115, 159, 160
   Homecoming, 108, 116, 117, 160
   A Solitary Blue, 160, 317, 335
Watson, Jane Werner, adapted by, *The Illiad and The Odyssey*, il. by Alice and Martin Provensen, 260
Westall, Robert, *The Machine Gunners*, 342
White, Anne Terry, adapted by, *Golden Treasury of Myths and Legends*, il. by Alice and Martin Provensen, 260
Willard, Nancy, *The Highest Hit*, il. by Emily Arnold McCully, 99, 100
   Household Tales of Moon and Water, 101
   Island of the Grass King: The Further Adventures of Anatole, il. by David McPhail, 100
   The Marzipan Moon, il. by Marcia Sewell, 103
   The Merry History of a Christmas Pie, il. by Haig and Regina Shekerjian, 100
   Sailing to Cythera: And Other Anatole Stories, il. by David McPhail, 100
   Uncle Terrible: More Adventures of Anatole, il. by David McPhail, 99
   A Visit to William Blake's Inn: Poems for Innocent and Experienced Travelers, il. by Alice and Martin Provensen, 93-98, 103-4, 159-60, 163, 259, 260, 308, 321
Williams, Vera B., *A Chair for My Mother*, il. by the author, 306-7, 321
Wolfson, George, edited by, *Shakespeare: Ten Great Plays*, il. by Alice and Martin Provensen, 260
Wrightson, Patricia, *The Ice Is Coming*, 340
   A Little Fear, 336

Yep, Laurence, *Dragonwings*, 315
Yorinks, Arthur, *It Happened in Pinsk*, il. by Richard Egielski, 300

Zemach, Margot, retold by, *It Could Always Be Worse*, il. by the reteller, 319, 329
Zindel, Paul, *The Pigman*, 335

Grateful Acknowledgment

is made to the following publishers, authors, artists, and agents for permission to quote and reproduce copyrighted material:

Illustration by Leo and Diane Dillon from *Why Mosquitoes Buzz in People's Ears,* written by Verna Aardema. Pictures copyright © 1975 by Leo and Diane Dillon. Reproduced by permission of the publisher, Dial Books for Young Readers, New York.

Illustration by Leo and Diane Dillon from *Ashanti to Zulu: African Traditions,* written by Margaret Musgrove. Pictures copyright © 1976 by Leo and Diane Dillon. Reproduced by permission of the publisher, Dial Books for Young Readers, New York.

Illustration by Peter Spier from *Noah's Ark.* Copyright © 1977 by Peter Spier. Reproduced by permission of Doubleday Publishers, New York.

Illustration by David Macaulay from *Castle.* Copyright © 1977 by David Macaulay. Reproduced by permission of Houghton Mifflin Company, Boston, and Collins Publishers, London.

Illustration by Paul Goble from *The Girl Who Loved Wild Horses.* Copyright © 1978 by Paul Goble. Reproduced by permission of Bradbury Press, New York, an affiliate of Macmillan, Inc.

Illustration by Donald Crews from *Freight Train.* Copyright © 1978 by Donald Crews. Reproduced by permission of Greenwillow Books, New York.

Illustration by Rachel Isadora from *Ben's Trumpet.* Copyright © 1979 by Rachel Isadora Maiorano. Reproduced by permission of Greenwillow Books, New York.

Illustration by Barbara Cooney Porter from *Ox-Cart Man,* written by Donald Hall. Illustrations copyright © 1979 by Barbara Cooney Porter. Reproduced by permission of Viking Penguin, Inc., New York.

Illustration by Arnold Lobel from *Fables.* Copyright © 1980 by Arnold Lobel. Reproduced by permission of Greenwillow Books, New York.

Illustration by Anita Lobel from *On Market Street,* written by Arnold Lobel. Illustrations copyright © 1981 by Anita Lobel. Reproduced by permission of Greenwillow Books, New York.

Illustration by Chris Van Allsburg from *Jumanji.* Copyright © 1981 by Chris Van Allsburg. Reproduced by permission of Houghton Mifflin Company, Boston.

Illustration by Marcia Brown from *Shadow,* translated and illustrated by Marcia Brown. Copyright © 1982 by Marcia Brown. Reproduced by permission of Charles Scribner's Sons, New York.

Illustration by Vera Williams from *A Chair for My Mother.* Copyright © 1982 by Vera Williams. Reproduced by permission of Greenwillow Books, New York.

Illustration by Molly Bang from *Ten, Nine, Eight.* Copyright © 1983 by Molly Bang. Reproduced by permission of Greenwillow Books, New York.

Illustration by Alice and Martin Provensen from *The Glorious Flight.* Copyright © 1983 by Alice and Martin Provensen. Reproduced by permission of Viking Penguin, Inc., New York.

Illustration by Trina Schart Hyman from *Saint George and the Dragon,* retold by Margaret Hodges. Illustrations copyright © 1984 by Trina Schart Hyman. Reproduced by permission of Little, Brown, and Company, Boston.

Illustration by Paul O. Zelinsky from *Hansel and Gretel,* retold by Rika Lesser. Illustrations copyright © 1984 by Paul O. Zelinsky. Reproduced by permission of Dodd, Mead, and Co., New York.

To Houghton Mifflin Company, Boston, and George Allen & Unwin (Publishers) Ltd., London, for permission to quote a passage from *The Return of the King* by J.R.R. Tolkien. Copyright © 1967 by J.R.R. Tolkien.

To Susan Cooper for permission to reprint "Newbery Award Acceptance," copyright © 1976 by Susan Cooper, from *The Horn Book Magazine,* August 1976.

To Mildred Taylor for permission to reprint "Newbery Award Acceptance," copyright © 1977 by Mildred Taylor, from *The Horn Book Magazine,* August 1977.

To Katherine Paterson for permission to reprint "Newbery Award Acceptance," copyright © 1978 by Katherine Paterson, from *The Horn Book Magazine,* August 1978, and "Newbery Medal Acceptance," copyright © 1981 by Katherine Paterson, from *The Horn Book Magazine,* August 1981.

To Susan Metcalfe for permission to reprint "Newbery Award Acceptance," copyright © 1979 by Ellen Raskin, from *The Horn Book Magazine,* August 1979.

To Joan Blos for permission to reprint "Newbery Medal Acceptance," copyright © 1980 by Joan Blos, from *The Horn Book Magazine,* August 1980.

To Nancy Willard for permission to reprint "Newbery Medal Acceptance," copyright © 1982 by Nancy Willard, from *The Horn Book Magazine,* August 1982.

To Cynthia Voigt for permission to reprint "Newbery Medal Acceptance," copyright © 1983 by Cynthia Voigt, from *The Horn Book Magazine,* August 1983.

To Beverly Cleary for permission to reprint "Newbery Medal Acceptance," copyright © 1984 by Beverly Cleary, from *The Horn Book Magazine,* August 1984.

To Robin McKinley for permission to reprint "Newbery Medal Acceptance," copyright © 1985 by Robin McKinley, from *The Horn Book Magazine,* July/August 1985.

To Leo and Diane Dillon for permission to reprint "Caldecott Award Acceptance," copyright © 1976 by Leo and Diane Dillon, from *The Horn Book Magazine,* August 1976, and "Caldecott Award Acceptance," copyright © 1977 by Leo and Diane Dillon, from *The Horn Book Magazine,* August 1977.

To Peter Spier for permission to reprint "Caldecott Award Acceptance," copyright © 1978 by Peter Spier, from *The Horn Book Magazine,* August 1978.

To Paul Goble for permission to reprint "Caldecott Award Acceptance," copyright © 1979 by Paul Goble, from *The Horn Book Magazine,* August 1979.

To Barbara Cooney for permission to reprint "Caldecott Medal Acceptance," copyright © 1980 by Barbara Cooney, from *The Horn Book Magazine,* August 1980.

To Arnold Lobel for permission to reprint "Caldecott Medal Acceptance," copyright © 1981 by Arnold Lobel, from *The Horn Book Magazine,* August, 1981.

To Chris Van Allsburg for permission to reprint "Caldecott Medal Acceptance," copyright © 1982 by Chris Van Allsburg, from *The Horn Book Magazine,* August 1982.

To Marcia Brown for permission to reprint "Caldecott Medal Acceptance," copyright © 1983 by Marcia Brown, from *The Horn Book Magazine,* August 1983.

To Alice and Martin Provensen for permission to reprint "Caldecott Medal Acceptance," copyright © 1984 by Alice and Martin Provensen, from *The Horn Book Magazine,* August 1984.

To Trina Schart Hyman for permission to reprint "Caldecott Medal Acceptance," copyright © 1985 by Trina Schart Hyman, from *The Horn Book Magazine,* July/August 1985.

To Janet A. Loranger for permission to reprint "Marcia Brown," copyright © 1983 by Janet A. Loranger, from *The Horn Book Magazine,* August 1983.